Sherpa

Sherpa

Stories of Life and Death from the Forgotten
Guardians of Everest

Pradeep Bashyal and Ankit Babu Adhikari

First published in Great Britain in 2022 by Cassell, an imprint of
Octopus Publishing Group Ltd
Carmelite House
50 Victoria Embankment
London EC4Y 0DZ
www.octopusbooks.co.uk

An Hachette UK Company
www.hachette.co.uk

This edition published in 2023

Text copyright © Pradeep Bashyal and Ankit Babu Adhikari 2023

Illustrations copyright © Jill Tytherleigh, 2023

ISBN 978-1-78840-334-4

A CIP catalogue record for this book is available from the British Library.

Printed and bound in the UK

10 9 8 7 6 5 4 3 2 1

Publisher: Trevor Davies
Senior editor: Pauline Bache
Copyeditor: Julia Kellaway
Design director: Mel Four
Typeset in 12.25/16pt Mrs Eaves OT by Jouve (UK), Milton Keynes
Cartography by Philip's, a division of Octopus Publishing Group Ltd
Illustrator: Jill Tytherleigh
Senior production manager: Peter Hunt

This FSC® label means that materials used for
the product have been responsibly sourced

To:
Sherpas,
our parents
and
Neilmani, Injina and Salina.

CONTENTS

KHUMBU REGION

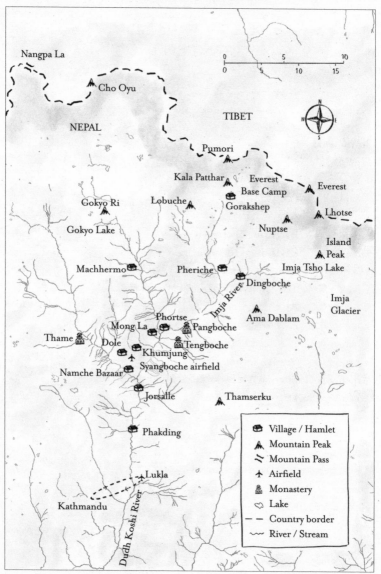

MAKALU REGION

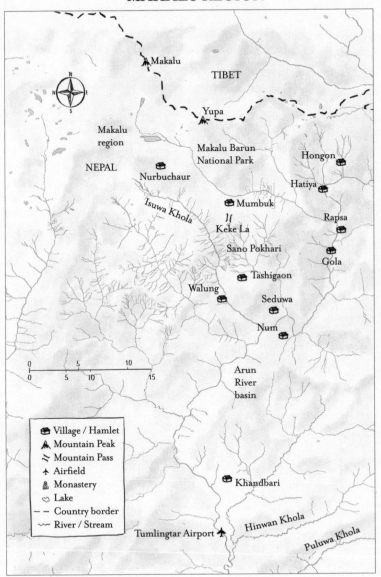

TIBET

Makalu

Yupa

Makalu region

Makalu Barun National Park

Hongon

NEPAL

Nurbuchaur

Hatiya

Isuwa Khola

Mumbuk

Rapsa

Keke La

Sano Pokhari

Gola

Tashigaon

Walung

Seduwa

Num

Arun River basin

0	5	10	
0	5	10	15

🏘 Village / Hamlet
🏔 Mountain Peak
≋ Mountain Pass
✈ Airfield
🏛 Monastery
🌊 Lake
– – Country border
〰 River / Stream

Khandbari

Hinwan Khola

Tumlingtar Airport ✈

Puluwa Khola

ROWALING REGION

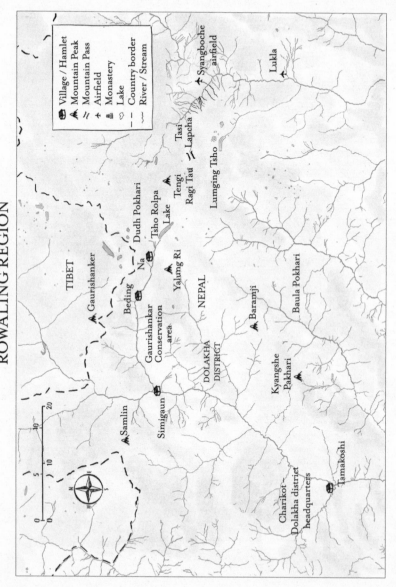

Legend:
- Village / Hamlet
- Mountain Peak
- Mountain Pass
- Airfield
- Monastery
- Lake
- Country border
- River / Stream

TIBET

NEPAL

DOLAKHA DISTRICT

Gaurishanker

Beding

Na

Dudh Pokhari

Tsho Rolpa Lake

Yalung Ri

Tengi Ragi Tau

Tasi Lapcha

Lumging Tsho

Syangboche airfield

Lukla

Gaurishankar Conservation area

Simigaun

Samlin

Baramji

Kyangshe Pakhari

Baula Pokhari

Charikot – Dolakha district headquarters

Tamakoshi

x

NEPAL AND SURROUNDING COUNTRIES

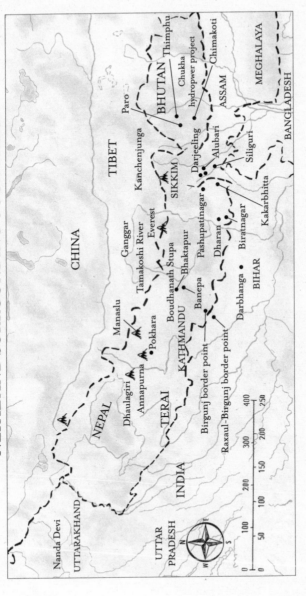

EVEREST – SOUTH FACE

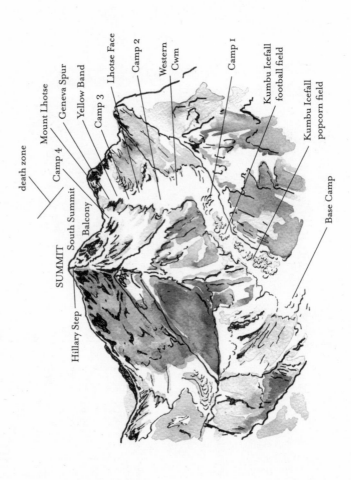

death zone

Mount Lhotse

Geneva Spur

Yellow Band

Camp 4

Camp 3

Lhotse Face

Camp 2

Western Cwm

Camp 1

Kumbu Icefall football field

Kumbu Icefall popcorn field

SUMMIT

South Summit

Balcony

Hillary Step

Base Camp

EVEREST – NORTH FACE

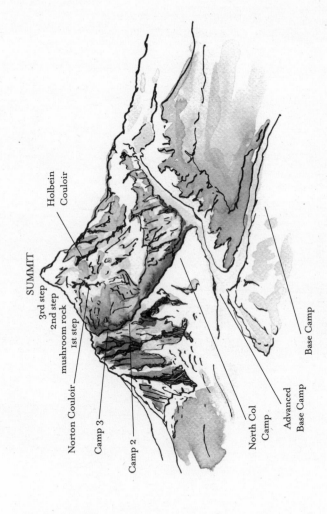

Holbein
Couloir

SUMMIT
3rd step
2nd step
mushroom rock
1st step

Norton Couloir

Camp 3

Camp 2

North Col
Camp.

Advanced
Base Camp

Base Camp

INTRODUCTION

Most major cities around the world stand below 50m (164ft) above sea level: New York and London are about 10m (33ft); Mumbai is below 20m (66ft); Tokyo, Paris and Cairo are about 40m (130ft); Sydney is below 5m (16ft) and Amsterdam is below 0m (0ft). In the faraway snow-land of Nepal, at over 5,000m above sea level, a city is reborn every year. This is Everest Base Camp – a tent-city standing on a glacier, where hundreds of people from all corners of the earth huddle up for most of the spring. Their destination, the highest point on earth, stands another several hundred metres higher, at 8,848.86m (29,031.69ft).

More than two-thirds of all those gathered in this tent-city belong to the Sherpa community, a Himalayan ethnic group of Nepal, numbering more than 150,000 in population. While most people are already exhausted by the time they reach Base Camp, Sherpas, who spearhead all the expeditions to the top of the world, are still surprisingly energetic and the sight of Sherpas fluttering in all directions is enough to fuel the oxygen-starved muscles of aspiring summiteers.

While some of the Sherpas will be seen cooking in makeshift kitchens, others will be training the foreign climbers, communicating in broken English. A few others will depart Base Camp to carry oxygen and other supplies to the higher camps; some will be planning their ascent; some will be seen praying to God in their local language; while others will be giving the much-needed physical and psychological impetus to a group of climbers about to begin an expedition.

On the way to the summit, Sherpas are the climbers' guardians, in charge of time and space. For their foreign clients, a Sherpa is their eyes on the mountain and, depending on the need, Sherpas become the climbers' weather experts, technicians and medics…and anything else needed for survival. In scenarios where a Sherpa senses a threat to the well-being of the expedition, he may even become the toughest boss one can imagine. It is a combination of all these traits that makes Sherpas, Sherpas.

This book is about these Sherpas, whose stories and role in mountaineering is largely untold. How do they function at the edge of life and death? Is it only due to their geographical and genetic benefits, or is there much more to it than that? What is at stake for these humble people? And what does it take for a normal human being to risk their life to make someone else's dream come true? This book seeks to answer these questions.

Those answers are abstract, dramatic and full of life. In telling these stories of extraordinary successes, and also failures and deaths, we will deal with a variety of ranges: the range of time – from as early as the first-generation climbing Sherpas in the 1930s and 1940s; the range of geography – covering key Sherpa hubs, from Khumbu to Rolwaling, and Makalu to Darjeeling; and, finally, the range of strange characters and their emotions, that can often feel like those from fairy tales. Through these characters, we present the Sherpas' oral history, their life and culture, myths and religions. This book takes you straight to the mountains, and into the homes and heads of the Sherpas.

Chapter I

FOOTPRINTS

Spring, 2019.

As with any other Mount Everest[1] expedition, Tendi's test as a Sherpa really began when he and his sole client left the relative safety of their tent in Camp 4 and plunged into the 'death zone'. Camp 4 is the last point on Everest where climbers can spend the night in a tent. Its flat space can accommodate a few hundred climbers with 'no risk of any avalanche'. It is also the point where high-altitude porters leave food, extra oxygen bottles and other supplies in preparation for an expedition.

Above Camp 4, where the death zone begins, there is nothing but hurdle after hurdle strewn with the footprints of those who have made the attempt before.

'One night of struggle between Camp 4 and the summit always feels like a lifetime to me,' Tendi told us.

Tendi Sherpa, an internationally-certified mountain guide, who has been on the summit of Everest (8,848.86m, 29,032ft) 14 times already by 2022, was guiding a 60-year-old American climber during one of the busiest periods the mountain had ever seen. On the face of it, his challenge was simple: to make sure that he and his client did not end up dead on the mountain.

---

1   The Nepali name for Mount Everest is 'Sagarmatha', literally meaning the head of the earth touching the heavens. The official Nepali name was given in 1956. In local Tibetan dialect, the mountain is named after the Sherpas' mother goddess – 'Chomolungma'. The popular name 'Mount Everest' was given after George Everest led a project measuring the height of the mountain for the first time in 1856. Before this, the mountain also had other names: 'Gamma', 'Peak b' and 'Peak XV'.

But how can anyone ensure anything in the 'death zone', at an elevation of over 8,000m (26,247ft) above sea level? The air does not have enough oxygen and any extended stay deteriorates bodily functions. Add to that the unpredictable wind and snow patterns, and climbers are left with severely impaired reactions – any miscalculation of even a single step can easily lead to death.

Try to imagine yourself struggling to push your body to the limit, when your heart feels like it is exploding and yet its pumping is barely enough to supply your oxygen-starved muscles. Even the supplementary canisters of oxygen are no magic solution. With every available resource, including the bottled oxygen, all that you can manage is to keep your body barely alive and still standing on your feet.

As the clock ticked past 9pm, Tendi and his client took steady steps along the 250-m (820-ft) vertical rock wall called the Triangular Face. Just above Camp 4, the sight of countless climbers' headlamps flickering on the steep mountain walls in all directions made it appear as if stars had fallen on the snow. The moon that evening was wide and bright when viewed from Base Camp, but the climbers up in the heavens could hardly see it, as thick fog, mixed with wind-blown snow particles, floated over their heads. As they walked on, their bodies were steadily warming up, although just thinking about the possibility that they might actually step onto 'the roof of the world' the next morning, sent chills down their spines.

It is not surprising that, with the climbers' excitement and keen motivation, honed through years of preparation, emotional investment in their dreams and material investment in resources, no one on the trail that night had any interest in the mystical atmosphere, the moon or the stars.

Just a few hundred metres away from their tents in Camp 4, Tendi and his client were already barely talking to each other; their breathing was starting to get heavy and they could feel their heartbeats in their throats. Their only mission was to get just a little further ahead. When climbing Everest, this is all you can think of.

The screeching of crampons on the rock and the sound of jumars moving over ropes in the climbing line mixed with the rhythm of the climbers' heavy panting. The windy snow slapped across their bodies and along the face of the mountain.

Tendi and his client crossed paths with some climbers who were just about to arrive at Camp 4 after scaling Everest. Tendi knew that they were running late and wondered what might have caused their delay. They looked to him like experienced climbers.

The time between 6 and 9am offers the best window for arrival at the summit. Summits made after 12pm are generally riskier because the winds become stronger in the afternoon. After reaching the summit, climbers should head back down to Camp 4 as soon as possible, to avoid any danger. For moderately skilled climbers, Camp 4 is four hours away from the top.

Tendi could feel the gravity of the ticking clock.

*

After about one and a half hours of difficult climbing on the Triangular Face, they came across a climber from Mumbai – Sharad Kulkarni – who was completely disorientated and distraught.

Sharad and his wife, Anjali, had separated in the climbing line while ascending Everest. Though Sharad managed to reach the summit, Anjali couldn't make it and, while heading down from the 'Balcony', had slipped several metres from the main line and couldn't be found. The Balcony is a brief resting place between Camp 4 and the South Summit of Everest, offering magnificent views of the lower peaks.

Sharad, who was several climbers ahead of Anjali, had been making unheeded appeals for the other climbers to pause their descent and help his wife, because he believed she was still alive. Tragically, her dead body was stranded in the snow, several metres above him on the same stretch. Sharad was utterly exhausted and devastated. For him, there was no last goodbye. Now Anjali was stuck forever somewhere between the Balcony and the South Summit. Everest had taken everything from Sharad…his crowning achievement was now a thing of grief.

Another few hundred metres above the Triangular Face, where a steep stretch leading to the Balcony began, Anjali's accident had led to a caravan of climbers, all aiming to reach the summit of Everest the next morning, stuck in an idle traffic jam. Energy-drained climbers, panting heavily, crawled like zombies, taking irregular steps completely out of rhythm. This 800-m (2,627-ft) one-way stretch is a knife-edge ridge, where climbers are faced with unpredictable changes in climbing conditions. The wind pattern and snowfall are never stable and climbers have to survive on a carefully calculated consumption of bottled oxygen.

Many blame this queue for the high number of deaths recorded in the mountain in 2019, which left 11 climbers dead in ice and snow. This year in Everest, which marks the exact border between Nepal and Tibet, nine climbers died on the southern side in Nepal, and two on the northern side in Tibet. Ten out of these eleven deaths were reported to have occurred in the death zone.

As the movement of upward climbers almost halted, Tendi stopped to wipe the mist from his glasses. It was about midnight and he sensed a threat to the well-being of his expedition, as, in his own words, 'waiting for the traffic to clear could take a lifetime'. *What if the jam does not clear in another couple of hours? What if they are unable to reach the summit in the wee hours of the morning, as planned? What if they are unable to get down to the safety of Camp 4 by noon? What if they are whipped by strong winds as they climb down later in the afternoon? What if they get stuck at a point where they can neither climb up, nor down?*

In a place with so many dangers, any delay in making a decision can be fatal. Tendi knew that he had to act quickly. Waiting for the jam to clear was simply out of the question. Every extra second spent within the death zone meant wasting precious bottled oxygen; even a minor miscalculation could easily cost them their lives. They couldn't even just return to Camp 4 and 'come back again tomorrow', as the weather on Everest is unpredictable. If climbers are unable to make their summit within the right time window, their chance might slip away forever. Even more critical is the energy factor. A journey through the death zone is not like a trip to the theatre, where people can easily come back the next day if it is fully booked. Every step you take requires ten deep, gasping breaths down to the bottom of your lungs. Your calf muscles are so tightly pulled together that you can feel the cramp in each of your steps.

'Can you imagine a rubber band stretched to its full extent, such that any extra stress or force will easily break it? In the death zone, our body is just like that. We have to keep functioning, but any extra stress can easily kill us,' Tendi said, explaining the torment.

At high altitudes, helicopters don't switch off their engines after landing and are in a hurry to take off as soon as possible, as there remains a constant risk of engine seizure due to the cold and limited oxygen. In Tendi's metaphor, the human body is just like that: 'If you walk too fast or stress too much, you are at risk of collapsing. If you are too slow or rest too much, your engines are also vulnerable, just like the helicopters'. This is a strange paradox.'

In a matter of milliseconds, Tendi cleared away all his doubts. What he was about to do would be no less than a miracle.

As always, Tendi was fully equipped with everything he needed to survive on the mountain. At an elevation where even a chocolate wrapper feels heavy, Tendi, who himself weighs about 70kg (154lb), was carrying almost 30kg (66lb) of extra weight, including supplementary oxygen bottles for himself and the client, extra oxygen regulators, chocolate, dry food, energy bars, water, basic medicines and an ice axe, together with the gear and climbing equipment on his own body. This included crampons, harnesses, helmets, a headlamp, a jumar, a pulley, a belay/rappel device, carabiners, batteries and a shovel. Although it isn't always a necessity, a length of 8-mm (0.3-in) rope, measuring 30m (98ft), is always part of Tendi's expedition gear.

As he pulled out the rope, Tendi fixed it on to his own suit at one end and the client's at the other. But his client, who was already panting heavily, was starting to panic. Their progress had been slowing as they made their way up the mountain, a potentially dangerous way to progress as it means climbers cool down and are exposed to the harsh elements.

The client repeatedly complained that his feet were freezing and that it was getting more and more difficult to breathe. Tendi removed the client's backpack, took out his oxygen regulator and cleared the frozen ice on the inner valve, which had been restricting free exhalation. For his freezing feet, Tendi loosened the client's bootlaces a little, asking him to move his toes and swing his legs to encourage blood flow. He also checked whether the harnesses, rucksack or tight-fitting layers of clothing were obstructing blood circulation in other parts of the client's body.

When the client was 'good to go', Tendi made signs with his hands, suggesting that they should take an alternative route. Left without any other possible choice, the client nodded.

The route up through the death zone, where Tendi and his client were stuck, has a main walking line on the ridges. This is fixed by a team of seasoned climbers, managed by the Expedition Operators Association of Nepal, who go to the summit during the first window every year. Other climbers follow the same walking route, using the ropes and anchors fixed on this line. These ropes and anchors are replaced every year.

Tendi hooked his client to an anchor in the main line, then stepped out of the main line and started overtaking the traffic, carefully walking along a knife-edge ridge, clinging on to the rope fixed to the main line.

Tendi climbed up until the 30-m (98-ft) rope between himself and the client felt tight. Now it was Tendi's turn to stop and attach himself to another anchor in the main line, as his client followed Tendi's footsteps on the alternative route, clung on to his rope and pulled himself up to the point where Tendi stood. Any miscalculation using this technique, known as 'short-roping', could easily kill them both.

'If I had even the slightest doubt that we would not be able to pull it off,

I would have just dropped the idea and thought of something else,' Tendi said. 'That day, I was 200 per cent sure that it would work.'

Their teamwork, repeated several times, meant that by 1.30am, the two had already overtaken the traffic jam. Both were now standing on the Balcony, looking down at the hundreds of climbers who were still stuck in the dark.

Well, that was good, Tendi thought and marched ahead for the final push to the summit that was about five or six hours away.

*

By 4am, both of them were standing on the South Summit of Everest, at 8,750m (28,707ft). If it were considered a mountain in itself, the South Summit would be the second tallest mountain on the planet, after Everest. Immediately after the South Summit, there comes a plunge of about an hour, after which the Hillary Step, a 100-m (328-ft) nearly vertical rock face to the summit of Everest, begins.

After what felt to Tendi like a lifetime, he finally took a selfie of his 13th Everest summit at 6.03am. The view was spectacular that day. The fog had cleared and, with a 360-degree view of the mountains, Tendi and his client could feel the first golden rays of sunlight emerging from behind the mountains to the east. While observing Everest from a distance and different viewpoints on the ground, people often get the sense that other mountains are taller than Everest. However, with standing on top of the world comes an alpine satisfaction that nothing else can really match the might of Everest. Tendi took off his helmet and oxygen mask for a few minutes, clicked selfies and made a short video of himself, expressing his feelings: 'It is an honour to be here again.'

'You see an ocean of mountains beneath you, and even the tallest mountains of the world look like tiny ridges from up there,' Tendi explained. 'You feel like spending hours and hours there, with gentle music and a beer in hand. But not everyone is like Babu Chiri Sherpa – there are limitations and you have to start your descent as soon as possible.'

9

In 1999, aged 33, Babu Chiri Sherpa set a record by spending 21 hours on top of the world without bottled oxygen. He made the summit of Everest his home by even erecting a tent in which to spend the night. Babu Chiri also had a record to his name for a speed ascent of Everest, as he took only 16 hours and 56 minutes to reach the summit in 2000.

'I was only growing up when Babu Chiri made such incredible trips, with all the limited gear and weather prediction facilities of that time,' Tendi said, in tribute to all the Sherpas who paved the way for younger guides like himself. 'I can only imagine what bizarre situations he would have got himself into and surprised humankind with, if only he was alive.'

Also known as one of the fiercest Sherpas ever born, in 2001, Babu Chiri fell off a crevasse in Everest's Camp 2 and died (see page 249).

*

As everything had happened within the planned timeframe, Tendi and his client slowly marched down, crossing all the milestones – the Hillary Step, South Summit, the Balcony and the Triangular Face – in another four hours. Tendi took another selfie at the safety of Camp 4 at 10.49am and crawled into his tent to rest.

While climbing up, Camp 4 is a milestone that marks the beginning of real hardship, as the remaining 800m (2,625ft) of the journey to the top require all of a climber's mountaineering skills, as well as their physical and mental strength. For a guide, the worry is not so much about the summit as it is about returning to Camp 4 safely.

Before heading up for the summit push from Camp 4, Tendi always caresses his sleeping bag, thinking that he might never be able to return to it and sleep inside the warmth of his tent. 'On the day of the final push to the summit, I tend to exaggerate my dreams and perceive them as a bad sign,' he said. 'But even if they really were a bad omen, I would not have the option to stop and not climb.

'As a guide, in the death zone, there is much more to just climbing. Above

8,000m (26,247ft), we have to take care of the clients like babies,' Tendi said.

No matter how fast a climber Tendi himself is, he has to follow the slower pace of his client. Every hour, he has to remind the client to take a moment and drink some water. Tendi carries the water bottle in the inner layer of his suit so that his body heat ensures the water does not freeze. Even if a client is not willing to stop for water according to Tendi's ticking clock, he sometimes makes it happen anyway – he has to become a 'tough boss'.

While climbing, Tendi also constantly pays attention to the client's breathing pattern. Whenever the panting starts to get heavy, he takes a moment to check the oxygen level and the regulator.

Since the oxygen supply is limited, climbers feel divided between climbing slowly and steadily, and increasing the pace, no matter what. As well as how hard it is to physically push your body into thin air in the death zone, any climbers on this trail continually undergo a tortured mental conflict of 'Yes, I can' and 'No, I can't'. Overcoming the challenges of the 'outer' Everest is one thing; above Camp 4, the 'Everest within' is equally hard to climb. Tendi therefore also makes sure to never miss out on complimenting his clients on their 'great achievement'. No matter how far away the peak of Everest is, Tendi constantly encourages his clients, saying, 'You're doing a great job. We're getting higher and higher. The summit is not very far from here. We can make it together.'

Alongside the magnificent view of the mountains, climbers also have to confront some of the most grotesquely tragic scenes one can ever experience in a lifetime, only escalating the psychological Everest within each of them. There are several points where a climber may have to pass by frozen dead bodies – other climbers who had stopped there, or fallen, many years ago – sometimes even having to step or jump over them. Even more common is the sight of Sherpas literally dragging the barely alive, unconscious bodies of their climbing clients, particularly while returning from the summit to Camp 4. For the same reasons that Camp 4 is known as the point where real hardships begin on Everest, while climbing down, it also represents the vital milestone of reaching safety.

Preparation for these dangers begins several weeks before the expedition, when Sherpas gradually acquaint the climbers with all the physical and mental hurdles they may encounter as they climb.

The process of physical acclimatization includes a stay of several weeks at Base Camp, at least one trip to the higher camps of Everest, including an overnight stay at Camp 2, and climbing practices in the nearby trekking peaks. At the mental level, Sherpas work to gain the confidence of their clients on the guardianship of Sherpas themselves, the top-notch climbing gear and equipment, and the fact that nobody is going to be left alone on the mountain.

'Throughout our several weeks of preparation, we make our clients aware of all the facilities, from fixed ropes and teamwork throughout the journey, to the availability of rescue, including helicopters, should anything bad happen on the mountain,' Tendi said.

'Above all, we make sure that the climbers understand that if anything is supreme in the mountain, it is their safety. We tell them how they can back out of the expedition any moment they start feeling unwell. Additionally, in order to gain their confidence in terms of safety, we tell them stories of how we have aborted missions from as high as a few metres below the top of Everest, depending upon the health of the client and changes in the climbing conditions. This is how climbers, including ourselves, build confidence with the mountain standing right before them.'

*

The Sherpas are a community of fewer than 150,000 people living within the borders of Nepal. Their primary home territory is in the Khumbu region, in the foothills of several mountains, including Everest.

While the mountains spread across a greater Himalayan range that forms almost all of Nepal's northern border with Tibet, the settlement of the Sherpa people stretches between the mountains of eastern and central Nepal – predominantly in the Khumbu region.

Most Sherpa villages are located between the altitudes of 2,000 and 5,000m (6,600–16,400ft). When observed from a distance, most of these villages can be found hanging by mountain balconies. The villages appear like fairy-tale settlements, as if painted on a canvas hanging on an urban wall. As you near them, you are welcomed by a view of fluttering prayer flags above your head and a meditative ringing of bells tied around the necks of grazing yaks and ponies. Then come the smiles full of greetings and the warm tea, from the people whose houses you enter.

As you become immersed in this 'fairy-tale' village, you realize that it is, in fact, very different from the one you read about in books. Here, what to the rest of the world are basics, are luxuries. All that grows in abundance at this altitude are nettle leaves. And, though potatoes are commonly grown, they do not grow in sufficient quantities, while millet grows only in the settlements at lower altitude. Subsistence farming at this altitude can never provide enough to sustain a family throughout the year. For this reason, until just a couple of decades ago, much of the struggle of Sherpa people was in ensuring they had enough food for survival. Other basic amenities, such as education and health, were never a priority.

Before 1951, Nepal was under autocratic Rana reign, ruled under ceremonial/powerless monarchs. The Rana regime was abolished in 1951, but the king remained and shared power with the people's government. In 1960, the king took absolute power, dissolving the multiparty system. As a result, the country did not have a liberal economic policy and any unchecked movement of foreigners was viewed by the palace as a threat to the king's direct control. Even though the first successful Everest expedition took place in 1953 – when Tenzing Norgay Sherpa and Sir Edmund Hillary reached the summit – Nepal allowed only one expedition per season, per route. Since only a handful of Sherpas would receive opportunities to take part in these once-a-year expeditions, climbing was never considered as a livelihood. However, democracy was established in 1990 and the direct rule of the king ended. Nepal then opened up to foreign tourists and the country adopted a liberal economic policy, under which the mountaineering industry got to explore its real potential. This was a key turning point for the livelihoods of Sherpa communities living in the mountains. As Everest expeditions increasingly adopted the structure and scope of commercial enterprises, the industry saw rapid growth.

From the 1990s, a larger number of Sherpas began to be regularly employed as porters and climbing guides. While Sherpa men would be busy climbing and trekking throughout the season, Sherpa women started running small hotels, eateries and lodges for tourists (see Chapter 6).

With this increase in their family income, Sherpas were gradually able to seek a better quality of life. At the very least, the priorities of the newer generations of Sherpas were scaled up from their struggle for survival, to a level that allowed for wider needs to be felt and addressed: primarily basic education and health facilities, among other much-needed community resources.

Nevertheless, owing to their extreme geographic and climatic conditions, accessibility and connectivity, for survival and growth, persist as major issues in most Sherpa villages. The majority of Sherpa settlements located at higher altitudes are still not connected to any road systems. Even today, most Sherpas get to fly in tiny airplanes and helicopters before they ever even see a road vehicle.

For their undisputed contribution in growing the Everest industry since the 1990s, Sherpas have been likened to several 'larger-than-life' stereotyped identities. Among other extraordinary metaphors, Sherpas have been labelled 'the X-Men of the mountains', 'the invisible men of Everest' and 'tigers of the snow'.

It is easy to see why many people believe that Sherpas are true superheroes, born to climb and to mastermind the strategy of ascent for other climbers.

Yet, no matter how convincing these assumptions may seem, Sherpas have not actually been mountain climbers since the beginning of their existence and, before the 1953 Everest expedition, were living in a completely different world, utterly unaware of the wonders that were about to ensue, changing their lives in their remote mountain homeland.

Even though it would take more than 40 years for the Everest industry to begin to flourish, the 1953 expedition had already marked the Sherpas' shift from the work of merely surviving, to their mission in spearheading the world's next big adventure.

*

The 1950s ushered in a pivotal time in modern world history. World War II had just ended and the Cold War between the former Soviet Union (USSR) and the USA was reaching its peak.

These two powerful entities were seeking to dominate each other on multiple fronts, including the war in the Korean peninsula and in the race to become the first explorers in space. While these two world powers were tussling, the grandeur of Great Britain's colonial past was slipping away. All over the world, former colonies were falling out of British control and into their uphill struggle to become both independent and stable. It was a challenging time for those in London, who presided over a decaying Empire, to keep its presence felt as a global power.

At the same time, Nepal was undergoing an equally dramatic transition. In 1951, the country made a decisive leap by ending 104 years of the autocratic Rana regime – the de facto rulers in the kingdom of Nepal. The Rana rulers were infamously obsessed with luxury and entertainment for themselves, to the neglect of the needs of their people.

During the 104-year reign of the Rana administration, the country had only a single school in the capital, Kathmandu. In that one elite school, attendance was restricted solely to the children of a few hand-picked aristocratic families. The Rana rulers are also said to have demanded a year's harvest of lentils from land owners throughout the country to construct a luxurious palace, Singha Durbar, which now serves as the Republic's main administrative centre. While the entire country grappled with extreme poverty, a lot of resources were spent on the Rana family's indulgences, such as foreign trips, a handful of cars imported from Europe, and the construction of palaces and statues of preceding Rana rulers and the kings still stationed at different locations in Kathmandu. Any form of protest or involvement in anti-Rana activities, politically or through art and literature, was persecuted and a number of anti-Rana political activists had been either exiled or sentenced to death.

By the time of the first successful Everest expedition in 1953, Nepal had only established official diplomatic relations with the UK, the USA, India and France. Nepal was not yet a member of the UN and passports were not even issued for the use of ordinary citizens.

There was much mystery surrounding the country's uncanny independence from the British colonial administrations that had governed the entire South Asian region – except for Nepal. Many people in India regarded Nepal as the ancient homeland of Hindu gods and goddesses.

The country was still closed to most foreign travel; its people and territories were known only among Indian and Tibetan travellers and traders, as well as by a few British bureaucrats, and limited research scholars who had obtained special permission to enter Nepal for approved pursuits.

In a strange turn of events, Britain, desperate to mark its presence as a global power during the volatile 1950s, was intently planning a mission to ascend to the highest physical location on earth – the peak of Everest.

Their mission was particularly critical because the UK's earlier attempts, both made by an expedition team under the leadership of George Mallory, beginning their ascents from the Tibetan side, had already failed, in the early 1920s. The second failed attempt had cost Mallory his own life and that of another British team member, as well as the lives of seven Sherpa porters, including those from Khumbu. It is still uncertain if Mallory made it to the top in his second attempt, as nobody knows if he died while ascending or descending Everest. The British made several other attempts during the 1930s from the north side and came back again in the 1950s after just over a decade of silence – this time approaching from the southern side in Nepal.

When Britain revived its interest in scaling the world's highest mountain, the Sherpas received global exposure for the first time ever. Somehow, they became part of London's quest to pull off a bold, high-profile bid to literally stand on top of the world.

*

Sometime during the last months of 1952, 19-year-old Kanchha Sherpa was grazing a herd of yaks in his hometown of Namche Bazaar, a village situated at an elevation of 3,400m (11,200ft), which is now popularly known as 'the gateway to Everest'.

Stricken by poverty and with no livelihood options to hand, Kanchha must have been wondering how he would eat that evening. Just then, he saw a couple of Sherpas dressed in western-style jackets and boots, possibly members of a Swiss expedition team who attempted to summit Everest in 1952.

Curious, Kanchha approached them and asked where they had found their outfits. The men told him that they worked for Tenzing Norgay Sherpa in the city of Darjeeling, the other side of Nepal's eastern border with India.

At that time, Tenzing Norgay, who grew up in Thame, a small village near Namche Bazaar, was living in Darjeeling. He had already been part of six earlier attempts made on Everest. In a 1952 Swiss expedition, Tenzing Norgay and climber Raymond Lambert had almost made it, reaching up to 8,595m (28,199ft), an altitude record at the time.

Hearing about Darjeeling and Tenzing Norgay, and having seen these men wearing 'nice' jackets and shoes, Kanchha was easily lured. He reflected on his own life in Khumbu and said to himself, 'I surely deserve better than this. If these men can, why can't I?' For Kanchha, his instant attraction to the Darjeeling dream was neither a result of the lure of adventure nor an expectation of money. All that he wanted was to escape the hardships of

Khumbu and see what life had to offer. That same day, Kanchha ran away from home and, after four days of walking, found himself at the doorstep of Tenzing Norgay's home in Darjeeling.

When Kanchha introduced himself, referring to his father whom Tenzing Norgay knew from Khumbu, it became easy to find a place in Tenzing Norgay's home. For the next three months, Kanchha helped out with household affairs – cooking and cleaning. One fine morning, Tenzing Norgay offered Kanchha an interesting job. He wanted him to take some *khaireys* (local slang for 'white people') to 'Chomolungma', the locals' name for Everest, named after the Tibetan mother goddess of the world (see page 51).

Interestingly, Kanchha did not know, at the time, that Chomolungma was the highest mountain on the planet. He felt instantly thrilled – not just because he now had a well-paid job that brought him 8 rupees per day (US$0.066 by the current conversion rate), but also because he would get to meet pale-skinned foreigners for the first time in his life.[2]

Approximately 300,000 Nepalis of various tribal groups, mostly from the mid-hilly regions of Nepal, had already fought in both world wars for Great Britain. However, their remote geographical location had prevented the Sherpas from having any opportunity to step onto the global stage. Before the Everest expeditions arrived on their doorstep, there was neither possibility nor reason for Sherpa villagers to come to the notice of the world.

Kanchha travelled with Tenzing Norgay to Kathmandu, where he first encountered English-speaking people. Back then, entering Nepal from Darjeeling was a long journey through several Indian cities. The most accessible entry point was the Raxaul-Birgunj border of Nepal and India. After entering Nepal here, the team had to walk several days across numerous hilly mountains to reach the Kathmandu Valley, the capital.

The team of Sir Edmund Hillary assembled in Kathmandu two

---

2   All rupees refer to Nepali rupees, unless otherwise stated.

days after Kanchha and Tenzing Norgay arrived. Kanchha recalls Sir Edmund Hillary as an extraordinarily tall person with brown hair and blue eyes.

The team, comprised of 400 porters from the mid-hilly region of Nepal, trekked all the way to Namche Bazaar. Kanchha remembers at least 25 porters carrying 30kg (66lb) of coins each – the field expense of that expedition.

For Kanchha and many others, the 1953 journey from Kathmandu to Khumbu stands out in their memory as the very first time Namche Bazaar saw so many foreign faces, all at the same time.

If you have ever visited Namche Bazaar, it might be difficult for you to mentally step into Kanchha's shoes and imagine how the village looked in the early 1950s, when it was very rare to catch a glimpse of even a single foreign face.

Nowadays, Namche Bazaar is a busy, popular and 'happening' town. It's a favourite spot for climbers and trekkers to stop and celebrate, both before and after their adventures up in the mountains. This is the place where international visitors can enjoy luxury services like the ones offered in Thamel – Kathmandu's busy downtown tourist haven – with amenities like tourist pubs, clubs, snooker houses, coffee shops and bakeries, as well as everything from cheap tea houses to opulent hotels.

Today, visitors unable to do a rigorous trek, or perhaps eager to get there faster, can take a direct helicopter flight from Kathmandu to Namche Bazaar, enjoy a champagne breakfast while gazing at the magnificent view of the mountains, including Everest, and return that same afternoon or stay overnight and return the following day.

All this, however, was far beyond the reach of Kanchha's imagination. He never envisaged that people could travel between countries that were separated by oceans – oceans whose existence he had only heard about in folktales. Before he left home to walk to Darjeeling, Kanchha was unable to even visualize a four-wheeled vehicle and he had never seen an airplane, not even high up in the sky.

In 1964, Sir Edmund Hillary built a short take-off and landing (STOL) airport in Lukla. Today, dozens of flights operate there on a daily basis. From Kathmandu it is about a half-hour flight to Lukla, from where the actual trekking in the Everest region begins.

Apart from the air route, the Khumbu Valley is completely cut off from the road network and, even today, the trek to Namche Bazaar from Lukla is a two-day journey.

*

It took 16 days for Kanchha's group of climbers and porters to arrive at Namche Bazaar from Bhaktapur, in the eastern Kathmandu Valley. All non-Sherpa climbers and porters were asked to return home, as their chance of being affected by high-altitude sickness was greater. The Sherpas and the yaks would take over from that point.

Some Sherpas, belonging to the village community of Namche Bazaar and nearby high-altitude villages, were hired as porters for three months. When asked about the excitement that the group of Sherpas felt during that time, Kanchha, who is now 89 years old, blushed and wasn't able to say much. His blushing told us all about how he felt at the time.

Despite their joy at having a well-paid job, an opportunity to see the legendary 'white people', be around them day and night, sample strange foreign delicacies and enjoy full stomachs, the Sherpas faced a remarkable series of hurdles.

First of all, although they were born and grew up in the foothills of the mountains, many of them had never been to the base camp area of Everest before. Unlike the British climbers, the Sherpas did not view climbing a mountain as a recreational pursuit, nor as a matter of national pride. For them, the glaciers had been left entirely untouched because these snow-covered peaks were known to be the revered abode of the gods. Moreover, many Sherpas thought that stepping upon the pristine mountain that embodied the power of the mother goddess would be a profoundly disrespectful, even sinful, act.

Nevertheless, motivated by the excitement of receiving 8 rupees per day, and thereby being able to support their families, the Sherpas made the difficult decision, accepted the job requirements, said their prayers and marched away to fulfil their mission.

Prayers are still a crucial part of every expedition in Everest. Just before the beginning of every climbing season, Sherpa priests conduct a massive *kshama puja* (prayers for forgiveness) at the base camp. Sherpas also visit and offer their prayers at Pangboche Monastery – the oldest in the entire region (see page 49) – en route to the base camp from Namche Bazaar.

*

The topography of Everest was as new for Kanchha and most of his fellow Sherpas as it was for the group of British climbers. None of them had any idea how cold it was going to be up there, how difficult the terrain would be or how they were actually going to climb the mountain. All that they knew from the 1951 British reconnaissance of Everest from the Nepal side was that it was altogether possible to take that route all the way up to the summit. The 1951 reconnaissance, which happened in autumn, and was led by Eric Shipton, had figured out ways through the zigzag of Khumbu Icefall to the South Col, mostly by observing the route from several nearby peaks and viewpoints including Pumori. In 1952, the Swiss expedition that almost made it to the summit, followed the same route identified as a potential by Eric Shipton and his team. As the air grew thinner with altitude, the tundra grew more compact until it disappeared completely by the time the 1953 team reached the site of present-day Base Camp – at around 5,364m (17,598ft).

After donning the loose-fitting mountaineering gear, made for a European frame, provided by the expedition team, the Sherpas made their first move above Base Camp.

Only a few minutes after leaving the safety of Base Camp, Kanchha's team came across a chunk of moving ice, something they had never seen before; they didn't know that such things even existed in the mountains. That place, known today as the Khumbu Icefall, is a treacherous 695-m (2,280-ft) moving river of ice, riddled with shifting crevasses, starting at the Lhotse Face at around 7,600m (25,000ft). The Icefall creates a major obstacle for climbers en route to Everest from Base Camp to Camp I, and some portions between Camps I and 2. It has so far claimed a quarter of all those who have died on the Nepali side of the mountain.

Kanchha and his team of Sherpas thought it would be impossible to cross this perilous stretch. 'The whole place was riddled with an extensive complex of snow, which was scary,' Kanchha told us. Despite the knowledge from 1951 reconnaissance and its tested evidence from 1952 Swiss expeditions, even the British climbers did not have black-and-white solutions to the massive problems they were facing at the Khumbu Icefall. 'The more we climbed up the Icefall, we were faced with never-ending riddles of deep crevasses and ice-seracs,' Kanchha said. 'Even the British climbers were taken by surprise, not having imagined they would come across anything like it. At that point, nobody knew how best to get past the Khumbu Icefall.'

The persistent Sherpas took around a week to figure out a viable route. However, there were still several deep crevasses along the way, and the expedition team had two ladders used for bridging the deadly gaps. 'It was not practical to re-use the same ladders again and again on different crevasses, as it was time consuming as well as risky,' Kanchha told us. Despite all their meticulous planning, including the purchase of sufficient supplies of gear, food and oxygen, the British team's calculation of the required number of ladders had failed to match the eternal challenge on the face of Khumbu Icefall.

The team came up with the idea of using tree logs to cross the crevasses. The next problem, however, was that no trees grow at that altitude. The nearest possible location to get the tree logs from was Pangboche, a village at around 4,000m (13,000ft) that houses the monastery where Sherpas say their prayers before their ascent.

For religious reasons, the villagers at Pangboche would not let the expedition team cut any trees in the village, so the Sherpas had no option but to return all the way down to Namche Bazaar to cut down pine trees and then carry them back up to the Khumbu Icefall (it is about a week-long journey from Namche Bazaar to Everest Base Camp). Kanchha and his team carried nearly a dozen pine logs to the Khumbu Icefall and used them to bridge the crevasses.

This is exactly what the designated 'Icefall doctors' do today on Everest. The Icefall doctors are experienced Sherpas best known for identifying a safe route before every expedition season, fixing that route with ropes, ladders and screws, and maintaining and repairing the route throughout the season against swift damage brought about by the shifting ice bulks. The work of these Icefall doctors is one of the most crucial preparatory tasks of every Everest expedition, especially as the safest route over the Khumbu Icefall is always changing, due to the constantly shifting location of crevasses in the slow-moving Khumbu Glacier.

According to recent studies, this movement of ice has increased over the years, due to climate change (see page 273). There are two established routes to the summit of Everest – from the Tibet and Nepal sides. But because of the increasing risks facing climbers at the Khumbu Icefall, some of the top western expedition companies have shifted their route from the one that starts in Nepal, on Everest's southern side, to the route that begins their ascent from the northern, Tibetan side. (More than a dozen other routes have been identified to date, but most of them have never been attempted.)

*

Despite successfully crossing the Icefall, Kanchha and the team of Sherpas still had a long way to go. The Sherpas were told that the higher they scaled the mountain, the higher their income would be; the heavier the weight they carried, the heavier the bag of earnings they would take home.

As Kanchha remembers, the team leader of the expedition, Colonel John Hunt, had made a point of ensuring that the expedition should not be adversely affected due to insufficiency of gear, food or oxygen, at higher altitudes. To implement this, he promised a bonus of 300 rupees for the Sherpas who could figure out an efficient way to transport and cache these essentials at the South Col, which stands at around 7,900m (25,919ft). In those days, the porters were not allowed to go above that point (see page 65).

Throughout the entire scope of their mission, the duties performed by Kanchha and his fellow Sherpas were key to the well-being and success of the expedition. Leaving the main climbers Sir Edmund Hillary and Tenzing Norgay behind, it was the Sherpas who climbed further up from every resting point, with loads of about 25kg (55lb) on their backs. Their job was to figure out the way forward, find another resting camp at the higher altitude, cache all the supplies there and come back again to guide Hillary and Norgay.

When the expedition reached Camp 4, the Sherpas were already exhausted. Kanchha remembers that he and his fellow Sherpas were unwilling to go any further. During three days of rest at Camp 4, Tenzing Norgay did all he could to cheer the Sherpas up.

'He made tea for us, gave foot massages and prepared us to go further up, encouraging us to continue exploring the way,' Kanchha told us.

Three Sherpas, including Kanchha, went up to another point above 8,000m (26,247ft), spending the night there. The next day, they climbed further up and securely erected a small tent and dropped off oxygen bottles, food, sleeping bags and other gear for Norgay and Hillary. Crossing off that last job on their list was a big achievement for Kanchha and his team.

As Kanchha and his small group returned to South Col then further down, Tenzing Norgay and Sir Edmund Hillary were carefully approaching the summit. After spending the night of 28 May 1953 at the very last camp, the next morning Norgay and Hillary went the rest of the way and, in the words of Hillary himself, 'knocked the bastard off'.

To this day, Kanchha still stresses his decisive role in the first successful summit: 'Hillary and Tenzing followed my footsteps and slept in camps that we erected,' Kanchha said. 'I still wonder how they figured out the rest of the way up to the summit. To me it looked impossible from where I had last stood.'

After this, Kanchha went on other Everest expeditions with different teams. But each time he went up there, his journey ended at the last camp and, despite being a pioneer who paved the way for the first successful expedition, he did not get a chance to scale the summit himself. A couple of years later, Kanchha's wife asked him not to go anymore, as they had already saved enough to open a hotel in Namche Bazaar.

Their hotel – the 'Nirvana Home Lodge' – is visible on the top-western end of Namche Bazaar's settlement on a sloped hill. Today, Kanchha spends much of his time in the hotel itself. Due to his own legacy, as well as his hotel's, which is one of the oldest in the entire region, Nirvana Home remains busy most of the time and requires reservations several weeks in advance. During winters, Kanchha lives in Kathmandu at his son's home, but as soon as January ends, his feet start getting itchy with the calling of home.

'I get a lot of visitors at Nirvana Home, and they ask me a lot of questions about my life and my role in the first successful expedition of 1953,' he told us. 'I don't have any hesitation in repeating my story as many times as I can. I find all the nostalgia very enjoyable.'

*

Almost 70 years after the first successful Everest summit in 1953, Everest has turned into an industry worth millions of dollars.

While Sherpas are still at the forefront of every expedition, they are now followed into the mountains by hundreds of climbers from all over the world. Scaling Everest might have been a matter of global pride for the UK in 1953, but it has now become a fairly common ambition for determined individuals from all over the planet, or at least for those with a taste for adventure.

Aside from the unprecedented growth of Everest expeditions into a huge industry, the advancement of Sherpas themselves can be seen on many other fronts. Contrasting with the utterly untrained and naïve workforce of the generation that Kanchha belonged to, the industry now has highly skilled, internationally-certified mountain guides like Tendi Sherpa.

Namche Bazaar, where formerly people barely survived on potatoes and millet, is now a bustling tourist hub where Sherpas cook all kinds of international delicacies in their kitchens. In just seven decades, Sherpa lives have undergone a striking paradigm shift, from neglected tribal villagers struggling for survival, to some Sherpa families running massive expedition companies that operate not just around Everest, but in mountain ranges on other continents, oceans apart.

Even Sherpa families who operated limited, seasonal businesses in Namche Bazaar or other nearby villages that are situated alongside popular trekking routes, have now bought a home for themselves in Kathmandu. Their children can be found studying at the finest schools in the capital, as well as at universities abroad. Many Sherpa families from the Khumbu region, which is still not connected to road networks, have nonetheless travelled extensively. Some have even resettled as far away as Europe and the Americas. A new generation of Sherpas have made their mark in the world, not only through climbing, but also in the fields of science, technology, the arts and business.

Since the growing mountaineering industry in Nepal requires more guides and porters than can be found among the limited number of ethnically identified Sherpas, highly motivated people from other ethnicities have also gradually begun to penetrate the mountain-guiding scene through advanced training. The fame of Sherpas is so prevalent in the mountains today that even the 'outsider' guides are commonly referred to as 'Sherpas'.

Up along the route to Everest, the resting camps that Kanchha and his folk explored after a great deal of hardship, are now jam-packed with climbers of every description, from all walks of life.

What does all this mean for Sherpas in general and for Nepal as a whole?

For Sherpas, the shift is from poor to rich, from bad to good. For Nepal, a region that was largely unheard of less than a century ago, the 'Everest industry' now generates millions of dollars in revenue every year. The tourism industry of Nepal today contributes around 10 per cent of the country's GDP (US$24 billion). Mountaineering and trekking are the two key pillars of the country's tourism. Above all else, Everest is one of the iconic factors that give this country global recognition.

However, the vivid changes omnipresent in the Everest world sometimes pierce Kanchha's heart: 'The changes may be good for the people, but not for the gods,' he laments. 'Can you see the bare black peaks of the mountains in this region? Those used to be covered with snow when I was young. This is a sign from the gods that they are angry!'

Chapter 2

ANGRY GODS!

On the morning of 18 April 2014, a few hundred metres away from Base Camp, Mingma Sherpa steadily walked through the treacherous Khumbu Icefall with around 30kg (65lb) of weight on his back supported by a strap around his forehead. His only mission was to get to Camp I before noon.

The caravan of about 50 Sherpas, including Mingma, had left Base Camp at around 2am. They had been sent to set up tents in the higher camps, dump supplies for climbers heading for the summit and return to Base Camp, only to go back again with more supplies.

When Mingma reached a region called the 'popcorn field' in the Khumbu Icefall, at around 5,800m (19,000ft), where blocks of randomly structured ice over snow resemble popcorn in a carton, he felt like taking a rest. He took off his load and leaned against an ice wall.

One of Mingma's friends had made it a little further up but was equally exhausted. He gestured to Mingma and invited him to join him for a cigarette. Mingma thought it was a good idea and moved quickly to make sure he got a puff or two.

As Mingma approached his friend, there was a sudden BANG...and then darkness.

'Fuck,' Mingma exclaimed, as he stopped in his tracks, flung himself down on the ice and gripped it in fear for his life. The ground beneath him vibrated like a motor engine. He became numb, his ears tingled and his feet felt colder than if they were bare in the snow.

The walking trail in Everest, especially during the early hours, is lit with the unidirectional beam of Sherpas' headlamps, resembling a snake's trail. The thud from behind suddenly obscured this vision. About 20m (66ft)

29

away from where Mingma had stopped to rest, all he could see was a thick storm of snow rising high into the sky.

In a matter of minutes, this stretch of the Khumbu Icefall, which shortly before had been buzzing with the sound of Sherpas, was filled with an infinite silence, broken only by the wind occasionally howling in Mingma's numb ears.

Mingma got back on his feet, jostled into the storm and joined some other Sherpas who were in a panic, figuring out their next move, waiting for rescue to come. As they waited, the Sherpas looked around to check whether anybody could be pulled out alive from the snow.

That day, a massive avalanche buried 16 Sherpas at the popcorn field, turning it into a sudden graveyard. The avalanche swept and hammered the Sherpas against the ice wall that Mingma had leaned on just minutes before – smoking had ironically saved Mingma's life.

The Icefall is usually considered risky because of its moving glaciers and shifting crevasses. However, the 2014 disaster was of a completely different nature – an avalanche dropping down from a higher wing of the mountain. A boulder of ice hanging on the west shoulder of Everest had already been alarming climbers for a long time. 'As we passed through that region, every time we would look up at the bulk of ice and calmly move on,' Mingma said. 'It looked horrible, but I never thought that it was going to kill us one day.' This bulk of ice looming over the popcorn field in the Khumbu Icefall was first recognized as a concern in 2012. That year, New Zealand climbing operator Russell Brice cancelled all expeditions of his company, citing the related risks.[1] Many criticized Brice for 'overreacting' because this kind of avalanche was incredibly rare in Khumbu Icefall. However, within two years, his worst fear had turned into a catastrophe.

Mingma was personally aware of this risk and the measures that were

---

1   Krakauer, Jon, 21 Apr. 2014, 'Death and Anger on Everest' *The New Yorker*. Available at https://www.newyorker.com/news/news-desk/death-and-anger-on-everest

being taken to avoid it. In 2014, the route that Mingma and his fellow Sherpas were treading in the Khumbu Icefall was slightly altered from previous years. Considering the risk, the walking line, which, in previous years, was closer to the wall with Everest's west shoulder looming directly over it, had been pulled slightly towards the centre. However, drifting the route too much towards the centre would expose the climbers to wider crevasses and avalanche threats from the face of Mount Nuptse (7,861m, 25,791ft) on the eastern side. Therefore, Mingma and his fellow Sherpas were confined to a very narrow stretch, making them vulnerable to any potential disaster.

When we interviewed Mingma at his home in Phortse village, at about 3,800m (12,500ft), in March 2021, he could vividly recall his first sight of the 2014 tragedy. He said the bodies of some Sherpas were half-pierced horizontally into the wall of ice, their stiff limbs sticking out just like nails struck into a wall.

This was one of the deadliest disasters ever recorded on Everest. Of the 16 Sherpas killed, three were swallowed into such depths in the ice that their bodies were never recovered.

Long before the rescuers arrived, Mingma and other Sherpas started shovelling the ice with their hands to take out the bodies and see if anyone had managed to survive the avalanche. After pulling out three dead bodies, the fourth one Mingma got his hands on was still just breathing: 'He was semi-conscious, mumbling something that I did not understand,' Mingma said.

Mingma's entire focus was on getting this Sherpa, apparently with a broken leg, to a rescue helicopter, by then operating from near the 'football field', a relatively wider stretch in the Icefall.

Mingma wrapped his hands around the Sherpa's shoulders to lift him up and dragged him steadily towards the football field, which he then discovered had already turned into a dead end. A chunk of ice, released by the avalanche, had sunk by several metres, blocking Mingma's way to the rescuers. The ropes fixed earlier in the route had already toppled under the ice. There was neither a ladder nor any hook to cling on to as they descended.

Had he been alone, Mingma would have taken a brave jump on the lump of floating ice, but the Sherpa dangling over his shoulder couldn't even walk, let alone jump.

Mingma had a few lengths of rope in his backpack. He took it out and looked around for anything to tie it to so that he could fix support for himself and the injured to climb down. There was a dead body nearby, buried upside down with his legs sticking out of the snow. Desperate to save the survivor's life, Mingma did not think twice about using whatever tools came to hand.

'I knew that if the tables had been turned, any other Sherpa would have done the same,' he said.

Mingma quickly tied his rope around one of the legs of the dead body and fixed support. Then, he lowered himself down slowly along the ice, the still-breathing body resting securely under his arm.

Eventually, after a tricky climb, he made it safely to the chopper at the football field. While the injured was flown immediately to Kathmandu, Mingma returned to Base Camp to rest. For days to come, he said he could feel his ears tingle with anxiety as if he'd been in a firefight and a bullet had narrowly missed him.

*

The base camp that Mingma returned to after the avalanche that day was by no means the same one he had left at dawn. Around that time in April, about a month before the summit window opens for climbers, Base Camp is usually in full swing. That year was no exception.

By that fateful morning of 18 April, all the climbers, supporting Sherpas, guides, managers and everybody else related to expeditions, had already arrived at Base Camp and assumed their respective roles.

The expedition season ideally spans a period of two to three months between March and May. During this period, Base Camp undergoes a complete makeover. The otherwise lonely glacier at over 5,000m (16,400ft), which is uninhabitable by any human standards, transforms into a city of colourful tents, accommodating over 2,000 people representing different walks of life.

For foreigners spending two to three months in this nook of the planet, the journey up to Base Camp is an adventure in itself. Let's digress a little and dive into this adventure, for thos who have possibly come from as far as Europe or the Americas to Nepal's Khumbu region.

As you board your flight to Kathmandu, you will start to get a sense of your destination.

The aircraft you board will probably be narrower and the services compromised compared to any previous commercial airline experience you have had. In a country of 30 million, which largely depends on an economy of remittance sent by about 3 million migrant labour workers abroad (India not included), these workers will occupy a significant number of seats on your flight.

After you have landed at Kathmandu's Tribhuvan International Airport, you will go through the tedious check-out process. You may have to wait a long time for your luggage, sometimes even getting into a bit of a bureaucratic struggle with immigration officers. Once your luggage has been retrieved, outside the airport you will weave through the chaotic road network of the city to your hotel.

After spending a couple of days in Kathmandu, you will find yourself in a tiny aircraft that can accommodate only about a dozen individuals. Your destination is the Tenzing–Hillary STOL airport in Lukla, considered one of the most dangerous airfields in the world.

The runway at this airport, which is a brief strip of just 527m (1,729ft) starting at the edge of a cliff on your approach, does not have any overshoot facility. Because of this, even when there is a strong

33

wind, no visibility or any other obstacles on the runway, once an airplane crosses the 'No Go' zone, it's only 'Go Go', with no chance of turning back. Pilots therefore claim that sometimes the survival rule in this airport is that you must be skilled enough to break the rules and improvise. Most flights in and out of Lukla are conducted before noon, as, during the afternoon, there is a high chance of blinding fog emerging up from the Dudh Koshi River, situated at the bottom of the hill on which the airport sits. Considering all the manual judgements involved, pilots flying to Lukla, no matter how experienced they may be in other places around the world, should have flown two years as a co-pilot there.

You are now in the Khumbu region, but your destination – Everest Base Camp – is still about a week-long trek from here. This is when you may start to appreciate that even a tiny country like Nepal, which is hard to spot on the globe, gets bigger and bigger day after day as you struggle to reach your destination.

The trail starts from Lukla, at 2,900m (9,500ft), on a rosy note. Immediately outside the airport, you will come across Lukla's thick market settlement. On both sides of the stone-paved trail of Lukla, there are shops, restaurants and pubs. While some trekkers like to spend one or two nights in Lukla before they head up, most people who land here in the morning leave the same day for Namche Bazaar, which is a two-day journey. On the first day, the trekkers will stop at Phakding or Jorsalle, tiny villages at lower elevations than Lukla.

Soon after leaving Lukla behind, you will enter Sagarmatha National Park, the highest conservation area in the world, of which Everest is also a part. The trail in the national park passes through thick rhododendron and pine forests and arrives at several tiny villages sitting by the Dudh Koshi River. At times, you will get the feeling of walking on a pilgrimage as you come across countless monuments, monasteries and even big rock boulders carved with Buddhist hymns and prayers. These monuments are placed in the middle of the trail with passing places on either side. It is believed that these prayers can bring good energies to those trekkers who put these monuments on their right side while walking.

On the second day, soon after leaving Jorsalle, the last village before Namche Bazaar, you are faced with a tricky uphill trail, damaged in many places by the caravans of mules transporting goods in the region. As you walk, you will encounter a number of these mule caravans, to which you should give way by squeezing against the sides of the path. In places, where there doesn't seem to be any space to give way to the caravan, trekkers are often seen panicking and jumping around, not knowing where to go. Sidestepping these mule caravans means that this uphill hike can take slow trekkers up to four or five hours.

Having finally completed this uphill section, you will be told that you have arrived at Namche Bazaar, but though houses and tiny villages start appearing, Namche Bazaar is still out of your sight. You ask someone, and they point to a hill towards the north, past which you are told is Namche Bazaar. You keep walking, but this last stretch – just 20 minutes of walking – feels like forever. Finally, as you make a turn towards the north on the trail and approach the hill that previously blocked your view, you get your first sighting of your destination. There it is – the mighty Sherpa-land with the same hustle and bustle of a metropolitan city, Namche Bazaar, standing at 3,400m (11,200ft).

Viewing Namche Bazaar from its southern approach on the Lukla side, the settlement looks crammed, with over 300 uniformly-designed tin-roofed houses huddled together in a sloped valley. Near the entrance are a beautiful monastery, an attractive water fountain and a stone-paved trail of stairs leading up to the main settlement area, with colourful prayer flags fluttering in the sky above you. As you sluggishly move your feet on the stairs, after entering Namche Bazaar, you will soon start experiencing a profound sense of satisfaction that you have made it this far. You will pass by happening pubs with music playing inside, teashops, bakeries, coffee shops, gear stores, and all manner of businesses. No matter how tired you may be at this point, you will be restless to get to your hotel as fast as you can, dump your bags and quickly come outside to enjoy the buzz of Namche Bazaar.

Normally, trekkers are advised to stay two or three nights here, to ensure that their bodies gradually acclimatize to the altitude. While in Namche Bazaar, they go for short hikes to a disused airstrip in Syangboche, sometimes up to Khumjung, and to a beautiful museum at the hilltop in Namche Bazaar itself. After two or three nights of rest in Namche Bazaar, trekkers buckle up for an even more adventurous journey.

Soon after leaving Namche Bazaar, you will start treading an altitude near 4,000m (13,000ft). The trekking hereon in is about gaining a few hundred metres of altitude every day. As you move up, the trees will gradually start disappearing and the air will start getting thinner. You will find it slightly difficult to breathe in the initial hours after starting to walk above 3,500m (11,500ft), but will soon adapt. You will tell yourself, 'Even the pine trees have acclimatized to the climate by reducing to dwarf shrubs. I can at least manage a few days with less oxygen to breathe.' Your stops before arriving at Everest Base Camp are the villages of Tengboche, Dingboche, Lobuche and Gorakshep, all of which offer largely basic living facilities.

Unlike in Namche Bazaar, you won't find elaborate breakfasts or an extended restaurant menu in these villages. They have no electricity and, if the hotels are packed, you will have to wait in a queue to charge your mobile phone and camera with solar-powered batteries. The dining hall is warm with a central metal stove burning wood and dung, which radiates heat into the room. In your bedroom, however, all you have to keep yourself warm is an abundance of blankets. You will be sweating all day due to extensive trekking, yet access to a hot shower is a luxury that could cost you several dollars. As the trekkers say, 'Well, you don't bathe when you are in the mountains.'

Nevertheless, if you still feel a connection to what you have come here for, you will realize how close you are to the mountains. After you cross Dingboche – one of the region's highest human settlements by Mount Ama Dablam (6,812m, 22,349ft) – your guide will start showing you the milestones of Everest: *'Can you see the Yellow Band over there on Everest?' 'That's the South Summit, the pointed peak a little below the main summit.' 'That is the area where camps are set on the mountain.' 'There they are! Take these binoculars. There are climbers walking on Everest.'*

In Lobuche, there is a space under the open sky preserved as a climbers' memorial, in honour of those who have died in the mountains. Families and friends of these climbers build a small stone wall in the name of the deceased person, and stack small stones together to give it the shape of a pyramid, making it look like a temple or monastery. Standing before this memorial, in front of the grand mountains that have been there for millions of years, you will be touched for a moment with a strange realization of how trivial life is. Yet, paradoxically, you are determined to achieve what you have come here for. When you look back at what you have left behind, you will feel proud. Yes, proud!

After completing this arduous journey, travellers finally enter Base Camp, sometime around late March or early April. By this time, this unconventional settlement will have already become a bustling hive of activity. Surrounded by snow-capped mountains and foothills, the travellers' first welcome sight will be of colourful tents and prayer flags fluttering above their heads. Base Camp will look like a flower garden planted on snow and ice.

Plunging deeper into Base Camp, there are restless people everywhere; each with their own reason for being there.

As for the Sherpas, they have a number of different roles. Some of them will be porters, carrying goods, gear and supplies all the way from Lukla. Some will be chefs and kitchen staff, unconventionally committed to treat foreigners to the best of global delicacies. Unlike chefs elsewhere, they won't be seen in white clean clothes and a hat. Rather, they will look like any other Sherpa, donning heavy snow boots, thick down jackets and a windproof cap.

Others will be climbing porters like Mingma, responsible for setting up camps, dumping supplies and guiding foreigners up to the summit. They will be doing much of the relentless back and forth along the summit route throughout the season.

Then there will be Sherpa Sirdars and Base Camp coordinators of different expedition companies, continually engaging with the aspiring climbers, dealing with their fear, excitement and all kinds of mental and physical ups and downs. ('Sirdar' is a title given to the head Sherpa in an expedition group and the Sirdar is responsible for managing all the other Sherpas in the team, including high-altitude porters.) While some of these clients will be experienced, others will be novices, all aiming to scale the summit of Everest.

Among all this hustle and bustle at Base Camp, there are medics stationed in several tents for those climbers who might fall sick in the process of acclimatization, and there will be music playing, with DJs putting on late-night parties for those climbers who still have the energy to dance.

*

Making a push for the summit is a process that requires meticulous planning and preparation. The most crucial part of this preparation is the need for climbers to fully acclimatize to the standards of the mountains. In doing so, throughout their several weeks of stay at Base Camp, the climbers are engaged in continuous training, making short hikes every day.

Before the summit window opens sometime in May, the climbers go up to Camp 2 and spend two or three nights there before climbing to touch Camp 3. In this pre-summit rotation, they also pass the dangerous Khumbu Icefall and return to the safety of Base Camp several times.

Base Camp is a unique place; a modern tent city seemingly as remote on earth as you could possibly be, yet connected with so many other places in the world. Climbers will be trying to speak with their families over internet phone calls, most of them sending pictures of the camp and sharing their experiences and stories.

Where there are stories to be told, there will also be friendships to be made. But these friendships will be like nowhere else in the world. Here, an American will be friends with a Sherpa. There will be Indians trying to tell their stories to Chinese; Chinese to Japanese; and Europeans to Asians.

With English as a common language connecting everybody, Base Camp plays host to several mutations of the tongue during every expedition season. The non-native English speakers will mix their broken English with their own native language, while native English speakers will import a host of new terms and expressions into their own vocabulary. As Everest weaves colours from all over the world in a single thread, language and nationalities dissolve under unified friendships and a collective goal. Though every climber at Base Camp will have their own stories to share about their journey and the process of acclimatization – some praising the work of Sherpas; others bitterly complaining that they are too strict – there are two things that everyone present at Base Camp has in common with one another: self-pride and motivation.

No matter how big a climbing celebrity a novice climber may be chatting to, the novice will be talking like a pro, bragging about how hard they have trained, how intricate their gear is and how sophisticated the Sherpas they are working with are. For the celebrity climbers already featured in the global media, Base Camp offers a peculiar niche – they can be in their ultimate element there, among the people who best understand them and their passion for mountaineering.

In the subconscious of Base Camp, if anything runs as high as Everest, it is confidence. Unless stricken to the ground with sickness, people are not willing to talk much about how tired they are or the challenges they face. This overshoot of motivation, however, is not an overstatement or exaggeration; it is simply a necessity to stay motivated in the face of what Everest will bring up as soon as they start climbing.

*

Just as the west shoulder of Everest dropped a massive rock of ice as big as a bungalow down upon Sherpas at the Khumbu Icefall in 2014, Tenzing Gyalzen Sherpa was on his way to Everest Base Camp from his home in Phortse. When he arrived in Pheriche, a tiny Sherpa village at 4,371m (14,340ft) on the way to Everest Base Camp, he heard a group of people talking about an accident at Khumbu Icefall that morning. A rescue helicopter was about to fly to Base Camp and Tenzing Gyalzen was offered a seat on board.

Utterly unaware of the scale of the tragedy that awaited him, Tenzing Gyalzen was looking forward to joining his expedition team and preparing accordingly for the summit of Everest about a month later. But when the helicopter landed at around 11am, the crowd at Base Camp was unusual.

As Tenzing Gyalzen peeked outside the chopper window, he was shocked to see the avalanche's aftermath – dead bodies were laid out one next to another, many of whom were familiar faces. One was the brother of Tenzing Gyalzen's friend.

Only four years into his climbing profession in 2014, Tenzing Gyalzen, who was then just 23, was frozen with fear. He could not get out of the chopper for several minutes. That day, he spent most of his time trying to console his friend who had lost his brother.

Between 6.45am, when the avalanche had struck, and 11am, when Tenzing Gyalzen arrived, the collective mood of the throngs at Base Camp had been subdued and restless. Several helicopters had arrived to help with the rescue, flying the perilous routes over Khumbu Icefall, but they were severely limited in what they could do. (Helicopter operations around Khumbu Icefall are forbidden unless there is an extraordinary situation, as vibrations can trigger the vulnerability of moving glaciers and ice lumps looming over the region.) They could not land at any point on the Icefall, and longline rescue, with people helping on the ground, was the only alternative.

In longline operations, rescuers drop down from ropes hanging from the helicopters. Anyone surviving on the ground is then fixed with the same rope or on the body of a rescuer and flown to safety hanging below the helicopter. At Base Camp, there was a pool of highly skilled rescuers from all over the world. Still, they could hardly help as the route up to the popcorn field where the avalanche had fallen that morning had been completely disturbed. Moreover, nobody knew how the avalanche had affected the moving glaciers or if there would be any subsequent shocks that could trigger another avalanche.

Even in regular times, the moving glaciers of Khumbu Icefall are stable only during the very early hours of the morning before sunrise. The rest of the time, especially when the sun is up, the glaciers are prone to shifting, and those at Base Camp witness avalanches at the Khumbu Icefall several times throughout their stay – they are a regular part of how the mountain functions. This is why people travelling from Base Camp to the summit prefer to leave after midnight.

'The restlessness of Base Camp that day was such that nobody knew the scale of the tragedy. Helicopters were busily transporting bodies, some dead and some alive,' Tenzing Gyalzen remembered. 'And there I was with other people, without any idea of what we should be doing.'

Sherpas who were stuck at the popcorn field did not have contact with their families. 'The families kept enquiring with us, but we simply didn't know whether their relatives were dead or still on the popcorn field,' Tenzing Gyalzen added.

Restlessness in the Sherpa villages was similar, but of a slightly different nature. People in the villages huddled around monasteries and lit butter lamps and incense sticks to appease 'the angry gods'. In Buddhist tradition, butter lamps are widely used in monasteries as an offering to the gods.

The Lama priests, who head the religious activities and offerings, read out hymns from Tibetan scriptures, and others repeatedly counted beads on their *japamala* with hopes of the safety of their loved ones in the mountains. *Japamala* is a string of beads commonly used for prayers in Buddhist traditions.

*

After the disaster of 18 April 2014, the following few days were quite eventful at Base Camp. This revered foothill at the top of the world was the venue for a host of Sherpa protests and negotiations. The entire Sherpa community was in favour of dropping all expeditions that season, demanding fair compensation to the families of the Sherpas who were killed in the avalanche.

The government, however, was primarily concerned about the permits it had issued to foreign climbers and the potential fallout from shutting down the mountain. The then-tourism minister, who had gone to Base Camp to negotiate with the Sherpas, later announced compensation of a meagre 40,000 rupees (less than US$400) per family, and pushed for climbing activities to resume straight away. However, as the Icefall doctors (see page 23) refused to do their job of fixing the routes that year, expeditions could not go ahead, regardless of what the politicians wanted.

The government placated their foreign customers by stating that the permits issued so far could be carried over for up to five years. However, as the expeditions were not formally cancelled by the government, a Chinese team summited Everest by flying directly to Camp 2 by helicopter to avoid the Khumbu Icefall. Many still question the legitimacy of this summit on ethical grounds, though, as the climbers had skipped a significant part of Everest.

That year, as the climbers mourned the deaths of 16 Sherpas, so did Chomolungma.

*

No one can forget 2014. Yet, a year later, Base Camp buzzed once again. Climbers from all over the world gathered there and the Sherpas donned their climbing shoes, all set to lead their parties to the summit.

In a place called Dole, at about 4,000m (13,000ft), on the popular Gokyo trekking trail, the sister of one of the 16 Sherpas killed in the 2014 avalanche was found hosting trekkers at her lodge with broad smiles. In the villages of Phortse and Thame, families of climbing Sherpas were found cautiously praying with butter lamps and Tibetan incense for the safety of their loved ones in the mountains. Despite all that had happened the previous year, the Sherpas, desperate to secure a livelihood after a year of inactivity, had no option but to be resilient and hopeful.

From our base in Kathmandu, we interviewed several Sherpas at Base Camp by telephone that year and they were primarily concerned about mitigating the risks of being at Khumbu Icefall. The number of pre-acclimatization rotations to the higher camps of Everest passing through the Khumbu Icefall region was reduced to only one. The rest of the acclimatization activities were shifted to other nearby trekking peaks like Mounts Pumori (7,161m, 23,494ft), Lobuche (6,145m, 20,161ft) and Kala Patthar (5,644m, 18,519ft).

All these strategies devised and implemented by the Sherpas were to avoid excessive risks at the Icefall for their clients. Nevertheless, the Sherpas still had the job of dumping supplies at the higher camps, doing a lot of back-and-forth through the Khumbu Icefall region. With expedition companies competing to please their clients with luxurious five-star service at the higher camps, loads on Sherpas' backs were ever-increasing. Beyond essential goods and supplies required in the expeditions, Sherpas were found carrying dining tables and chairs.

Many Sherpas were still putting themselves at considerable risk, waking up at midnight and disappearing into the maze of ice in the darkness. Nima Sonam Sherpa, in his early 50s, was one of them. On the snowy day of 25 April 2015, after lunch, Nima Sonam was about to go to sleep in his tent. His friends were glued to one of the continuous card games that went on in the kitchen. It was about two or three weeks before the summit window could possibly open. For this reason, everyone at Base Camp was calm and in energy-saving mode.

Suddenly, at 11.55am, Base Camp shook unusually. At first, many feared another avalanche at Khumbu Icefall. The tremor stopped after about a minute. Nima Sonam rushed out of his tent and, along with everyone else, gazed up at the Icefall.

'Surprisingly, Khumbu Icefall stood calm and composed,' Nima Sonam told us. 'Then I figured that it was an earthquake. In a matter of seconds, when I turned my head away from the Icefall, I saw a massive avalanche sweeping towards Base Camp from Pumori like a football rolling down a hill.'

An earth-shattering bang, as if a bomb had exploded nearby, quickly caught up with what he was seeing. Nima Sonam recalled it as the most horrifying sound he has ever heard.

'The avalanche swept past, cloaking me in a thick storm of snow particles and dust. I covered my face with my jacket, clutched on to an iron stand of my broken tent and tried to stay as steady as possible against the swirling wind,' Nima Sonam said. 'I saw the avalanche destroying everything at Base Camp. The wind, mixed with snow particles and rocks, was so strong that it easily ripped the tents apart, scattering all the goods and equipment here and there. If I had not held on, I would have also been easily swept away. All that I had in my mind at that moment was that I should somehow try to survive. The wind kept hitting me, but I stayed as firm as I could and gripped the stand more tightly. While I was making every effort to keep myself alive during those seconds, I also thought the world was about to end and that nobody was going to survive. The wind's impact was so immense that I blacked out at some point. When I finally regained consciousness, the storm had gone and I was still alive.'

Nima Sonam came to and looked around. There was chaos at Base Camp. The avalanche had swept away most of the tents. Survivors were running here and there, not knowing what to do. Several people – both Sherpas as well as foreign climbers – had gone missing. Nobody at that time could even guess the scale of the casualties.

To make it even worse, aftershocks were still shaking the ground every now and then, scaring everybody to the core. People were literally holding each other's hands to stay upright against the wind.

The 7.8 magnitude earthquake killed at least 9,000 people across Nepal that year. While there are dozens of other fatally risky places on Everest, 22 people died in the 'safety' of Base Camp alone after the earthquake triggered an avalanche at Pumori.

In the immediate aftermath of the quake, Nepal, being one of the poorest countries in the world, was in complete shock. The government just didn't know how to react.

Unlike the Khumbu disaster of 2014, the Base Camp avalanche did not garner as much attention, as rescue helicopters needed to be deployed all across the country. Under such circumstances, Nima Sonam and other survivors like him started their own search-and-rescue operation.

Nima Sonam still vividly remembers how hard he tried to save someone from under the snow. He'd managed to prise him out from the ice. 'Just as I was about to take him to a rescue helicopter, the man succumbed to his injuries,' he said. 'All that I could do for him was cover his body with a shawl.'

*

The havoc of the earthquake and the uncertainty that followed was on a different scale at the higher camps in Everest. When the earthquake struck, at least 170 people were stranded in them. Ten-time Everest summiteer Nima Chhiring Sherpa, in his early 50s, had reached Camp 2 that day. After the earthquake struck, as nobody knew how the routes might have been affected, people at the higher camps stayed where they were, waiting for rescue to arrive.

When the helicopters finally came, petrified foreigners were prioritized for lift-up from Camp 2, while scores of injured were being rapidly airlifted from Base Camp itself. At the same time, Nima Chhiring and his fellow Sherpas were abandoned to make their own way down the mountain.

Left with no choice, Nima Chhiring and his friends started descending carefully.

Talking to us in his hometown of Phortse, Nima Chhiring recalled how terrifying it was to pass through the Khumbu Icefall that day, as he and his fellow Sherpas knew that the moving glaciers had become severely unstable due to the earthquake and its aftershocks.

'More than anything else, I was worried about home. Phone networks were disturbed by the tremor and there was no way to check up on anyone. The same day of the earthquake, after arriving at Base Camp from Camp 2, I rushed back to my village,' Nima Chhiring said. For an average trekker, Phortse is a two-day trek from Base Camp. That day, Nima Chhiring did it in about nine hours.

The earthquake destroyed hundreds of thousands of houses across the country. The houses in Sherpa villages in the Everest region, mostly made of mud and stone, were no exception.

When asked if he was annoyed at not being evacuated by helicopter from Camp 2 that day, Nima Chhiring only smiled, with no words to complain or express his grudge. Instead, there was something else that was disturbing his peace of mind. While he was on the way back home from Base Camp, a series of questions haunted him: *What is happening: an avalanche last year, and then an earthquake this time! Why did people have to die in the safety of Base Camp? There are other places in the death zone and Khumbu Icefall, which are a hundred times riskier! Is there a message for us climbers in these two consecutive disasters? This must be a calling from the mountains to stop this adventure once and for all. No way! What will I do if I stop climbing?*

Disasters like this always take people by surprise, and as Nima Chhiring highlighted, the tragedies at Everest in 2014 and 2015 were mostly unexpected. In 2014, Khumbu Icefall showcased an avalanche, a disaster utterly different than those associated with shifting glaciers and crevasses. In 2015, another avalanche triggered by an earthquake transformed the safety of Base Camp into a graveyard in minutes. Many took this as a sign that mountain climbing was a business that was bound to turn ugly sooner or later. It prompted several veteran climbers and guides, mainly from the Sherpa community, to quit mountaineering forever.

Nevertheless, expeditions are still happening and Sherpas like Nima Chhiring, Nima Sonam and Mingma are still climbing, despite the death and destruction they have witnessed.

Yet, the questions that crossed Nima Chhiring's mind on that fateful day, remain unanswered. Could answers be found in the region's oldest monastery in Pangboche, at 4,000m (13,000ft), on the way to Everest Base Camp?

*

One fine morning, over 350 years ago, three brothers believed to have supernatural powers – Lama Sangwa Dorje, Khenwa Dorje and Rolwa Dorje – arrived at Thame after crossing the Nangpa La, a pass separating the Khumbu region of today's Nepal and Tibet. The brothers, originally from Khumbu, had gone to southern Tibet for Buddhist studies, returning with a vow to establish monasteries in the region.

It is believed that, on their arrival, the brothers had a friendly competition showing off their powers. In his demonstration, Rolwa Dorje held on to a thick iron rod, twisted it together with both hands and turned it into a tight-rope. Then, Khenwa Dorje stacked grains of rice lengthways, one on top of another, and surprised everyone with the balance he could maintain. When it came to Lama Sangwa Dorje's turn, he just smiled, looking at the rays of sunlight beaming into the room through a window. He caressed his shawl and threw it over a thin shaft of sunlight. What happened afterwards shocked everybody in the room.

The shawl hung upon the sunlight, fluttering peacefully in the air, and Lama Sangwa Dorje himself rose off the ground and flew away.

Popularly known as the monk who could fly, Lama Sangwa Dorje hopped from one mountain to the next, carefully taking a bird's-eye view of the Everest region, searching for a suitable place to settle down for the rest of his life. While Lama Sangwa Dorje soared the skies, Khenwa Dorje stayed in Thame itself, later building the Thame Monastery, while Rolwa Dorje travelled to Rimijung and later established the Rimijung Monastery.

Meanwhile, Lama Sangwa Dorje flew all over the region, unsatisfied with several places he visited. However, as he flew past the current Phortse village, Tengboche grabbed his attention. He glided down to this flatland by the Imja River and landed gracefully on his feet.

Although Lama Sangwa Dorje did not choose this place for his permanent residence, in 1919 locals founded Tengboche Monastery there, preserving a rock where Lama Sangwa Dorje's landing had left a footprint. Tengboche Monastery today remains the most active monastery in the region.

Lama Sangwa Dorje once again took to the skies and travelled northeast from Tengboche. When he arrived where Pangboche village is situated today, the landscape simply fascinated him – the flatland, also by the Imja River, is more extensive than Tengboche and a look towards the north from Pangboche offers a magnificent view of the mountains, including Ama Dablam and Everest.

Lama Sangwa Dorje instantly fell in love with the place and came to rest there, gliding down and landing on his behind this time, again leaving a permanent mark. Near Pangboche, Lama Sangwa Dorje found a cave, today known as Nangajong, where he meditated – in body, speech and mind – for several months.

According to Sherpa folklore, during this time, Lama Sangwa Dorje found two peculiar companions. One was a yeti (a Sherpa word for 'wild man of the mountains'), a mythical snow creature that served the revered Lama with warm water and herbal tea. Another was the statue of Gombusungjen, a Buddhist God, who flew from a temple in India and arrived at the cave to meet the enlightened Lama.

During their stay at the Nangajong cave, Lama Sangwa Dorje befriended the God and convinced him to stay at Pangboche in a monastery he was about to build. After Gombusungjen agreed to stay and bless the region and mountains, Lama Sangwa Dorje established the Pangboche monastery right over the rock imprinted with the mark of his behind.

At the monastery, Lama Sangwa Dorje placed a sacred statue of Gombusungjen and the skull of his yeti friend, who had died in an avalanche. An American television channel featured the 'original remains' of the yeti in the 1990s, after which they are said to have been stolen. Later, in 2011, a pilot from New Zealand made replicas of the stolen remains and handed them over to the monastery.

During our conversation with the locals of Pangboche, we observed a subtle unwillingness to talk about the yeti remains being replicas. While the world sees ancestral remains of a mysterious creature whose existence is debatable, the locals of Pangboche and the entire Everest region have a different outlook. They simply like to hold on to their story of how the friendship of the yeti and Lama Sangwa Dorje stands for the sanctity of Sherpa communities and their religion.

Because Pangboche was the place chosen by the revered Lama Sangwa Dorje, the site today holds significant value, not just for the Sherpas, but for mountain climbers from all over the world.

Until his death in 2018 at the age of 87, the most senior-ranking monk in the entire region – Lama Geshe of Pangboche monastery – would bless thousands of climbers on their way to triumphing Everest and other mountains. Despite several technological advancements in the global climbing scene over the last three decades, the blessings from Pangboche have always remained the climbers' steady and reliable source of safety in the mountains.

For climbers passing by, Lama Geshe would offer solace to their anxiety. In his abode at a hilltop in Pangboche, he would receive visitors, look them in the eye and pass on to them much-needed comfort to relieve their fear of the mountains. His friendly gestures, the aroma of incense in the room and the sprinkling of sacred waters upon climbers queuing up for blessings, all re-created the legacy of peace and protection from the times of Lama Sangwa Dorje.

The Lama would also tie a talisman – a sacred yellow and red thread – around the necks of the climbers and give them a few grains of enchanted rice. By hurling the rice grains against a potential threat like an avalanche up in the mountains, the climbers could supposedly save their lives.

While many literally came here for blessings with the hope of supernatural safety and protection, others simply stopped by to observe this customary process of spiritual acclimatization to the mountains.

It is impossible to know or measure the quantitative results of these blessings from Pangboche. What is universally understood, though, is the feeling of well-being and contentment that the climbers, be they Sherpas or foreigners, found in Pangboche at the feet of Lama Geshe.

*

In 2021, when we arrived in Pangboche seeking answers to the existential questions of Nima Chhiring, Lama Geshe had unfortunately already passed away. In his place was the revered Lama Ngawang Paljor, who was carrying on the tradition of Lama Geshe in offering blessings from Pangboche to climbers passing by.

On a windy afternoon, when we entered his room, he snacked on milk tea and beaten rice. He gestured for us to be seated on a bench by the window. We silently waited until he finished his meal, wiped drops of tea from his long goatee, looked at us and asked which mountain we were headed to. He had clearly mistaken us for climbers.

When we told him we were not there to climb, he said, 'There have not been many this year. How bad is this disease in Kathmandu?', referring to the COVID-19 pandemic.

That afternoon we spent many happy hours listening to his stories of Lama Sangwa Dorje and Pangboche monastery. He also told us how the Sherpas regard different mountains as the God of their respective clans and how, intrinsically, the prayers and blessings at the monasteries are connected with the act of climbing mountains.

When we asked Lama Ngawang Paljor how the blessings have failed to be effective against the recurring disasters and the lives lost every now and then in the mountains, he said the deeds of humans have greatly angered the gods.

'No prayers or blessings will work when the gods are angry and want to send us a message,' he said.

When he was younger, before he became a monk, Lama Ngawang Paljor was himself involved in trekking as a porter. Recalling his trips to Everest Base Camp and the Annapurna circuit past the city of Pokhara in western Nepal, he expressed deep concerns over the ever-increasing onslaught and offence in the mountains and, in return, the melting of glaciers.

'Ever since the climbing started, all people have been doing is disrespecting the gods and their values; smoking and drinking in the mountains, littering everywhere, cutting down trees and killing animals in the sacred forests all affect the sanctity of the region,' he told us.

He recalled with disgust an incident that had happened several years ago when climbers had slaughtered yaks at Everest Base Camp for meat. 'They don't kill animals anymore in the mountains, as it is banned these days, but a single act of filth was enough to remind the gods how selfish humans have become. That's what brings bad times in the mountains sometimes, killing several people.'

Everest – 'Chomolungma' in Tibetan – is believed to be the home of Miyolangsangma, the goddess of inexhaustible giving, food, prosperity and abundance. Miyolangsangma is one of the five long-life sisters. They originally belonged to the shamanic traditions of the Bon religion, which was prevalent in the Himalayan region before the spread of Buddhism.

In the 8th century, the five sisters, then known for their demonic activities, were introduced to Buddhist principles by Padmasambhava, also known as Guru Rinpoche, a Buddhist mystic who introduced Tantric Buddhism to Tibet. Because of their extraordinary abilities, the five sisters were given the responsibility to protect Buddhism.

Now revered as the resident goddess of Everest and the entire Khumbu region, Miyolangsangma's figurative manifestation in Buddhist art holds a special connection with the affluence that Everest has brought to the whole region.

In a 2019 article by the late H E Tsem Rinpoche, the Abbot and reincarnate Lama of Tengboche Monastery describes Miyolangsangma as a beautiful goddess with orange skin who rides a red tiger and dons colourful garments made of silk.[2]

The article states, '. . . she holds a bowl of food in her left hand and a mongoose that spits out jewels in her right. She exudes an air of stern benevolence as if requiring that her beauty and generosity be reciprocated with respect and offerings.'

For this reason, for all that Miyolangsangma has to offer, Sherpas believe that climbers should be gentle as they climb the mountain and respect the aura of the goddess with humility and thankfulness.

---

2 Tsem Rinpoche, H E, 13 Jun. 2019. Miyolangsangma, the goddess of inexhaustible giving. Available at https://www.tsemrinpoche.com/tsem-tulku-rinpoche/ buddhas-dharma/miyolangsangma-the-goddess-of-inexhaustible-giving.html.

According to Tsem Rinpoche, at Everest, 'the karmic effects of one's actions are magnified and even impure thoughts should be avoided to prevent climbing mishaps and accidents'.

In the Sherpa community, the first successful Everest summit of 1953 is believed to have been possible only with the blessings of Miyolangsangma upon Tenzing Norgay Sherpa. In his memoir, Tenzing Norgay himself expressed his thankfulness to Miyolangsangma for welcoming him and Sir Edmund Hillary and showing them the route to the top.

Therefore, for anyone spiritually connected with the mountains like Lama Ngawang Paljor, Tsem Rinpoche and Tenzing Norgay, because of all that Miyolangsangma has given to this region, what humans have done to her will not be tolerated.

'All we can do is pray to her, please her and ask for her blessings,' Lama Ngawang Paljor said, with a somewhat disconcerted look.

*

While it's possible to see how humans may have angered the gods, on the other side of this, is the equally valid pursuit of the Sherpas, like Nima Chhiring, who put themselves at the mercy of Miyolangsangma and Lama Sangwa Dorje to alleviate their deprivation. Nobody can better understand the Sherpas' desperation in climbing the mountains than the first-generation Sherpas, who started climbing simply with the hope of receiving some decent food to lessen their hunger, warm clothing offered by foreigners during expeditions and a little money to sustain their families.

Although, as we have seen, many Sherpas have given up climbing in response to the recurring disasters and deaths, and what many believe to be a message from the gods to let the mountains rest, for most Sherpas this is simply not an option and, despite making only a meagre sum of about US$3,000–4,000 per expedition, there is no alternative livelihood.

The climbing industry, which is at its absolute peak today in terms of technology and material safety, is finally recognizing that these pursuits have raised the fury of the gods, and has been making subtle efforts to return to the values of the mountains and, hence, appease the gods.

For instance, while the number of aspiring Everest summiteers is growing every year, there are constant efforts from all quarters to clean up the mountains. Until a few decades ago, and even during the early 2000s, littering was a major concern in Everest, as well as other mountains. Very few cleaning campaigns were conducted back then, and the climbers were not as aware of the harms of littering as they are today.

The government of Nepal has now made it mandatory for all climbers to carry down their litter along with an additional 8kg (18lb) of waste, including empty oxygen tanks, kitchen waste, batteries, food wrappers, cans and faecal matter, among other things, otherwise they will lose their deposit of US$400. The government also pays for empty cylinders, which Sherpas in particular are interested in carrying down. While a number of climbers have been following this regulation, in the absence of proper monitoring, many still do not bother.

In addition to these measures, the Nepal army, with the help of Sherpas, carries out massive cleaning campaigns every year. There are also several charities that are interested in cleaning up the thousands of kilos of waste that have been abandoned in Everest over several decades. The government of Nepal spends nearly US$10 million cleaning Everest every year. However, there are criticisms that these cleaning campaigns are focused on lower altitudes of Everest, while higher camps are neglected. Alongside these efforts, the Sherpa families have been doing all they can to satisfy the gods through their rituals and unconstrained prayers, and, interestingly, the number of climbers seeking the blessings of Miyolangsangma at the doorstep of Lama Sangwa Dorje's monastery in Pangboche is also growing.

*

Rotating a *Mane* (Buddhist prayer wheel) installed in his living room in Thame – a Buddhist gesture of humility to the gods – Sirdar Mingma Chhiring Sherpa, 90, a first-generation Sherpa, sounds somewhat annoyed when someone asks him if the activities in the mountains may have angered the gods resulting in deaths and disasters. As if to make the gods grasp the extent of desperation that the Sherpas are still in, he said, 'I don't think there is any valid reason for the gods to be angry with us.' His eldest son Lakpa Rita Sherpa, a 17-time Everest summiteer, quit the climbing profession after the avalanche of 2014.

Sirdar Mingma's youngest son, Kami Rita Sherpa, holds the record for the highest number of Everest summits. We met him at Boudhanath Stupa, a celebrated Buddhist shrine in Kathmandu, a few days before he embarked on his Everest mission in 2019.

Despite his record number of 26 summits, and his unmatched knowledge of Everest, Kami Rita believes that it is his luck and blessings that have been protecting him to date. No matter the number of summits he has in his résumé, he offers his prayers to Miyolangsangma before each and every ascent.

While others in the queue to the summit are manically documenting their accomplishment in photos, Kami Rita holds back for a moment before putting his last step on the top. The most celebrated Sherpa, Kami Rita gives thanks to the mother goddess, gets down on his knees and touches the ground of Everest with his forehead asking for forgiveness for all his offences.

'To date, I think, she is appeased,' Kami Rita contemplated.

Chapter 3

BECOMING SHERPA

One chilly morning, some 70 years ago, as the snow on top of Mount Kongde Ri (6,187m, 20,299ft) was about to be transformed by the golden rays of dawn, Sirdar Mingma Chhiring Sherpa and his friends, carrying buckwheat and corn grain on their backs, walked past their home in Thame and quickly disappeared behind the mountain.

Their families back in Thame, a tiny village of fewer than 25 households at the foot of Kongde Ri, squinted to discern the movement of Sirdar Mingma and his friends as they grew smaller and smaller and finally disappeared.

At around dusk they arrived at a glacier in the foothills of Nangpa La (see page 47). Acclimatizing to the extreme altitude and cold, the Sherpas camped on the glacier for the night.

As the night wore on and it started getting colder, the Sherpas wrapped their traditional Bakkhu tunics (Sherpa attire made of yak wool) and Docha (Sherpa shoes made of animal hides and wool) as tightly as they could to stay as warm as possible. It would be several decades before the first Sherpas got their hands on down-filled jackets, lightweight, warm climbing shoes and tents made of lighter material than canvas, among other comforts. Besides the heat of their own bodies and their clothes, the Sherpas did not have any other form of heat. All they had to eat were thick buckwheat chapatis and dry chutneys of salt and chilli wrapped together in little handkerchiefs. As Sirdar Mingma ate, he was concerned more about the number of chapatis he had in stock than the cold.

This night on the glacier was the first of their seven days of hardship before reaching Tibet and then finally returning home.

'I don't remember what we did throughout the night, but I do remember getting hardly any sleep on the glacier,' Sirdar Mingma, now in his early 90s, recalled in an interview with us at his home in Thame in 2021. 'It was tough on the snowy days, both to survive, as well as to navigate, as we did not have anything like maps or a compass. Back then, we used to have a lot of snow.'

Early the next morning, they would cross the Nangpa La pass at 5,800m (19,000ft) and climb down to the vastness of Tibet, where they would get to spend nights in Dharmashalas, makeshift resting points with stone roofs and half walls.

For several centuries before the Everest region got a taste for mountaineering, Sherpas survived on their trade with Tibet. They exchanged their grain for salt and brought it back to Khumbu and other lower regions in the mountains of Nepal to exchange it for more grain once again. The surplus of grain and salt sustained their lives, but they rarely had full stomachs.

Much of what Sherpas are known for today – their skills in ripping the mountains apart – can be quite easily connected to how their forefathers sought their livelihood as traders, by navigating through the imposing mountains and finding their way into Tibet.

*

On the fourth day after they left Thame, Sirdar Mingma and his friends finally arrived in the Tibetan town of Ganggar in the Tingri region. They exchanged their grain for Tibetan salt at the exchange rate of 1 *maana* Tibetan salt for 2 *maana* grain in volume.[1]

Although the governments on both sides had issued a special border trading permit for Sherpas and Tibetans, the trade was never fair, according to Sirdar Mingma. First, the glory of salt and its preciousness was such that

---

1   1l (1.75pt) = 1.75 *maana*.

Tibetans never needed to travel to Khumbu for trade, as it was always the Sherpas who arrived on their doorsteps to exchange grain for salt.

Moreover, according to what Sirdar Mingma recalls, the measurement of grain and salt was openly unfair. 'Our grain would always be heaped up like a small mountain in the measuring basket, while the salt was always tightly measured, only up to the designated mark,' he said. 'We were exploited because of our humble circumstances. No one from our groups ever raised a voice against this exploitation.'

Apart from salt mines, Tibet also had a unique tradition of harvesting salt by pouring the brines collected from salt mines and ponds into saline fields and evaporating them in the sun until the process of crystallization was complete. This ancient technique of salt production since the Tang Dynasty (A D 618–907) is still preserved in Tibet today.

Back home, some Sherpas traded with people belonging to other ethnicities, mainly Rai, from the lower mountains of Nepal. While some Sherpas themselves descended from Khumbu to mid-hilly regions around Shorung for more lucrative barter deals, some even made it as far as Darjeeling, about 200km (124 miles) east of Khumbu, across the Nepal–India border. From Darjeeling, the Tibetan salt would make it to some parts of northern India and West Bengal.

Sherpas' trade and employment in Darjeeling can be traced back to as early as the 1880s. In his 1993 book, Stanley F Stevens cites the 1901 Darjeeling district census – the first one taken – evidencing the presence of 3,450 Sherpas then residing in Darjeeling.[2]

Although some of his friends had been going to Darjeeling for trade during the mid-1900s, Sirdar Mingma only went to Shorung and other surrounding mid-hilly regions of Nepal. He recalls his best barter deal was there at 5 *maana* grains for 1 *maana* salt. His friends, who went to Darjeeling

---

2   Stevens, S. F., 1993. *Claiming the High Ground: Sherpas, subsistence, and environmental change in the highest Himalaya*. University of California Press.

and other lower regions of Nepal, slowly explored other areas of trade with Tibet, which included iron and some luxury western watches, then available in India and highly in demand among Tibetans.

*

By the late 1940s, Darjeeling, which was ten days by foot from Khumbu, was becoming increasingly popular as 'the land of dreams' among the Khumbu Sherpas.

This allure resulted from the exposure of some Sherpas to Darjeeling and other parts of India's West Bengal for trade. The stories of railways, vehicles, foreigners, good food and a more manageable lifestyle were more than enough to attract young Sherpa boys and girls. Thus, many Sherpas, including Sirdar Mingma, ran away from home to pursue glories in this Indian hill station, which the British rulers of India also regarded as their summer capital.

In the late 1940s, at the age of 19, Sirdar Mingma left home with some of his friends. He walked for ten days and arrived in Darjeeling for the first time. (Today, travelling from Khumbu to Darjeeling by road takes three to four days, as there is no direct connection. People from Khumbu must journey all the way to Kathmandu, before taking the highway to Nepal's eastern border and then travelling another whole day to arrive at Darjeeling.) Sirdar Mingma recalls his early days in Darjeeling when he was employed as a porter and a railway track labourer. Some of his fellow Sherpas also started pulling rickshaws.

Sirdar Mingma's life took many exciting turns in Darjeeling. One day, after two years in this new-found hometown, he happened to encounter a group of girls speaking the language of the Khumbu region.

He approached the girls to talk and instantly fell in love with one – Pasang Diki Sherpa – who would become his wife, and who, when we interviewed Sirdar Mingma, actively participated in the conversation and served us tea.

Just like her husband, attracted by the tales of Darjeeling, Pasang Diki had left home with her friends, an all-girl group. Later, when people they met in the villages objected to unmarried girls travelling like that, some of the girls disguised themselves as men and trod the rest of the journey as couples.

Pasang Diki considers herself lucky to have met Sirdar Mingma as soon as she arrived in Darjeeling.

'He was already well-settled with a rented room and a daily wage, which was sufficient,' she said.

The two were married within a year, and started living a happy romantic life in their little paradise. Sirdar Mingma also met Tenzing Norgay Sherpa in Darjeeling. By then, Tenzing Norgay was already a big name in the mountain-climbing scene, as he had attempted an ascent of Everest several times with foreign teams.

In 1953, when Tenzing Norgay scaled the summit of Everest with Sir Edmund Hillary, his fame skyrocketed, and so did his stature and influence in Darjeeling. As he originally came from the Khumbu region, Tenzing Norgay had great respect for the Sherpas arriving in Darjeeling. Even before his 1953 summit, he was regarded by many fellow Sherpas as their job-provider – several Sherpas would regularly arrive in Darjeeling seeking the one who was named Tenzing Norgay. They would appear before him, innocently hoping for a better life altogether, without knowing anything about trekking or mountaineering. This connection between Sherpas from Khumbu and trekking jobs in Darjeeling makes the city a little-known epicentre for the rise of Sherpas in Nepal's mountain-climbing scene.

Tenzing Norgay found trekking employment for several Sherpas and was hugely concerned about the well-being of his people in Darjeeling. He even took Sirdar Mingma to a climbing school in Kerala, southern India, and trained him there. Both Sirdar Mingma and his wife Pasang Diki recall Tenzing Norgay as a very helpful person. To check on how his people were doing, he would randomly step into Sherpas' rented rooms in Darjeeling, asking for evening-time tea.

Sirdar Mingma recalls his first experiences of trekking in local peaks near Darjeeling and Nepal's Mount Kanchenjunga (8,586m, 28,169ft) that borders both Nepal and India. At that time, his daily wage was 4 Indian rupees (equivalent to 6.4 Nepali rupees, US$0.05), excluding meals and accommodation.

During Sidar Mingma's initial days of trekking and mountaineering, when he got to wear warm jackets, eat good food and sleep inside a tent, he reminisced about his days of struggle back home and on the Nangpa La trading route to Tibet.

Dealing with high altitudes with loads of supplies and rucksacks on his back seemed too easy, but was nonetheless rewarding, for Sirdar Mingma. By then, he realized he had already become a mountain-climbing Sherpa a long way back when he first crossed Nangpa La into Tibet with sacks of grain on his back.

*

After spending seven years in Darjeeling with his wife and two daughters, Sirdar Mingma started feeling homesick. His parents were growing older and sending messages with trading Sherpas, asking him to return to Khumbu. All this time, Sirdar Mingma had known that Darjeeling could never be his permanent home and, moreover, he wanted his daughters to grow up in their own homeland. Sometime in the mid-1950s – he cannot recall the exact date – he left Darjeeling with his family.

At this time, the construction of Nepal's first major highway still wasn't complete and the country didn't have a public bus service until 1959, so Sirdar Mingma and his family had to travel via several Indian cities and enter Nepal through the Birgunj border point. Birgunj, a Nepali town bordering India on the southern plains, is still a major trading post today. From Birgunj, the family got a lift on a small truck to Kathmandu and then travelled on foot to Banepa, a little town on the outskirts adjoining Kathmandu Valley to the east. Khumbu was 14 days' walk from Banepa and Sirdar Mingma hired a couple of porters of Tamang ethnicity, who lived in Nepal's mid-hilly regions, to help his family on the journey.

*

When Sirdar Mingma and his family arrived back home in the village of Thame, many pre-existing models of Sherpas' lives had started to undergo some significant changes. After the successful Everest summit of 1953, the region had begun to attract expeditions, employing several Sherpas.

The Khumbu region was also slowly getting a taste for trekking. At the same time, while Sirdar Mingma was still in Darjeeling in the 1950s, as China slowly increased its surveillance activities in Tibet, the trade terms were starting to be revised according to Chinese interests. When China took complete control over Tibet in 1959 and the Dalai Lama fled to India, things further worsened for Tibetan and Sherpa traders.

This development essentially brought the trading activities in Nangpa La to a near halt. Around the same time, the easy and cheaper flow of Indian salt had been affecting the demand for Tibetan salt in both Nepal and bordering Indian cities. Moreover, the Sino–Indian war of 1962 widely affected the previous trading connections between India and China, with Sherpas acting as a bridge between them.

'In the immediate years after my return to Khumbu, there was a paradigm shift in our lives. Mountaineering and tourism had begun to emerge as a substitute for the livelihood that we earlier sought through trading,' Sirdar Mingma recalled. 'When China closed Tibet to foreigners, all the expedition attempts on Everest from the northern side shifted to Nepal. That's when we became the first generation of Khumbu Sherpas to start expeditioning on Everest. With this, the future of Sherpa communities and the tourism of Nepal were both about to change.'

Things generally became easier in Nepal after the country opened to foreigners and started issuing visas after the coronation of King Mahendra in 1955. While the first tourist hotels were opening in Kathmandu, mountaineering activities were slowly and steadily growing in Khumbu.

Talking with us for a magazine interview in 2012, Inger Lissanevitch recalled how King Mahendra's father, King Tribhuwan, quickly dismissed any tourism ideas in Nepal, even until the early 1950s. ' "We don't have anything to show to the foreigners. There are no proper roads and shopping malls as in Calcutta",' Inger recalled King Tribhuwan saying.[3]

Inger and her husband Boris Lissanevitch, who ran a hotel business back in Calcutta, had befriended King Tribhuwan during his visit there. The King later extended a special invitation to Inger and Boris, after which the couple decided to stay in Kathmandu permanently. When Inger and Boris came to Nepal in the early 1950s, there were fewer than a dozen cars in Kathmandu, and everything was carried physically over the mountains by porters, as there was no driveable road connecting Kathmandu.

Soon after the couple started The Royal Hotel, the first tourist hotel in Nepal, in 1955, the travel agent Thomas Cook asked if they could manage a couple of days' tourist visas for three groups of tourists travelling the world on the famous Cunard Line's Caronia cruise. No access had been granted in Nepal before that, so the Lissanevitch couple talked it through with their friends in the government and made sure the first tourists to Nepal got visas upon their arrival. The coronation of King Mahendra had already taken place by then, and the first newcomers were even granted a royal reception.

Life magazine ran an article on 28 March 1955, with its lead sentence reading, '. . . the irrepressible stream of tourism, which has upset many a sanctuary, finally broke into remote Nepal'.[4]

*

With the introduction of tourism to Nepal and emerging global interest focusing on Everest, Sherpas from Sirdar Mingma's generation started getting occasional jobs in different expedition teams. It was easier for Sirdar Mingma to find employment in these expeditions, as he had some prior

---

3   Baniya, R. and Bashyal, P., 4 Nov. 2012. 'Boris Ki Rani'. *Nepal Magazine*, Kantipur Publications. Available at https://pradeepbasyal.blogspot.com/2013/01/blog-post_8.html.

4   *Life*. 28 Mar. 1955. 'A cook's tour into Kathmandu'.

experience in trekking and mountain-climbing from his time in Darjeeling. Like many of the first-generation Sherpas we met in Khumbu, Sirdar Mingma went up to Camp 4 several times, but never reached the summit.

Back in the 1950s, the Sherpa guides and porters were only allowed to go up to the high camps near the South Col, from where the foreign climbers would go further up by themselves. Interestingly, none of the first-generation Sherpas ever expressed a desire to summit Everest with their clients. 'During our times, summiting Everest was never a priority among us. We still did not know what records meant and why the foreigners were so obsessed with climbing the mountains,' Sirdar Mingma said. 'We were happy as long as we got paid for our work.'

Sirdar Mingma went to Everest and several other trekking routes throughout Nepal until 1992, when he took retirement at the age of 62. Throughout his career, he served several expedition groups as a lead Sherpa guide, for which the villagers called him by his rightful title 'Sirdar' (see page 38).

For the first-generation Sherpas, including Sirdar Mingma, a role in the gradually increasing number of Everest expeditions meant opening a new avenue for upcoming generations. However, as expeditions were still not as frequent as they gradually became in the decades that followed, for the first-generation Sherpas, mountain-climbing opportunities were still very limited. 'It was not the money that lured us. As porters, we could only earn enough to sustain the basic needs of food, clothes and shelter for our families. More than money, expeditions attracted us for warm clothes, shoes and food,' Sirdar Mingma recalled.

By the time Sirdar Mingma retired, his sons – Lakpa Rita Sherpa and Kami Rita Sherpa – had already been introduced to the climbing business. His elder son Lakpa Rita is a celebrated mountain climber who has been on top of Everest 17 times. He is the first Sherpa to summit the highest peaks in all seven continents, popularly known as the 'Seven Summits'. He took retirement from climbing in 2014 and settled in Seattle, USA, with his family. Now he manages and operates expeditions from Base Camp every season. Sirdar Mingma's younger son, Kami Rita, scaled the summit of Everest for the first time two years after the retirement of his father. By 2022, he held a world record of 26 Everest summits.

To Sirdar Mingma, the gallantry of his sons in the mountains makes him realize how swiftly things have progressed in the mountains. From crossing over Nangpa La on the way to Tibet to his sons making and breaking records at Everest and peaks worldwide, he said, 'Sometimes, I wonder how all these became possible in one lifetime.'

*

Mingma David Sherpa, 32, shares two things in common with the veteran Sirdar Mingma.

First, as is evident, is his name.

Second, are the mountains and the acts of mountaineering, which Mingma David has taken far beyond what Sirdar Mingma's generation could even think of back in their heyday.

Before he entered his 30s, Mingma David had climbed all 14 of the 8,000-m (26,247-ft) peaks across the globe, making him the youngest person ever to do so. With eight Everest summits to his name, the world also knows Mingma David as a fierce Sherpa who was a member of the first successful winter expedition of Mount K2 (8,611m, 28,251ft) in Pakistan in 2021.

K2, the second-highest peak on the planet, is known as a hostile mountain that kills one out of every four climbers attempting it. The 2021 winter expedition, which Mingma David was part of, was so risky that climbing guide and writer Freddie Wilkinson noted in the *New York Times* that it was 'the last great prize of high-altitude mountaineering'.[5]

5   Wilkinson, F., 23 Jan. 2021. A summit of their own: A Nepali team climbs K2. *New York Times*. Available at https://www.nytimes.com/2021/01/23/opinion/k2-nepal-himalayas-everest-mountain-outdoors.html.

With all that he has achieved at such a young age, it is easy to assume that Mingma David must have been climbing since his childhood. Yet, quite surprisingly, his journey in mountaineering started when he was 17 years old. What's equally interesting is his transition from a typical schoolboy at a village far away from Kathmandu, at the foothills of Kanchenjunga in far-eastern Nepal to a mountaineer.

In 2007, when 17-year-old Mingma David left his home in Lelep of Taplejung District to visit Darjeeling during his annual school break after Grade 9, he was sure he was going to Darjeeling and nowhere else.

This was a year after the decade-long armed Maoist civil war had ended in Nepal, costing the lives of more than 17,000 people. As he transitioned from primary to secondary school throughout the conflict, Mingma David recalls how the school mostly acted as a Maoist breeding ground. The militants would organize cultural shows and meetings two to three times every week.

'Before the war came to an end in 2006, my education at the village was disproportionately affected as we would not have any classes in school whenever the Maoists came and carried out their activities,' he said. 'I was happy that the Maoists would no longer be affecting the school as I prepared for the national board exams of Grade 10 that year [then known as the School Leaving Certificate (SLC)], after my return from Darjeeling.'

The SLC is a key education milestone, also referred to by many in Nepal as an 'iron gate'. It is the basic qualification for any menial clerical jobs in offices and, culturally, people even take this milestone as a means to judge a young person's qualities: 'Have you passed the SLC?' For Mingma, therefore, the SLC represented a milestone, after which he would be able to make a basic living and even contemplate higher studies.

Mingma David was honest when he promised his parents that he would return home in less than two weeks and continue his schooling. Around the same time, Mingma's elder sister, who lived in Kathmandu with her husband, had come to Taplejung to visit her parents. When she returned to Kathmandu, her parents asked her to accompany her brother Mingma David up to district headquarters in Phungling, where the siblings would part ways.

The remote village of Lelep, a Himalayan settlement close to Kanchenjunga, is still deprived of a driveable road. Back in 2007, the villagers had to walk about 12 hours to reach Phungling, from where Kathmandu is an overnight bus journey.

While on their way to Phungling, Mingma David's sister suggested that he come to Kathmandu with her instead of Darjeeling. With no way of communicating with his parents back home, Mingma David had to make this decision by himself. As he had no specific plans in Darjeeling, he readily agreed and boarded a bus to Kathmandu with his sister. This was his first time travelling in a vehicle. Throughout his journey on the night bus, Mingma David dreamed about Kathmandu – its temples, roads, buildings, hotels – and the people he would see there.

Mingma David's sister showed him around the city, and the two weeks quickly passed. Finally, it was time for him to return home and continue his education. However, life had different plans for him. As the country took its baby steps into a new transition after the Maoist civil war, many things had already changed or were swiftly evolving.

In 2007, the world's last Hindu monarchy struggled to keep its position, while the rebelling parties, including the Maoists, were adamant about overthrowing it. While Mingma David strolled around the streets of Kathmandu with his sister, the country was preparing for the Constituent Assembly elections the following year. Against this backdrop, an appetite for national representation, which the Maoist war had successfully inculcated among different marginalized groups and communities across the country, had started to come to the fore.

The Terai region of Nepal – the southern plains bordering India – was already experiencing spiralling violent protests and Mingma David's way back home to the remote village of Lelep was due to go through this fire. However, as all movements were halted due to strikes imposed by several groups demanding their rights for national representation, Mingma David was stuck in Kathmandu and therefore would miss his admission into Grade 10 back home. Despite the protests and demonstrations happening all across the country, Mingma David could think of nothing else but the promise he had made to his parents, which was now broken.

*

Three months went by and Mingma David was starting to believe he would never be able to take the SLC that year. His life in Kathmandu was slowly becoming mundane. He had nothing much to do except help his sister's family with the daily chores and go on short walks in the morning and evening. One day, a distant family relative, a trekking guide, visited his sister's home. That visit over lunch landed Mingma David his first job as a porter trekking to Poon Hill (3,210m, 10,532ft) near Pokhara.

Following that, the short treks up and down routes like Poon Hill, mainly in the hilly regions near Mount Annapurna (8,091m, 26,545ft), continued. Consequently, Mingma David started making about 5,000 rupees (US$50) per trip.

As Mingma David was educated up to Grade 9, he knew basic mathematics. Cashing in on that skill, he upgraded himself to 'trip accountant', keeping a record of bills and expenses. Compared to his fellow porters, Mingma David was also skilful in conversing with foreigners in manageable English and taking orders for restaurants.

However, Mingma David questioned his self-worth every time he went trekking as a porter and menial accountant, when he was supposed to have been at secondary school doing his national board exams. He craved something to make him feel more worthy. Driven by this desire, in 2009, Mingma David enrolled at a private school in Kathmandu in order to sit the board exams the following year without actually taking any formal classes.

At the same time, he had been looking out for climbing opportunities in the mountains, an area in which he considered he was already experienced.

He got in touch with Dorjee Khatri, then a three-time Everest summiteer, who came from Mingma David's home district of Taplejung. Dorjee Khatri was also a close family friend of Mingma David's parents. As Mingma David did not have any climbing experience or training, Dorjee Khatri managed to get him in his team as a porter and kitchen staff member in one of his Mount Manaslu (8,156m, 26,759ft) expeditions in 2009.

Manaslu in Western Nepal is known as the 'killer mountain' for its highly technical climbing track and notorious record of deaths.

'That was my first opportunity in the mountains, and my work was supposed to be limited only up to the base camp,' he said. 'But I believed from the very beginning that I belonged higher.'

It was this belief in himself that led to an extraordinary and unprecedented opportunity for Mingma David in Manaslu. One of the high-altitude porters in the team fell sick at the base camp and could not go up to Camp I to dump supplies. Mingma David saw an opportunity and asked Dorjee Khatri if he could take the sick Sherpa's place. Although reluctant, Dorjee Khatri had no other option. He asked Mingma David whether he could really pull off the task. When Mingma David showed confidence, he finally embarked on his first high-altitude trip to the 5,800m (19,000ft) Camp I at about 3am.

From what Mingma David recalls, the journey was cold and lonely. 'It had been snowing for over a week when we arrived, so there was thick snow on the surface, but there were only a couple of crevasses on the way, which made my trip a lot safer,' he said. 'There were no major jeopardies that I had to face. That job was a test that I passed with flying colours.'

His first trip up to Camp I on Manaslu, which took him only about four and a half hours, was also a milestone that earned him the trust of Dorjee Khatri, his mentor who later showed him the rest of the mountaineering world.

Back in Kathmandu, Mingma David faced a dilemma.

First, while he was preparing hard for the national board exams in 2010, he also got basic mountaineering training. Then, he started searching for a better climbing opportunity. The government had marked 2011 as a 'tourism year', with a campaign aiming to bring 1 million international tourists to the country, which provided a good opening for Mingma David.

'I was at a crossroads back then. If I failed my exams, the back-up I had planned was mountaineering and the other way round. But, in any case, I had to make one of these work for my future,' Mingma David said.

If he didn't pass the SLC, and also couldn't make it in the mountains, Mingma David's future was bleak. He would either have to take a labour job in the Gulf or continue as a menial porter in trekking and climbing.

The following year, Mingma David received a call from his mentor Dorjee Khatri. A large group of about two dozen British climbers had made a booking for an Everest expedition from the Tibet side.

For that expedition, the company wanted to hire as many as 70 Sherpas, including porters, kitchen staff and high-altitude guides. After his convincing performance in Manaslu the previous year, Mingma David quickly got a placement.

As a high-altitude Sherpa, he had the promising possibility of guiding clients up to the top of Everest. (In that expedition, one Sherpa guide was entitled to accompany two of the clients up to the top, unlike the widespread practice these days of appointing at least one Sherpa per client.)

Life tests people in strange ways. If he were to go to Everest that year, Mingma David would have to, once again, forfeit his exams. With his life at a crossroads, Mingma David made a brave decision and headed north to Tibet.

*

From the northern side in Tibet, Everest begins at Advanced Base Camp (ABC) at around 6,500m (21,000ft), roughly equivalent to Camp 2 of

Everest from the Nepal side. Owing to relatively more accessible geography on the northern side, ABC can be accessed by yaks, which are often used for transporting goods.

After his first few steps from ABC on the way to a higher camp at the North Col to drop off supplies, Mingma David realized that getting an opportunity and pulling it off were two completely different things. He had learned how to wear crampons and other gear during his basic mountaineering training in Kathmandu after his return from Manaslu. However, when he had to actually walk on snow and ice wearing the crampons and with seven oxygen tanks (weighing 4kg – 8.8lb – each) on his back, he stumbled and fell down several times.

During his first ascent up to the North Col, Mingma David was left far behind by the other Sherpas travelling with him.

'I would start having panic attacks even when another member of my team was just a little way ahead of me,' he recalled. 'I started getting a headache and the nausea of altitude sickness, and as I sluggishly moved up, there were tears rolling down my cheeks.'

Mingma David completed his first trip to the North Col and back to ABC in great mental and physical distress. But, after that, each trip became slightly more manageable than the previous one.

Dorjee Khatri was taking care of Mingma David as if Mingma was his client, monitoring what he was eating to how much water he was drinking, which was a huge source of comfort for Mingma David, as well as helping to boost his confidence.

During one of the regular trips up to Camp 3 – the last camp beyond the North Col and Camp 2 – one of his fellow Sherpas suddenly fell ill. As helicopter rescue was not available at that point, Mingma David and other group members were asked to carry the suffering team member back down to ABC.

The challenge was to return back up to Camp 3 in time to make the final push to the summit. This was his first time in the mountains without his mentor and Mingma David, once again, reflected on the board exams he had abandoned.

'We were all so exhausted, but we hardly had any time to rest. We left ABC and embarked for Camp 3 at dusk,' he said. 'Had I not dropped my exams back in Kathmandu, I might have dropped the summit of Everest that year. Now I had no option but to push myself to the limit and be at Camp 3 and join the rest of my team, no matter what.

'I undertook that as a challenge. I could feel the burden of duty to ensure I returned as I was trusted with the task of getting two clients to the summit,' he said.

All of Mingma David's motivation came from his losses and challenges, and he got back to Camp 3 just in time, but the overnight journey was arduous, without any moments to pause or rest along the way.

'Whenever a colleague overtook me and went a few steps ahead, I would conclude that I was already too slow,' Mingma recalled. 'I would push my feet a little harder along the trail to overtake the member ahead of me, but all in vain. I still kept walking. That day, it was as if my only purpose in life was to get to Camp 3 as soon as I could. If I rested, I thought, I would be resting for all my life, letting a rare opportunity slip out of my hands. I just kept moving my feet swiftly, panting and feeling the pounding of my heart up to my throat.'

The critical journey from ABC to Camp 3 was also like a mirror to Mingma David and, as he walked, he saw a clear reflection of his own strengths: 'There were times when I thought I would collapse. However, falling down would have been too costly as I could not afford to collapse and let that opportunity get away. I pushed myself beyond what I thought was my limit, and still kept walking, without falling down. Then I realized how I could make treading a difficult journey like that a new normal in the mountain-life that I was looking to join.'

The following morning, when the sun rose, Mingma David could see one strong member of the team almost near Camp 2. Mingma David was second in line, while two others were a little way behind him. They arrived at Camp 2 at around 8am. Dorjee Khatri himself had come all the way down to Camp 2 to receive Mingma David and the other Sherpas with warm water and juice. After resting for about an hour at Camp 2, they headed for Camp 3 and arrived there by noon. 'I miss a mentor like Dorjee in every expedition,' Mingma David told us, remembering Dorjee Khatri, who died in the 2014 Khumbu Icefall disaster (see page 29).

That night, while the team rested at Camp 3, a storm broke parts of the tent. 'Others were panicked by that incident,' Mingma David said, 'but as I was naïve about the tantrums of nature in the mountains, I thought it was what usually happens in this place, so I slept like a baby that night.'

The following day, the team scaled the summit and returned safely, and Mingma David's mountain journey began from the top of the world. Standing at the summit of Everest, Mingma David had achieved his biggest dream at that time. His dilemma about his future and career had somehow subsided, as an Everest summit in his résumé would land him jobs in the mountains even if he never passed the SLC.

'Above everything, it all felt like a miracle to me,' he said. 'In any other profession I could imagine, there would always be a higher aim. On the top of the world, I literally had no higher place to be. I still cherish this feeling, each time I go climbing.'

*

In 2013, Mingma David had just descended to Base Camp from his first Nepal-side summit of Everest, when he heard about two rescue operations desperately seeking Sherpas.

A Bangladeshi climber had died somewhere above 8,000m (26,247ft) on Everest. An operation was about to begin to bring his body down. In another disaster on Mount Dhaulagiri (8,167m, 26,795ft), there was chaos. Several climbers had already died in a storm and operations were underway to rescue any survivors. A Spanish climber, along with a Sherpa guide, were still believed to be alive, stuck somewhere between 7,000 and 8,000m (23,000–26,250ft). Unfortunately, the rescuers deployed on the mountain were unable to locate them due to poor weather and zero visibility.

Mingma David had to choose between the two operations.

He chose the rescue of potential survivors on Dhaulagiri. However, because of the bad weather, a helicopter came only on the third day after Mingma David had arrived at the base camp. When he landed at Camp 2, travelling over 322km (200 miles) west of Everest, the missing, supposedly still alive, had been stuck already for four days. As the ground rescue team had no clue about their whereabouts, a longline rescue operation was planned (see page 41).

Mingma David, who was completely new to and untrained for such an operation, should have been the last choice for a risky longline rescue. However, out of all the Sherpas available, he was considered the most eligible as he was the smallest and lightest. Also, he was well acclimatized with high altitude as he had returned from the summit of Everest just a few days previously. Mingma David had no idea how he was going to make it through the thick cloud of snow, torturing cold and invisible knife-edge ridges. Nevertheless, he did not back out.

His struggles started immediately after he took off along the ridgeline of Dhaulagiri, hanging by the helicopter. 'Soon after the helicopter took off, with me hanging on the rope, the wind started hitting me very badly. I had tied my glasses behind my neck, but the wind was so strong that it easily peeled off the glass covering my left eye. My cheekbones hurt with the slapping of the wind as if someone had hit my face with a metal rod,' he recalled. 'The fog was also really thick and I couldn't see anything. I closed my eyes, clenched my teeth and kept praying that the helicopter would not crash.'

The longline flight was only about five minutes, but it felt like a lifetime to Mingma David. 'I have never had a longer five minutes in my life,' he said.

It was already dark when he dropped above 7,000m (23,000ft) on Dhaulagiri near the mountain's last camp – Camp 3 – hanging by the rope. A few minutes after he jumped off the rope and landed, he was joined by a Spanish doctor, who was also dropped there. The doctor was a seasoned climber, who had already ascended 14 mountains across the world. Not knowing if they would actually be able to spot the stranded climbers, Mingma David moved up, carefully taking his steps on the snow, as even his fog lamp struggled to light the way ahead.

'As I started walking, everything suddenly felt easier, as I was in control of my own body, unlike when I was hanging by the helicopter,' he said. Mingma David slowly marched uphill from a point about 200m (660ft) below Camp 3, carefully trying to spot any footprints on the ground. However, there were no tracks that he could follow, since any that had been left from several days ago would have been covered in snow already. Mingma David looked back to consult with the doctor, but was surprised to see that he was no longer following him. *He must have stopped at one of the tents in Camp 3,* he thought. On his own, relying on what he had been briefed on, he just ploughed ahead, hoping to locate the climbers somewhere on his way. After about two hours of searching above Camp 3, he finally saw some movement on a rock face a little above 7,400m (24,300ft) – a shadow cast by his fog lamp.

When he eventually reached the stranded climbers, the Spanish climber had already died, but the accompanying Sherpa was still alive; devastated, terrified and starving, but alive. Mingma David quickly gave him some juice and snacks, and told him that he would now be rescued.

'The Sherpa had already almost lost consciousness. He had no strength mentally or physically,' Mingma David recalled. 'In the dark, I could hardly see his face, but I clearly felt his trembling as I patted him on the shoulder to give some confidence.' After a few minutes of Mingma David's efforts to comfort the devastated survivor, he stood up and the two slowly headed towards Camp 3.

'I held his hand as we walked down. From several days of being stranded on the mountain, his body had frozen, and he stumbled a few times as we tried to move. However, thankfully, apart from mental and physical exhaustion, he had no major injuries.'

On the way, they met other members of the ground rescue team and found a tent at Camp 3 in which to spend the night. When the helicopter arrived the following day, Mingma fixed the survivor on the rope and facilitated the longline rescue. The rescuers headed down further and boarded another helicopter near Camp 2, and returned to the base camp.

Mingma David's first experience in a rescue was later recorded as the highest longline rescue ever conducted. From then on, however, Mingma David kept wondering how the Sherpa whom he had rescued had been able to survive without any major health issues despite spending four consecutive nights under open sky that high on the mountain, while his Spanish client had succumbed.

'I am still surprised how he did not get any frostbite,' Mingma David recalled. 'I later learned that he was totally fine after just two days of treatment at a hospital in Kathmandu!'

*

By now, Mingma David had taken his name in mountaineering beyond just counting the number of summits. Whenever there was the need for a never-been-done-before rescue operation, Mingma David was the name on everyone's lips.

On 19 May 2016, Mingma David was resting in his tent at Camp 4 after summiting Everest. Just as he was falling asleep, he was disturbed by a hullaballoo outside his tent. He crept out to see what had happened and discovered that an Indian climber – Chetna Sahoo – and her Sherpa guide had become stuck near the South Summit, deep into the death zone. Her husband had just arrived at Camp 4 and been told about his wife's situation.

He was utterly devastated, hopeless and helpless. The Sherpa guides of the team were unable to go back to rescue the climbers as they had just returned, and were exhausted and completely out of breath.

Mingma David and some other Sherpas stepped into action and headed towards the South Summit, wholly aware of what it meant to try to rescue someone from the death zone at that point in the day. 'When we left Camp 4, it was already evening, and we knew that our rescue operation was going to stretch very long into the night,' Mingma David told us. When he left Camp 4, the slower climbers were just arriving there, after their Everest summit that morning, while many were still on their way. At the same time, climbers aiming to reach the top the next morning were starting to leave the camp.

The knife-edge walking trails on Everest, which are primarily one-way, are usually prone to crowding at this time. Above all, undertaking a back-to-back journey in the death zone is considered foolish even for the highly experienced Sherpas, so getting the survivors back to the safety of Camp 4 from the South Summit was going to be very challenging for Mingma David and his fellow Sherpas.

It is usually seven hours' walk from Camp 4 to the South Summit. However, that day, as they had to save two lives, the team of rescuers completed that journey in about three and a half hours. When they finally reached the South Summit at 8,600m (28,200ft), Chetna and her Sherpa were still alive.

Chetna had run out of oxygen several hours previously and her Sherpa guide had given her his half-used canister. Without oxygen and movement for several hours, Chetna's guide was starting to pass out, while the oxygen that Chetna had been taking was about to finish.

First and foremost, Mingma David and his friends gave new oxygen tanks and snacks to both of them. Then, after a couple of minutes, the Sherpa got back on his feet. However, Chetna had already given up and wouldn't budge.

'We tried to motivate her by telling her how desperate her husband was at Camp 4 to meet her, but she still wouldn't move,' Mingma David said. 'Only after we mentioned her children back in India, did she show some movement.'

The arduous task now was to bring her down as soon as possible, as there was no way she could survive there any longer.

Only barely conscious, it was clear Chetna could not walk, so the Sherpas employed all the rescue techniques they had learned throughout their careers on Everest. At times, they carried Chetna. When they were themselves too exhausted, they simply dragged her barely breathing body. They had to make sure that the movement was uninterrupted as even 15 minutes of being stationary in temperatures between -20 and -30°C (-4 to -22°F), could easily freeze them to death.

After more than seven hours of rescue, the team finally arrived at Camp 4 at around 5am the following day.

Every single person at Camp 4 lauded the team for all their efforts. 'Everybody was cheering and wanted to talk with us about what happened,' Mingma David recalled.

However, he and his friends, who were on the verge of collapse due to extreme exhaustion, could no longer talk to anybody. As others took over the work of saving Chetna, Mingma David sneaked into his tent and quickly fell asleep with his harnesses and boots still on. When he woke up, the sweat on his feet had already frozen and it took several other Sherpas to help him remove his boots.

Chetna's dreams of climbing Everest made at her hometown, Odisha, a coastal state in India, had somehow been fulfilled. However, if it wasn't for the astonishing skill, perseverance and bravery of Sherpas like Mingma David, Chetna would never have been able to reunite with her husband and later tell her children what she saw from the top of the world.

From a young boy torn between sitting the school board exams and pursuing a career in the mountains, Mingma David has now made a big name for himself in the climbing community. He had already come to the world's attention by becoming the youngest Sherpa to climb all 14 of the 8,000-m (26,247-ft) peaks across the world. In particular, his K2 feat of 2021 proved that he was one of a kind. He also owns an expedition company in partnership with the climbing sensation Nimsdai Purja.

For all that he has already achieved by his early 30s, Mingma David is a unique character. He is non-assertive and softly-spoken, and unlike many Sherpas who speak Nepali with a particular Tibetan accent, his is distinctive. His looks are fairly different than most of the Sherpas too. He has such a lean build that anyone would hardly imagine him making the impossible possible in the mountains. Yet, he has crafted miracles. With a long career still ahead of him, nobody knows what this petite Sherpa has to offer the world.

*

In the late 1990s, Panuru Sherpa, a mountain-climbing guide from Phortse, and his wife Pasang Diki, came to Kathmandu with their young son, Lhakpa.

The Sherpa couple had dreamed of a different life altogether for their first child – a life far away from the mountains – so they enrolled Lhakpa in a Tibetan school in Kathmandu's Kapan, an area with a strong Buddhist–Mongol settlement.

Lhakpa had already attended kindergarten at the local school in Phortse, and should have therefore started his education from Grade 1 at this new school. However, as he still could not recognize the English alphabet, the school admitted him to kindergarten.

Lhakpa's parents returned to Phortse after dropping Lhakpa off at the school. The young boy would now stay in the school hostel for the next ten years, at least, unless he passed the national board exams of Grade 10 (see page 67). Kathmandu, just 160km (100 miles) away from Phortse, was a whole different world for Lhakpa. The distance, that requires three days of travel in flight and trekking, comes with a vast range of diversity, from climate to culture; the altitude alone between the two places differs by almost 2,500m (8,200ft).

As he grew up, Lhakpa gradually got accustomed to the ways of Kathmandu. He made new friends from different walks of life and prioritized schooling and having a good time in the hostel. Lhakpa's focus was not tethered to the mountains and mountaineering, which his father rigorously followed back in Phortse. At the hostel in Kathmandu, Lhakpa was outside the lure of the deadly profession of mountaineering.

For several years while he was in school, Lhakpa was unaware of the recklessness of the mountains and mountaineering. Even until his early teenage years, all that Lhakpa knew was that his father would come to Kathmandu twice every year – at the beginning of spring and towards its end.

At the beginning of spring, his father would receive his clients and arrange for climbing permits and gear, and then, later, he'd come to see off the clients at the end of the season. Lhakpa particularly liked his father's trip to Kathmandu at the end of spring, as he would get to spend more time with him. On top of this, there would be all kinds of colourful chocolates in his pocket! Lhakpa did not realize that these chocolates meant celebrations of successful expeditions.

'I realized much later what my father's spring trips were all about,' Lhakpa said to us in an interview in Phortse in 2021.

To Lhakpa's delight, his father would also show up sometimes during the winter season. He had no idea about the extra-hard work mountaineers like his father had to go through during winter expeditions.

*

In the winter of early 2021, one of the world's busiest trekking routes of Khumbu had turned into a ghost trail. Due to the impact of COVID-19, most of the hotels were shut, and only a few Nepalis and a handful of foreign tourists could be seen travelling in the region.

Moreover, spring was about to begin and the Sherpa community was still uncertain if any expeditions would happen that year. After a nearly 12-hour arduous journey from Namche Bazaar, we arrived in the typical Sherpa village of Phortse, in the lap of the beautiful Mount Thamserku (6,608m, 21,680ft). The village is famous for having an Everest climber in each household. Some of the families even have three generations of Sherpas who have been going to the mountains to seek a decent livelihood.

It was already dark and windy. The snowy trail that we had been treading was slippery and full of mule dung. Taking slow steps on the side of the trail, we clung to anything we could hold on to. We heard drum beats from a *gumba* (a local term for monasteries) in the distance and realized that we were almost there.

Phortse welcomed us with evening-time prayers drifting from the gumba.

Making our way through thick fog with the help of headlamps, we arrived at the hotel of Panuru Sherpa, the respected mountain climber who runs an academy called Khumbu Climbing Center (KCC) in Phortse.

As soon as we entered the home, Panuru's wife and 25-year-old Lhakpa started making us comfortable with hot water, tea and Syakpa, a kind of Tibetan soup. We asked for Panuru and learned that he had gone to Namche Bazaar for some work related to a gumba under construction in Phortse.

We seated ourselves close to the cooking stove used for both cooking and heating the room. As we sipped our tea, Lhakpa, a thin young man with thick spectacles dressed in trousers and a down jacket, was doing the dishes and preparing food together with his mother. While the mother was regularly conversing with us, Lhakpa was silent and went largely unnoticed. We could guess from their movements that Lhakpa might be the son of the family. However, we were only sure about that when Panuru came home the following day and Lhakpa called him 'Papa'.

During our several days' stay with Panuru's family, Lhakpa showed us around Phortse. There are monasteries at all ends of the village, which sits

Climbers queued up in the death zone of Everest. The death zone is an area more than 8,000m (26,247ft) above sea level, at which point most climbers require bottled oxygen. Here delays can prove fatal. Photo courtesy: Tendi Sherpa.

Climbers walking along knife-edge ridges in the death zone of Everest. Photo courtesy: Tendi Sherpa.

Namche Bazaar, the gateway to the Everest region. Photo courtesy: Pradeep Bashyal.

Kanchha Sherpa holding a picture from 1953 Everest summit expedition, which he assisted as a 19-year-old. Photo courtesy: Kanchha Sherpa Foundation.

Tendi Sherpa in action on Everest. Photo courtesy: Tendi Sherpa.

Tenzing–Hillary Airport, also known as Lukla Airport. Photo courtesy: Pradeep Bashyal.

Everest Base Camp. Photo courtesy: Pradeep Bashyal.

The village of Pangboche.
Photo courtesy: Pradeep Bashyal.

The town of Phortse, a two-day trek from
Everest Base Camp.
Photo courtesy: Pradeep Bashyal.

Khumbu Icefall with Everest Base Camp at its foot.
Photo courtesy: Kuntal Joisher.

Lama Ngawang Paljor at his
residence in Pangboche.
Photo courtesy: Pradeep
Bashyal.

Pangboche Monastery.
Photo courtesy: Pradeep Bashyal.

Mingma David Sherpa, who climbed
14 8,000m (26,247ft) peaks before
the age of 30. Photo courtesy:
Mingma David Sherpa.

Nima Chhiring Sherpa of Phortse,
who was stuck between Camp
2 and Camp 3 when the deadly
earthquake of 2015 struck.
Photo courtesy: Pradeep Bashyal.

Sirdar Mingma Chhiring
Sherpa, a first generation
trekking Sherpa, rotating the
prayer wheel at his home.
Photo courtesy: Ankit Babu
Adhikari.

Panuru Sherpa and Lhakpa Sherpa, father and son
climbers on Everest. Photo courtesy: Lhakpa Sherpa.

A Stupa (or Chorten) in Thame on the way to Thame Monastery. These tiny Stupas can be found all over the entire Khumbu region.
Photo courtesy: Ankit Babu Adhikari.

The village of Thame. Photo courtesy: Pradeep Bashyal.

View of Phortse from Mong La.
Photo courtesy: Pradeep Bashyal.

Training gear and equipment at Khumbu Climbing Center in Phortse. Photo courtesy: Pradeep Bashyal.

Jamling Tenzing Norgay Sherpa at his family's private museum. Photo courtesy: Pradeep Bashyal.

Statue of Tenzing Norgay Sherpa in Namche Bazaar. Photo courtesy: Pradeep Bashyal.

Kushang Dorjee Sherpa at his home
in Darjeeling.
Photo courtesy: Pradeep Bashyal.

Kushang Dorjee Sherpa's mother at her
village home in Nurbuchaur of Makalu
region in Nepal.
Photo courtesy: Salina Bhattarai.

Kushang Dorjee Sherpa's home in Nurbuchaur.
Photo courtesy: Ankit Babu Adhikari.

on sloped terrain. Towards Phortse's east, Thamserku, considered one of the most beautiful peaks, emerges every morning with the sun, and gets quickly cloaked in fog before noon.

There are nearly one hundred households crammed together in this tiny village. While most of the houses are modern structures made of stone, steel and wood, there are also some old Sherpa houses, reminiscent of the typical lifestyle and Sherpa economy before the rise of the climbing industry. Lhakpa guided us to some of these houses, upon our request, to meet some climbing Sherpas from the older generations.

One morning, we visited one of these old houses to meet a climbing Sherpa in his late 80s. The two-storey house had an animal shed together with a storage corner for food and supplies on the ground floor. The upper storey was a long, single room, with a fireplace at its centre, and a bed in one corner by the window facing Thamserku towards the east. When we arrived, it was almost 8am and the old Sherpa was still asleep, while his wife was lighting the fireplace to roast potatoes for breakfast. The Sherpa woke up once we'd arrived and, at the very first sight, gave us a long, wide smile, showing us his toothless gums. It was evident that he was elated to see visitors in his home. He quickly put on a jacket, one that he must have preserved from one of his early mountain expeditions.

Though he went to Everest several times in his youth as a high-altitude porter, he does not remember how far he went up the mountain or how many times. He does, though, recall that he retired after he got caught in an avalanche, during which a number of his friends died. However, he does not remember which year or how many people died in that avalanche. When we asked the old Sherpa if he made a good living out of climbing, he proudly said, in a broken Nepali accent hard to decipher, which Lhakpa was continuously translating for us, 'I guess so. I built a new home in Phortse, where my son and his family live now. My wife and I live in this old home. We love it here.'

By now, the wife had finished roasting the potatoes and the old man joined us by the fireplace for breakfast. Before he took his first bite, he coughed and spat on the ash by the fireplace, quickly covering the phlegm with ash, rolling it on the ground like a tiny ball and throwing it in the fire. Having seen that, for a moment, we did not feel like eating anything, but as that would have been disrespectful to the wise souls there, we gracefully munched the breakfast of roasted potatoes with several rounds of Sherpa tea.

There was another old Sherpa who Lhakpa took us to meet, this time in a hotel run by the family. When we arrived, the Sherpa was glued to a game of wrestling on the TV, something that we rarely saw in all of Phortse. The old man had hearing problems and did not seem too bothered about entertaining us, so we quietly slipped out of his room, without disturbing him too much. Another Sherpa who Lhakpa took us to explained how he once went up to the base camp of Everest as a porter, and ended up donning a crampon left there by a climber, simply out of curiosity. A foreign climber in the team was impressed by his enthusiasm and decided to take him higher up.

After taking us to a number of old Sherpas in Phortse, Lhakpa said, 'I really enjoyed visiting these veterans with you guys. I learned things that I had never heard before.'

Lhakpa, usually shy and composed, does not mingle easily, so it was difficult to get him to open up. As Everest is a common topic of discussion in Phortse, we asked Lhakpa if he ever wanted to be on top of the world like his father. He surprised us with his answer: 'I have already been there, done that.' We were startled to hear that Lhakpa had already climbed Everest at such a young age. We decided to save that conversation for a little later, probably over dinner that night at his home.

*

Much of Lhakpa's life in Phortse is occupied with helping his mother with household chores. His day starts by releasing the yaks in the shed out to the ground for grazing.

The home has several rooms for tourist accommodation. The flush in the toilets in the rooms freezes in the mornings, so Lhakpa also makes sure the back-up jerrycans have enough water in all of the rooms.

The villagers keep the seasonal harvest of potatoes in underground storage. Every other day, Lhakpa examines the repository and makes sure the potatoes are okay. As we saw on our first day in Phortse, Lhakpa is clearly passionate about helping his mother in the kitchen and it is one of the few places where we saw Lhakpa kidding around and cracking jokes with his mother.

One day over lunch, when Lhakpa told us that his phone had broken during a training session at the climbing centre, his mother looked at him and said, 'Thank God the mountains have not broken your bones like your phone.' To us, this was a somewhat melancholic statement, but the mother and son burst into laughter.

Lhakpa's extraordinary bonding with his mother made us ask them, 'Have you two always been like this?' Lhakpa looked into the eyes of his mother and said with a hint of wit, 'Have we? You guys left me alone when I could not even walk properly.'

The mother looked at her son and replied with the same candidness: 'We just meant to give you a better education for your own future.'

We realized then that Lhakpa is a small package with many surprises. This boy of 25, who had grown up and experienced the urban life of Kathmandu, was now glued to peaceful Phortse, the mountains and his mother's kitchen.

*

Panuru's family tried as much as they could to keep Lhakpa away from the mountains and mountaineering. However, it was not enough to escape the fact that little Lhakpa, growing up at a school hostel in Kathmandu and later even studying at a higher secondary campus, belonged in Phortse.

Lhakpa's school used to close for a month every year during the winter season so that children from mountain communities could be reunited with their families. As trekking and mountaineering business is rare during the winter season, Lhakpa never got a chance to become acquainted with the mountains as a child, so much so that when climbing came into his mind, he assumed it must be like climbing a vertical wall with ropes from the bottom to the very top.

Once, Panuru appeared at the school with facial bruises, which he could not hide. When Lhakpa asked his father what had happened, Panuru told him that he had been in a minor bike accident. It took several years for Lhakpa to learn that Panuru's facial bruises were marks of injuries from an avalanche, and he had even undergone several weeks of treatment at a hospital in Kathmandu. We asked Panuru if he remembered this particular avalanche, but he replied, 'There was one in 1996, when an avalanche had swept me 200m (656ft) in the snow on the northern route of Everest, but I don't know if Lhakpa remembers that one, as he was too young back then. I think the accident that Lhakpa mentioned must have been a minor one, which is quite common up there.'

As Lhakpa transitioned from primary to secondary level, he was known among his friends as the boy from the village with Everest climbers in every household. As he grew up into a teenager, his curiosity about the mountains was only amplified and he slowly started to understand more and more about mountain climbing. 'I will summit Everest at least once in my lifetime,' he told himself. This all-consuming ambition was something born from his growing self-belief.

During the winter break when Lhakpa was in Grade 8, a group of climbing trainees at his father's KCC in Phortse planned to exercise on a nearby icefall. Lhakpa went there with his father and did some ice-climbing himself for the very first time.

This was a step closer to achieving his dream of climbing Everest one day and, after returning from that break, Lhakpa started visiting a wall-climbing facility in Kathmandu, a common pastime usually done for recreation. It was at this facility that he learned the skills needed on the mountain. Lhakpa was dedicated to developing his mountain craft and, despite the growing distractions of young adult life, such as restaurants and movies, he would always put in hours at the wall.

'No matter what, I never missed my weekly practice in wall-climbing,' he told us.

One day, Lhakpa's uncle presented him with an opportunity to get that bit closer to his dream.

*

In the spring of 2010, having completed his secondary school exams, he had gone with his father to Everest Base Camp to help coordinate an expedition. He was accompanied by his uncle as his father had to go and receive some clients elsewhere. While at Base Camp, his uncle invited him to join a separate expedition on Mount Lobuche East, a relatively small trekking peak at 6,119m (20,075ft).

As Lhakpa had not prepared himself to go anywhere above Everest Base Camp, he was not sure initially. Moreover, he had not had any proper training so far, and there was no insurance or salary.

'You can imagine how unprepared I was to climb any peak,' he said. 'I did not have any climbing shoes, which is a basic requirement for any climber.'

But the opportunity to achieve his first milestone in mountain climbing was too great for him to pass up. Lhakpa called his father in Lukla and asked if he could accompany his uncle to Lobuche Peak. Panuru did not object as he knew Lobuche was relatively safe for a first-time climber. Lhakpa then asked to borrow his father's climbing shoes, which had been transported to Base Camp along with other goods and equipment, to which Panuru agreed. And so Lhakpa literally and metaphorically climbed in his father's shoes and made a round trip to Lobuche Peak – a huge leap towards realizing his Everest dream.

Lobuche Peak is considered a trekking peak that offers a great starting point for mountaineering skills, without too many risks involved, as there are very few crevasses and avalanches. The mountain gives aspiring climbers good exposure to the mixture of rock, snow and ice-climbing, and the use of technical skills, such as rope-climbing, and proper mountaineering gear, such as climbing suits and crampons. Some expedition companies even include Lobuche Peak in their trekking itineraries.

Lhakpa did not face any hurdles during his Lobuche summit. 'I had thought it would be difficult at some point,' Lhakpa said, 'but it was a piece of cake; not too exhausting. The summit of Lobuche Peak intensified my mountain dreams, and I became more determined than ever to climb Everest one day.'

Back in Kathmandu, Lhakpa joined the higher secondary school and started attending the Nepal Mountain Academy (NMA) for a certified basic mountaineering course. By now, he had moved out of the hostel and was living with a relative. Lhakpa recalls how disconnected he was from his studies, instead wanting to either hang out with friends or learn mountaineering.

'After my Lobuche summit in 2010, all that I had in my mind was mountains. The school I was in did not have anything to offer to satisfy my actual urges,' he said. 'With each passing day, I started missing the mountains more and more.'

This brought him back to Phortse, to his best possible mountaineering teacher...his father.

Although Panuru had initially planned for a different life for his son, he accepted the reality when he sensed Lhakpa's desperation for the mountains. He trained his son at his own climbing school – including advanced wall-climbing, rock climbing, use of gear in the mountains, rope fixing, rescue operations, ice-climbing, and much more – and made a competent climber out of him.

After the ban on Everest expeditions due to the disasters in 2014 and 2015 (see chapter 2), Panuru finally offered Lhakpa his big break. He asked his son to join his team on an Everest expedition from the northern side in Tibet.

Initially, Panuru had planned to shadow his son on the mountain, guide him thoroughly and, above all, ensure his safety. However, things don't often go as planned in the mountains.

When the time came for the final summit push, Panuru could not shadow his son in the death zone, as he had to attend an emergency at ABC. As things had already gone too far, there was no way Panuru could retract his son from the death zone without going for the summit. However, Lhakpa was not as anxious as his father. He kept going higher and higher, deeper and deeper.

'I had worked very hard to prepare myself for this summit and, with or without my father, I had to do it anyway,' Lhakpa told us. 'It was definitely exhausting in the death zone. At times, the knife-edge ridges on the mountain scared me to the bone. However, I just kept looking upward, and didn't look back until I was standing at the summit.'

Finally, at the age of 19, as Lhakpa lived his school dream, he also became another son of a climber from Phortse to have made it to the summit of Everest. Since then, he has climbed Everest twice, the last time being in the spring of 2021. He has also climbed several other mountains including the highly technical Ama Dablam and Cho Oyu (8,188m, 26,864ft).

*

We asked Lhakpa if he ever missed his life in Kathmandu. He had a simple answer to that – not that much.

He added, 'Here in Phortse, I may not be going to the mountains every day, but I am closer to it. It is not the same in Kathmandu.'

Rather than thinking too much about all that he may be missing, Lhakpa is focused on developing his own understanding of the mountains. In his view, keeping the body comfortable and knowing one's own limit in climbing is the key to becoming a good mountaineer.

In December 2021, we met Lhakpa again, in Kathmandu. This time, the otherwise reserved Lhakpa seemed more comfortable with us, thanks to a series of phone calls and social media chats we had had in the run up to our visit.

When we met him, Nimsdai Purja was the talk of the town, with a Netflix documentary about his summits of fourteen 8,000-m (26,247-ft) peaks around the world. Lhakpa had watched the documentary the previous day, and shared his thoughts with us: 'Nimsdai says nobody can beat him in the mountains.' Lhakpa has his own reservations about that: 'Mountains and the act of climbing are not about beating anybody. Moreover, we are still young and in the game,' he said.

He had come to Kathmandu to purchase a mountain bike, which he wanted to take all the way to Phortse. He had his own plans with the bicycle. 'I am planning to summit Manaslu, descend on a snowboard, then cycle all the way to Kathmandu, possibly next year, if everything goes well,' he told us. Lhakpa had grown up skateboarding in the streets of Kathmandu and is fairly skilled on a snowboard as well. Descending Manaslu was a dream that Lhakpa had woven together with one of his friends from Phortse, who had unfortunately passed away during ice-climbing training near the village. At his young age, with his mountaineering career yet to flourish, Lhakpa is tremendously burdened by this dream and is determined to achieve it one day, for his friend. 'I will start cycling and preparing myself for this mission this year,' Lhakpa said.

However, Lhakpa is yet to share his mission with his father Panuru, who at the time Lhakpa met us in Kathmandu, was in North Carolina, in the US. Panuru had been using the mountaineering off-season in Nepal as an opportunity to expand his network in the US, and also make some extra money by guiding his previous clients to different trekking and mountaineering locations there. He had been living with one of his sponsors, helping him with the household chores as well.

Lhakpa showed us some video footage of his father skiing in the US. 'He is teasing me all the time by sending me these little clips,' he chuckled.

'I don't know how he will react when I share my plans about the snowboard descent from Manaslu.'

After Panuru returned from the US in January 2022, we met him in Kathmandu at a restaurant with a wall-climbing facility. When we arrived, Panuru was hanging on the wall like Spiderman. The city's youngsters seemed awestruck with his skills, not knowing that Panuru was then a 16-time Everest summiteer (he summited again in the 2022 climbing season). His daughter, Lhakpa's younger sister, also named Pasang, was there too, clapping as her father crawled up a difficult section on the wall. Herself a roll ball player who also has an interest in basketball, Pasang studies at a college in Kathmandu. The father and daughter were due to leave for Phortse the day after we met them. Ice-climbing training was going to kick off later that month and she would be one of Panuru's students this time.

Mindful not to reveal Lhakpa's outrageous Manaslu plans, we asked Panuru what he felt about his son's climbing skills. 'I am his teacher, and I know all his strengths and weaknesses. He has a lot to learn, but at this stage, I can be confident that he is a better climber than myself,' Panuru said. 'He is young, passionate and full of technical skills. He is a complete climber and can excel if he keeps up with his passion.'

Panuru recalled how he prepared his son in the mountains during some of his initial ascents. 'My son was a lucky student, for I was there as his mentor in the death zone of Everest,' Panuru said, recollecting all the simple questions Lhakpa would ask in the tent before sleeping: *Papa, how long will it take tomorrow? Will it get colder than this, Papa? How is the way? Is it too difficult?*

Beyond all Lhakpa's curiosities, Panuru was also constantly reassuring him by telling him about the rescue facilities and back-up support that the climbers had in the mountains, in case of a disaster or an accident.

'The first and second time we were in the death zone together, it was difficult for him. When he was too exhausted, I helped him by carrying his backpack,' Panuru said. 'But he has never been a disappointment. He climbs as if he has it in his blood.'

We asked Panuru if he wanted his son to pursue world records by doing unusual stunts in the mountains. 'I have played it safe all my life and I want my son to do the same. That is the most mature outlook one can take in climbing, as nobody can challenge the magnificence of the mountains.'

Panuru is a modest Sherpa who does not really believe in the illusion of world records. For the safety of his clients, he has aborted missions several times from even just a few hundred metres below the top of Everest. 'Safety is the key. If you are alive, you can always come back next time,' he told us.

When we met Panuru, Lhakpa was off on an advanced mountaineering training course in Rolwaling Valley. Still unaware of his son's plans to descend Manaslu by snowboard, Panuru said, 'He has bought a snowboard and a bicycle. I don't know what he is up to. I have told him that he can take the bicycle, but not the snowboard. Snowboarding is enjoyable, but risky, and if he starts snowboarding, he might lose his focus on climbing.' When asked if he would take Lhakpa's bicycle to Phortse the following day, Panuru laughed and said, 'It's all his load and I am not going to take it. Let him carry that all by himself.'

Desperate to break the status quo of safe, modest and mature climbing his father has been teaching climbers all his life, Lhakpa wants to try new things, strengthen his résumé with a higher number of summits, become an Internationally Certified Mountain Guide (IMG) and travel the world. On top of all this, he wishes to continue helping his mother in the kitchen, where both the windows offer him a magnificent view of the mountains.

*

As the global interest in mountaineering continues to grow, so too do the dreams and ambitions of the Sherpas. From Sirdar Mingma becoming one of the first-generation climbing Sherpas driven by the need for survival and a livelihood, to Mingma David giving it his all to become well-known across the world and Lhakpa taking his baby steps into the world of mountaineering, Sherpas continue to be drawn to the mountains, one generation after another, yet for vastly different reasons. Even those Gen-Zers – like Sirdar Mingma's grandchildren – who may not be willing to risk their lives and suffer in the mountains and whose parents have tried to divert their interests away from climbing, may well get the urge one day, pack their bags and stand on top of Everest, for climbing is simply in their blood.

Chapter 4

REVISITING TENZING NORGAY

In downtown Darjeeling, by a narrow British-era road leading to a highway connecting other nearby districts, there is a house with a street-facing wall that has a circular stone badge embossed with the date – 29 May 1953. That's when Tenzing Norgay Sherpa and Sir Edmund Hillary reached one of the planet's final frontiers – the top of Everest. The badge has a carving of Everest detailed with camps set throughout the route; the Nepalese, Indian, British and the United Nations' flags hoisted together on top; images of two ice axes crossed over one another forming an 'X' and a climbing rope. This is the house of Tenzing Norgay, the game changer in the world of mountain climbing. With his feat, the little-known tribe of Sherpas discovered their unique purpose in mountaineering, which continues to shape the global climbing scene even today. Tenzing's house is a common landmark for local taxi drivers and tourists. Some passers-by even take a moment or two to quickly click their picture with this house in the background.

This small Indian hill town is often characterized by its 19th-century British infrastructure, a northern view of the mighty Kanchenjunga – the world's third highest peak – the still-functioning steam engine railway line that attracts tourists from all over the world, and several lush tea estates hundreds of years old. Among Darjeeling's identities is the legacy of Tenzing, who is dearly remembered here as an undisputed hero. His glories are proudly talked about, and preserved so well, that his Darjeeling connections continue to shape how people throughout the world perceive the work and glories of Sherpas.

*

One morning in September 2021, we arrived at the premises of the Gymkhana Club, a government-run elite sports facility in Darjeeling. As we slowly entered one of the covered halls of this British-built century-old heritage building, where a game of badminton was underway, someone on the court called to us, 'Are you looking for something?'

'Jamling *dai*[1],' we replied, unsure if the man would know the person we were looking for.

A tall man with his hair in a ponytail, who was walking towards the exit door of the hall, looked back at us and volunteered: 'He is at the tennis court. Follow me. I am also headed there.' Across the street, we followed the man through a small iron gate to the tennis court. There were not many people there. One man, stretching, immediately caught our eye.

We recognized Jamling Tenzing Norgay Sherpa from the very first look, not because we had met him before, but because we had seen Tenzing, his father, several times in photographs and documentaries. The most popular images of Tenzing are characterized by his typical Sherpa eyes, the thin layers of skin on both sides of his cheeks etched with wrinkles due to relentless smiling. As Jamling grinned, stretched and practised his tennis shots, he very much resembled his father.

We greeted Jamling and he greeted us back, gesturing with his racquet to a bench outside the dressing room. As we sipped tea and watched Jamling play, we also carefully observed the certificates of sports championships named in honour of Tenzing, hanging on the walls of the tennis court. Soon after he finished his first game, Jamling came running towards us. The man, now in his 50s, was fit and looked much younger than his actual age. 'I am sorry to keep you guys waiting,' he said, panting. He ordered a cup of tea for himself and asked us how things were in Kathmandu.

Of all Tenzing's children, Jamling is the most visible bearer of his legacies. He is a mountaineer himself, and reached the top of the world

---

1   A Nepali term for elder brother.

in 1996. He operates a mountaineering company and often accompanies his clients in trekking and climbing. In Darjeeling, he has forged quite a reputation. He chairs the Gymkhana Club and is looked up to for motivational leadership coaching. 'I feel alive when I am outdoors,' he told us, which reminded us of an emotional expression of his father in his autobiography: '. . . there (in the mountains), life is too real and death too close'. [2]

As we conversed with Jamling, we were focused on seeing Tenzing through his eyes. Jamling's sportsmanship, leadership, assertiveness and love and care for the Sherpa community, which, in his own words, his father regarded as an extended family, all resemble his father's well-documented characteristics. Over tea at the tennis court, we asked Jamling to help us understand his father as much as possible. In response to this, without a second thought, he invited us to his home the very next day.

The following day, we took a walk from our hotel, asking local taxi drivers the way to Tenzing's home. Jamling had scribbled a map on a napkin for us, but we wanted to see how widely Tenzing's legacy still lives on in Darjeeling. Following the way the taxi drivers showed us, we arrived at Darjeeling's downtown square called Chowrasta, from the Mall Road side where the Gymkhana Club is also situated.

Towards the other end of Chowrasta are two footpaths – one leading to the old Sherpa settlement in Toong Soong, and the other leading towards the main market area and Gandhi Road, where Tenzing's house is located. After about 30 minutes of walking, we were finally outside the main gate.

At the entrance to the property, built on steep land, begins a staircase beside the wall with the embossed badge. The staircase leads up to a complex of houses spread across the entire range once owned by Tenzing, and now inherited by Jamling. At the top of the staircase is a courtyard in front of the main residence, where Jamling and his two gentle dogs received us.

---

2   Ullman, J. R., 1955. *Man of Everest: The Autobiography of Tenzing*. Pilgrims Publishing.

After his 1953 feat, this house offered inspiration to several young Sherpas from the Khumbu region, who would randomly show up at the courtyard in groups in search of mountaineering work.

Tenzing received everyone gladly and offered a place for them to stay in his house. 'Especially in the years after 1953, my dad was very particular about keeping himself grounded,' Jamling said. 'He did not want people to think that he had evolved into a celebrity. Sherpas from Khumbu loved Tenzing as their man and would fully rely on him. My dad also thought the same and would let them do so. From its earliest days, this house has accommodated at least 500 Sherpas, if not more.'

Jamling straightaway led us to the family's personal museum, a two-storey hall connected by an indoor staircase. Entering this museum was like walking into a time machine, which took us back to Tenzing's heyday. The museum houses Tenzing's personal gear – from his climbing suit to the heavy oxygen cylinders made of iron, which he carried on his back during the 1953 Everest mission.

We tried lifting one of these and quickly realized how hard it must have been to carry these cylinders filled with oxygen at that altitude. In 1953, the oxygen tanks weighed 10kg (22lb) each, a significant improvement from earlier versions from the 1920s that would weigh up to 15kg (33lb). Oxygen cylinders have now evolved into several times more efficient and manageable units made of lighter metals like titanium and alloys. They are as light as 3.5kg (7.7lb) today.

This colourful museum from the black-and-white era also has a rich collection of Tenzing's personal cameras that he took on several of his expeditions. There are accolades from all over the world – from the US to the (then) USSR – including personal gifts from political and public figures, Tenzing's photographs, news clippings and other keepsakes.

One major attraction in the museum is a couple of coats hanging on a wall by the staircase. The coats, wrapped in transparent plastic covers, actually belonged to the first Indian prime minister Jawaharlal Nehru, who gifted them to Tenzing during one of his trips to England. The museum, so rich and vibrant with a proud era of mountaineering captured so well, is, like any other personal museum, an account of Tenzing's personal history and achievements.

While we travelled back in time at the museum, Jamling has his own way of looking at it. For him, the museum brings a feeling of nostalgia for a time when few people loved to explore the unknown and but permanent precedents for generations to come. 'My father was one of them. With each passing moment, I am more and more convinced that he is the first Sherpa who climbed because he was following his passion,' he said.

*

29 May 1953.

The world that Tenzing descended to after reaching the summit of Everest was no longer the same one that he had left behind on his ascent. In one of the world's most astonishing occasions of overnight celebrity, the limelight of the world had suddenly fallen upon this regular man who belonged to a previously unheard of mountain tribe. Tenzing had clearly pushed the potential of what a human could achieve beyond any known limits.

As the world was taken aback with the achievement of this humble Sherpa man and the media everywhere jostled to reach Tenzing, his schedule started to become tightly packed with back-to-back foreign trips. He was congratulated by the British Queen at Buckingham Palace, and Indian prime minister, Jawaharlal Nehru, befriended him to the extent that he partnered with Tenzing in establishing the Himalayan Mountaineering Institute (HMI), a climbing school in Darjeeling.

With all this global attention, Tenzing's life – and his family's lives – changed beyond recognition. From his struggles to make ends meet, Tenzing had suddenly started 'thinking about income taxes'. [3] He shifted

---

3   Ullman, J. R., 1955. *Man of Everest: The Autobiography of Tenzing*. Pilgrims Publishing.

from Toong Soong to his new luxurious mansion in an expensive neighbourhood in Darjeeling's downtown. Despite its close proximity to the tourist hubs, Toong Soong is a somewhat isolated settlement, with narrow roads, buildings with old, rusty and damp walls, budget guest houses, dark alleys and untouristy shops along the streets.

Even today, Toong Soong remains a Sherpa hub in Darjeeling. Toong Soong had, and still has, a particular character that offers a Sherpa a homely connection: a majestic, unhindered view of a mountain range towards the north that includes Kanchenjunga and spreads across India and Nepal. Standing today in Toong Soong and facing the vastness of the northern mountain range, it is not too difficult to understand why the first Sherpas migrating to Darjeeling from Khumbu's mountain villages would have settled here. This was probably why Tenzing, even after shifting to his new mansion, kept going back to Toong Soong to meet his people almost every day, whenever he was home in Darjeeling on a break from mountaineering.

Adding to the list of Tenzing's post-1953 wonders, he enrolled his children at St Paul's, one of the most expensive British-era private schools of India. This is particularly remarkable given that they were the first Sherpa kids to attend an expensive private school.

With his success, the Sherpas, who were previously just the fortunate employees of infrequent foreign climbers, started imagining themselves in a much broader picture and looking up to Tenzing's haul as a goal to which they could aspire.

However, all of Tenzing's material gains after his summit did not sufficiently speak of his character. The twists and turns of his life, and the figurative ups and downs along the adventurous path that he chose to tread, offer a largely unheard-of and almost mythical narrative. His determination to push his limits, despite the series of fateful circumstances that unfolded throughout his pre-1953 life, which could have been enough to make him want to quit climbing, was the quality that projected an abstract, larger-than-life character on to this 172-cm (5-ft 8-in) ever-smiling Sherpa.

*

Having been born after Tenzing's death and having grown up hearing his legend mixed with facts, fabrications and fairy tales, we were about to follow the trail of his footprints: from Nepal's Khumbu region to India's Darjeeling. As we crossed the bordering Nepali town of Pashupatinagar and stepped into India, it didn't feel as if we had arrived in a foreign country. Nepal and India share an open border and the nationals of the two countries can freely travel across it without providing any official paperwork.

In our three-hour ride from Nepal's bordering airport to Pashupatinagar, we followed an uphill trail of tea estates, which did not leave us even after we crossed the border. Unlike other Nepal–India borders that mostly exist in vast agricultural plains, people living on both sides of this hilly eastern border speak Nepali as their primary language – another factor that blurred the political delineation of territories for us. For as long as it has been known, the Nepal–India borders have remained the same.

Towards the plains, where half of Nepal's population resides today, there used to be lush green forests, deemed unsuitable for living in due to the hot climate and related fatal diseases like malaria and leishmaniasis, more commonly known as *kala-azar*. During Tenzing's lifetime, when less than 5 per cent of the country's population was literate, it was normal practice for Nepali men to travel across the border in search of their fortunes. Even today, hundreds of thousands of Nepalis continue to escape Nepal's poverty, finding themselves menial jobs mostly as security guards, kitchen helpers and labourers in different Indian cities.

Nepali people's cross-migration to India also gave them a chance to find employment in the army, particularly in the Battalion of the Gurkhas, who were named after the well-known hometown of Nepal's first king. Before the partition of British-India, Nepali men would often make it as far as Lahore, a practice so well-documented in the oral tradition of Nepal that especially people from the older generations commonly identify Nepali people working in foreign countries as '*lahures*', even today.

From older times, there is a particular image of *lahures* returning home during festivals – dressed in fancy, colourful outfits, sunglasses and with radios hanging from their shoulders. These *lahures* would bring toffees to distribute among villagers and would also be loaded with cash to be spent in gatherings of friends and families. This image as a reflection of the prosperity and good fortune awaiting them in India would easily attract young Nepali men: one generation after another. At the sight of a *lahure* returning to their village, young Nepali men working in the fields would make hasty plans to discover their own fortunes in India, and with these impulsive decisions, would run away from their homes the very next day.

The story of Tenzing was somewhat similar.

At the age of 13, he stepped out of his family home in Thame and walked for more than two weeks to get to Kathmandu, where he was able to see for himself a glimpse of just how prosperous life could be outside Khumbu. The mountain villages in Khumbu were far from the reach of regular *lahures* and lucrative army jobs. Nevertheless, during his travels outside of Khumbu, Tenzing had met *lahures*, especially men from other Mongol-origin hilly ethnicities like Rai, Limbu, Magar and Gurung, who were widely recruited in the British Army.

While people from these Mongol-origin ethnicities were believed to be brave, strong and resilient, Sherpas were yet to be tested and nobody knew of their particular strengths.

By then, the early expedition attempts on Everest had already taken place in the 1920s from the Tibetan side. Some of the Khumbu Sherpas had also taken part in these expeditions and even died in accidents. Tenzing's generation was somehow aware that foreigners were planning an ascent of Everest. They had heard about Darjeeling and that the expeditions were planned and commissioned there by the British. 'By virtue of the possibilities of work closest to their capacities, Darjeeling offered Sherpas what other parts of India offered other Nepalis including *lahures*,' Jamling said, recalling his father's breaking out of the cocoon. Born several years after Tenzing's 1953 feat, Jamling has invested a significant part of his own time in trying to fully understand his father. 'My father must have been smart enough to sense this opportunity in Darjeeling,' he added.

In 1933, a group of several Sherpa boys and girls started planning for an escape to Darjeeling. Tenzing was part of this secret mission. As recalled by Tenzing in his autobiography, the group's leader was Dawa Thondup, who seemed to have fair knowledge of Darjeeling and expeditions that were about to happen, even though he had never been there himself. Still, Dawa Thondup's influence and whatever little knowledge he had was more than enough to fuel the excitement among local boys and girls.

The escape from home involved over a month of meticulous planning for food and shelter on their way, finances and the route to take. Regarding their finances, there was no way any of them were going to carry any money. All that this company could manage was clothes, blankets and food sufficient to sustain them throughout the journey. Tenzing also managed to sneak out a blanket from his home. The arduous journey from Khumbu to Darjeeling took them through jungles, valleys, steep ridges, rivers and tiny Nepali hamlets on the way. As this group of adventurers pushed into the unknown, Tenzing must have been weaving little dreams of prosperity for himself. He could surely not have known the reality of what lay ahead for him.

*

In 1933, when Tenzing set foot in Darjeeling, a British expedition team there was regrouping after the great loss, in an Everest attempt in 1924, of two of the most competent British climbers – George Mallory and Andrew Irvine. For all its uncertainties, the Mallory-Irvine expedition is believed to be the one that got the closest to the summit prior to the Tenzing-Hillary feat of 1953. Members of that expedition at the lower camps of the northern side of Everest have been reported to have seen Mallory and Irvine making a push for the summit from their final camp. However, as the duo disappeared in bad weather, there is no evidence, nor any certainty, as to whether they had made it to the top or not, whether they disappeared on their descent. Mallory's body was found on Everest 75 years later in the spring of 1999, at 8,140m (26,706ft). Irvine is still missing.

The same year the British were preparing to return to Everest after nine years of silence, Tenzing had also come a little closer to the climbing hub of Darjeeling, but not close enough to find his way straight into the climbing team. Like most of the migrants of that time, he got a job looking after cows and a potato field in a small place called Alubari – literally meaning potato field in Nepali – on the outskirts of Darjeeling.

Still very far from the Darjeeling glories he had dreamed of when leaving home, in Alubari, Tenzing's life was not much different than in Thame. His work was to look after the cattle, cut grass, collect fodder, grow potatoes and simply survive. 'I still remember my father sharing with us his days of struggle in Alubari,' Jamling recalled. 'Although he was in a loving family, his time in Alubari could never quench his thirst beyond leaving home and coming this far. From the very beginning, he wanted to be an explorer and kept seeking mobility throughout his life.'

Just as Dawa Thondup had hinted back in Thame, the same year they arrived in Darjeeling an expedition kicked off. 'An expedition used to be such a big thing back then that absolutely everybody would be aware of it,' Jamling told us, showing photos of Sherpas being recruited in one of the early expeditions near the Mall Road in Darjeeling. In one of the photos, Tenzing stood in line with other fellow Sherpas to be recruited in an expedition as a porter.

In Alubari, when desperate Tenzing heard an Everest expedition had finally arrived in Darjeeling, he got in contact with Dawa Thondup and asked for his help in getting recruited for the expedition. Dawa declined the request citing his young age and inexperience. However, an adamant Tenzing would not give up. He decided to find his own way onto the recruitment line.

Tenzing made preparations. At that time, he had long, braided hair, because of which, many confused him for a woman. He cut his hair short and, to leave a more mature impression on the recruiters, also managed to don Nepali dress. Cutting his hair could have been a smart move. However, the decision to dress in Nepali attire proved counterproductive. Tenzing looked like a man from a non-Sherpa ethnicity and, without any prior experience in climbing, he was rejected.

As he recalls in his autobiography, he returned to Alubari with his head down and in utter disappointment. Soon after this rejection, Tenzing learned that there was a rumour about him back in his village in Khumbu. A couple of boys who had run away from Thame and met Tenzing in Darjeeling told him that people back in the village, including his own family, had come to believe that he may have died, since he was completely out of contact and there was no news concerning his whereabouts.

While entering Darjeeling from Nepal, Tenzing had deviated from his group and got lost near the border. A local man rescued him and returned him to Alubari, and for several months before Tenzing met Dawa Thondup during recruitment, he was out of touch with his group.

Distraught by the bad luck in trying to get on the expedition, the news from home must have made Tenzing homesick. He quickly packed his bags and headed north to his village, without any promises of coming back to Darjeeling. After returning to Thame, his family were so happy to see that he was still alive and had returned home. Tenzing's village life got back to normal and he started helping his father with herding the yaks.

In the summer of 1934, Tenzing followed the tracks of his ancestors, accompanying his father to Tibet across Nangpa La to trade salt for grain. To Tenzing's embarrassment, the expedition team that had rejected him back in Darjeeling was camped near the village where he arrived with his father for trading. That very moment, deep down somewhere in his heart, Tenzing felt that the expedition was where he truly belonged.

After returning home from the salt trade in Tibet, his father offered him an opportunity to go to Tibet again – the life of a trader awaited him.

However, he was already bitten by the climbing bug, so Tenzing again packed his bags and headed south to Darjeeling, to try his luck one more time. This time, Tenzing had a clearer mission. He did not go to Alubari, but went straight to Toong Soong, where other climbing Sherpas of that time had settled. He made friends with Ang Tharkay Sherpa, a contemporary veteran, who had already been part of an unsuccessful German expedition on Kanchenjunga in 1931 and the British attempts on Everest in 1933 and Mount Nanda Devi 'East' (7,817m, 25,646ft) in 1934, also unsuccessful. Tenzing secured a place in Ang Tharkay's home, where he would help the family with any household work.

With Ang Tharkay, Tenzing got a little closer to climbing and the related knowledge and skills. The Sherpa community and some of the foreigners who keep track of climbing history recognize Ang Tharkay as an unquestionable mountain warrior, one who could have easily been in Tenzing's shoes with a little cosmic adjustment of time and space.

Throughout the years of active climbing attempts on Everest and other mountains from the 1930s to the 1950s, Ang Tharkay and Tenzing grew together, first as porters then gradually as climbing Sherpas and then Sirdars (see page 38) in different expeditions across various mountains.

Ang Tharkay, particularly, was the favourite of Eric Shipton, for his dependability, composure and mature outlook. In 1937, Ang Tharkay was the Sirdar in Shipton's exploration survey trip near K2 in today's Pakistan and the following year on Everest. He was also a Sirdar of the French expedition team that made a successful summit of Annapurna in 1950, the first 8,000-m (26,247-ft) peak ever climbed, for which Ang Tharkay became the first Sherpa to bag a European honour – the Légion d'honneur. In 1951, when the British expedition team of Eric Shipton attempted Everest from the south side, Ang Tharkay was the Sirdar of the party. The group was detained by Chinese armed forces and Ang Tharkay, who knew the local Tibetan dialect, haggled the price of their release from 10 rupees to 7. While Ang

Tharkay was bargaining loudly, helpless Shipton had been praying for the cost of their freedom not to exceed his own estimate of 1,200 rupees.

In 1953, if Eric Shipton had led the British attempt on Everest instead of Colonel John Hunt, Ang Tharkay would possibly have replaced Tenzing. In 1953, while Tenzing headed towards Everest, Ang Tharkay went to Dhaulagiri in western Nepal. His extraordinarily long mountaineering career continued until 1978, when at the age of 70, he went on an expedition to Dhaulagiri with the French, as a Sirdar.

There are several occasions when the statures of Tenzing and Ang Tharkay have been compared. A 1954 profile of Tenzing by Christopher Rand in the *New Yorker*, quotes an Indian reporter in Darjeeling:

> 'Tenzing is debonair and smiling; Tharkay is quiet and sure. Tenzing has the unquenchable fire of adventure in his eyes; Tharkay's gaze reflects a solid dependability, like Everest. Tenzing's disarming has the piquancy of spiced humour; Tharkay's few comments are seasoned with a wisdom as old as the mountains he climbs.'[4]

*

In 1935, soon after Tenzing had married Dawa Futi, a Sherpa woman from the Khumbu region who had run away to Darjeeling, there was another expedition – a reconnaissance on Everest, led by Eric Shipton.

Tenzing stood in the recruitment line again, along with Ang Tharkay. Ang Tharkay was already Shipton's first choice. This time, Tenzing also was fortunate as Shipton decided to take him in even though he did not have any certificates of previous experience on Everest. There were other senior, experienced Sherpas in the line, but Tenzing simply got lucky.

Tenzing's first time on Everest was about exploration of different

---

4   Rand, C., 28 May 1954. The story of the first Sherpa to climb to the top of Mt. Everest. *New Yorker*. Available at https://www.newyorker.com/magazine/1954/06/05/ tenzing-of-everest.

approaches from the western face of the mountain and discovering more about the climatic conditions during monsoon. The expedition set up a camp at the North Col, but had to retreat owing to risks of an avalanche. During the 1935 reconnaissance, the team also found the body of Maurice Wilson and his diary. Wilson was attempting a solo ascent of Everest in 1934 and had died above Camp 3.

The 1935 reconnaissance was special to Tenzing for one more reason. When the expedition had camped in Tibet, his father came all the way from Thame, crossing over Nangpa La, to the campsite, just to meet his son. This was the first of only two reunions that Tenzing had with his father after he left home for Darjeeling for the second time. The second reunion happened during their 1938 attempt, also in the mountains.

Tenzing again went to Everest in a 1936 British expedition as a high-altitude porter. The expedition had to be aborted due to an unusually early monsoon. After the 1936 expedition, Tenzing got a chance in Shipton's team to explore Garhwal, a Himalayan region in north-western India. The 1936 trip to Garhwal took Tenzing across several major Indian cities like Calcutta and Delhi; he travelled by train for the first time and felt the real heat of the plains. 'My father was a well-travelled man. He had equal respect for all the mountains and, throughout his lifetime, went across most of the mountains spread from Bhutan, Tibet and Nepal to Pakistan and Afghanistan,' Jamling recalled. 'His extensive travel across the Himalayas, even before 1953, had given him a close understanding of mountains and of the act of climbing. That must have prepared him, in some part, for Everest.'

In 1938 again, Tenzing's time on Everest did not prove lucky, as the team under the leadership of H W Tilman had to retreat due to bad weather conditions and limited predictability. Nevertheless, some remarkable achievements had been made. The company, of which Tenzing was also a part, had made it up to Camp 6 on Everest, the highest thus far, for which he was awarded a 'Tiger Medal' along with other Sherpas of the team. (Back then, there were no permanent camps and expeditions had to set up their own as they climbed.) Showing us the tiger medal, Jamling contemplated, 'Although unsuccessful, the attempt of 1938 had brought them several times closer to the top of the world. This must have fuelled the determination of my father.'

After Tenzing's first three attempts on Everest in the 1930s, the global political scene started to worsen with the start of World War II, followed by Indian struggles for independence from British rule. Just as the mountaineering world saw a slack, Tenzing went through a major tragedy in his life, with the death of his first son, aged just four, due to blood dysentery.

After 1938, there was a 13-year-long silence in Everest, before another British attempt was made in 1951. In the war years, as the fate of expeditions became uncertain, Tenzing went on to explore a different career path. In the early 1940s, Major Chapman appointed Tenzing as his batman – a personal servant of high-ranking army officials at that time. With his wife and two daughters, he followed Major Chapman from Darjeeling to Chitral, in present-day Pakistan, where he spent another five years far from the hustle and bustle of mountain expeditions.

Tenzing's time in Chitral saw another major tragedy. In 1944, his wife Dawa Futi succumbed to illness supposed to have been induced by climatic shocks, leaving behind two daughters aged just four and five. In 1945, after the death of his wife and when the Indian independence movement was at its peak, and debates around India–Pakistan partition were gaining significant momentum, Tenzing gathered up his two little daughters and headed towards Darjeeling.

The journey was rather arduous. Owing to political tensions, the trains were all packed and Tenzing could not get a ticket. Thankfully, he had an old military uniform gifted by Major Chapman. He dressed in the army outfit and hopped into the military compartment of a train with his two daughters. Tenzing had managed to carry with him some expensive stones widely available in Chitral, and was able to make quick money by selling them in Darjeeling.

'Several years away from mountaineering, and having lived through two major tragedies of his life – the death of his son and wife – my father had every reason to quit mountaineering once and for all,' Jamling recollects. 'However, for someone who had decided a long way back in 1934 that trading was not his cup of tea and that he belonged to the expeditions, the "call of the mountains" would never go away.'

For Tenzing to be ready to climb Everest, he still needed a solid emotional support system, to somehow make up for the tragedies he had suffered with the losses of his son and wife.

After his return from Chitral, in 1945, he worked as a labourer, repairing railway tracks in Darjeeling. It was here that Tenzing met Ang Lhamu, a milk vendor in a nearby market. A relationship ensued between the two as they bargained over the milk price almost every day. They eventually got married, and Tenzing finally filled the emotional void in his life.

While it may have just meant his second marriage for Tenzing personally, Buddhist spiritual interpretations of Tenzing's and Ang Lhamu's lives offer a larger mystical story, directly relating to how the universe had been conspiring for Tenzing's achievements of 1953…

*

The exact date of Tenzing Norgay's birth is mired in uncertainty.

For much of his life, there was no need to recollect his date of birth. However, when he reached the top of the world in 1953, the world was interested in knowing and documenting every aspect of his life. People from his parents' generation told him that he was born in the Rabbit year. In the Tibetan calendar, years are said to be controlled according to one of 12 animal signs: Mouse, Ox, Tiger, Rabbit, Dragon, Snake, Horse, Sheep, Monkey, Rooster, Dog and Pig.

Tallying this information with the Western calendar, Tenzing figured out that he might have been born in 1914. However, the calculation has its own margin of error as, in a cycle, a Rabbit year had also occurred in 1906 and 1926, but at the time of his calculation, Tenzing thought he was not as old or young as someone born in 1906 or 1926 respectively. He was also told that he was born in the best mountain weather. Best weather in the mountains is towards the end of May, which is also the ideal time to go climbing. With these pieces of information, recollecting that Tenzing was born in late May and coinciding his assumed birth time with the day he went on the summit of Everest, his birthday was set as 29 May 1914.

At the time of his birth, Tenzing was named Namgyal Wangdi by his parents. Later, they brought him to visit a revered Lama, who consulted his scriptures and declared that the child was an incarnation of a wealthy man of the same district, and therefore should be named Tenzing Norgay, literally meaning 'wealthy and fortunate follower of religion'.

The Thame locals told us a popular folktale about Tenzing. The same year he came into this world, hundreds of yaks were born in his family, signifying that Tenzing was born with good signs of high achievements. After his birth, his family, which was previously mired in poverty, started rearing 300–400 yaks at a time.

In another similar story we heard from the older generation in Thame, as a young boy, Tenzing was once looking after yaks in a grazing field. It was a bright, sunny day and Tenzing fell asleep on the ground. When other fellow herders took notice of him, he was still asleep and there was a huge snake standing on its tail, creating a shadow right over his head. This particular story holds significance in Hindu religion, as the snake is one of the favourite animals of Lord Shiva, who resides in the mountains.

Tenzing's son Jamling shared with us one more story, at his office in the same building that houses their museum.

Jamling was born to Tenzing and his third wife Dakku, after the death of Ang Lhamu in 1964. He had no children with Ang Lhamu and, before she died, she is said to have arranged for his third marriage with Dakku, her cousin/sister. In one of her conversations with her son Jamling, Dakku had told him that their family holds a sacred connection with the mountains and the mountain goddess Miyolangsangma.[5] She had also asked Jamling to visit a high-ranking Trulshik Lama meditating in the mountains in Solukhumbu of Nepal. (Solu and Khumbu make up the district of Solukhumbu, which hosts Everest and several other mountains in the range. The mountainous region that begins in Lukla is referred to as Khumbu, which is still not connected by road. Meanwhile, Solu, which is situated at a lower altitude below Lukla, is accessible by road and connects the region with other neighbouring districts.)

After Dakku died, Jamling took himself to the doorstep of the revered Lama in Solukhumbu, during one of his trips to the Everest region in 1995, a year before his own summit. During their conversation, the Trulshik Lama revealed his acquaintance with another senior holy man called Ladakh Lama, who, in the 1930s, had prophesied that a local man from the mountain tribe of Sherpas would climb Chomolungma first.

Trickling down his further interpretations of Tenzing, the Lama also told Jamling that his father was meant to be that man. He particularly referred to how Tenzing was destined to be deviated from anything he tried to do outside the mountains. 'My encounter with the Trulshik Lama rang bells in my mind,' Jamling told us. 'I came to recollect how my father, as a child, had run away from a monastery where he was being trained to become a monk. Despite all the major hurdles he faced in life, he was committed to the act of climbing. He went to many places, but always came back to the mountains.'

Throughout the entire Everest region and among all the Sherpas, Tenzing is believed to have been shown the way up to the summit of Chomolungma by its resident goddess Miyolangsangma. Jamling's encounter with the Trulshik Lama only added weight this particular belief. The Lama told Jamling that Tenzing's second wife, Ang Lhamu, was herself

5 Tenzing Norgay, Jamling and Coburn, Broughton, 2001. *Touching My Father's Soul.* 2001.

a manifestation of Miyolangsangma, whose sole purpose was to nurture Tenzing towards his cosmic mission. 'I am very much convinced that my father came to this world with a purpose, and so did Ang Lhamu. She was with him even when he made it to the top,' Jamling said.

*

Soon after he returned to Darjeeling, in 1947, Tenzing attempted Everest with a Canadian-born mountaineer, Earl Denman, but returned without success. He also made contact with Swiss expeditions and quickly gained their trust. In that same year, the Swiss made him Sirdar of their Everest expedition and later, in 1952, considered Tenzing a key member of their team for the final summit push. This decision proved fruitful as the team reached up to 8,595m (28,199ft), the highest ever recorded, that year.

After reaching such a height with the Swiss team, Tenzing's stature as a Sherpa saw a sharp rise in the alpine community, and the King of Nepal even honoured him with a prestigious national award.

After getting so close, the Swiss were pretty sure they would make it in their next expedition booked for 1956. The French were also in the game, and had already booked the spring of 1954 for their expedition. Therefore, for the British, who had been in the race for a long time already, the only chance to be the first to reach the top of the world was in 1953. They had been closely observing how things had unfolded for the Swiss in 1952 and the key players of that team, including Tenzing.

Before this, the British expeditions, with their own colonial glories and backgrounds, had never recognized a Sherpa as a major climber. For them, Sherpas were just the obedient, fierce porters who could help them in the high altitudes, not fellow climbers who could even devise strategies up in the mountains.

In the months after returning from his 1952 expedition, Tenzing suffered from malaria and was admitted to a hospital in the Indian city of Darbhanga in Bihar. When the British approached him to join their expedition, not as a porter, but as an equal climber this time, as with the

Swiss, he was bed-ridden, had lost a lot of weight and was weaker than ever before. However, being Tenzing, there was no way he would resist the mountain's call. He was already committed to go with the Swiss team in 1955, but he decided to take a chance with the British as well, in 1953.

Most of the British Everest expeditions before this point were led by veteran Eric Shipton, a lenient and easy-going leader. However, as the British were in a neck-to-neck competition with the French and the Swiss, they decided to have on board a much more uncompromising war hero, Colonel John Hunt, as the leader of the 1953 expedition. John Hunt divided the climbers in his team into pairs – the first to attempt were Tom Bourdillon and Charles Evans; Tenzing Norgay and New Zealander Sir Edmund Hillary were second in line; and then Wilf Noyce and Mike Ward were the third pair.

As the pairs approached the higher camps from the base camp of Everest, Hillary survived what could have been a fatal incident. Somewhere near the Khumbu Icefall, he slipped into a crevasse, pulling with him his partner Tenzing, who was attached to the same rope. Promptly, Tenzing pulled out his ice axe and hit it against an ice wall, creating an anchor and thus saving them both from the fall. In this quick action, Tenzing lost one of his gloves. We had seen the other one – a whitish woollen glove – sitting in a museum with rest of Tenzing's gear. The lone glove tells the visitors a story of Tenzing and Hillary's friendship beyond the summit of Everest. Both have detailed this incident of survival as a key event in their friendship, bonding and mutual trust throughout the expedition and even beyond.

The 1953 British expedition was meticulously planned. Altogether, eight camps had been set up to the South Col and, as per Hunt's plans, the first pair of Bourdillon and Evans could start their assault from the last camp at the South Col. The first assault was a modest one as Hunt's aim with this pair was to reach up to the South Summit, if not the top. If Bourdillon and Evans failed to scale the summit, the second team of the strongest climbers in the pack – Tenzing and Hillary – would launch another assault.

Things unfolded exactly as Hunt had predicted. The team of Bourdillon and Evans reached the South Summit on 26 May, but had to stop 100m (328ft) below the top as Evans had issues with his oxygen valve. Evans and Bourdillon were using experimental closed-circuit oxygen equipment. Nevertheless, the first pair was able to tip off Tenzing and Hillary about the landscape they had seen over the South Summit – a rock step with a thin layer of ice and snow. With this valuable insight of the geography that they were about to approach, Hunt's second pair, who had the conventional open-circuit oxygen equipment, began their assault. For this stronger pair most likely to make it to the top, Hunt's meticulous planning included setting up a ninth camp a little below the South Summit, an area that Tenzing had already noticed during his attempt with the Swiss the previous year. Tenzing and Hillary spent a night at this last camp near the South Summit and made their final push, reaching the summit of Everest on 29 May, just before noon.

*

Despite being born over a decade after his father became a sensation, Jamling has an uncanny recollection of how his family was obsessed with mountains, occupying most of their time with talk about mountains and mountaineering, from chats over the dinner table to annual festivals. Jamling told us with a light humour, 'Most of the time, my father was in the mountains. When not in the mountains, at our home, he would be surrounded by people related to the mountains. No matter how busy he was, my father used to organize his timetable like in the military, and would make sure he had time for the family. He would tell me stories, but all of those would be about the mountains. Sometimes I feel I have known the mountains long before I came to know myself or my family.'

Jamling's recollection, however, is mixed with the burden of legacy that came pouring down on his shoulders at a very young age. Despite being enrolled in one of the most expensive private schools of India, it did not take too long for Jamling to realize that he wanted to be in the mountains, just like his father. Soon after completing Grade 12, Jamling presented himself before his father in his office, by the present-day private museum of the family, and said, 'Dad, I want to climb Everest.'

Having seen the struggles of the mountains all his life, Tenzing did not want his children to face the same hardships he had endured… 'He rejected my plea. And once he said "no", I didn't have any option but to quietly leave the room,' Jamling said. 'Instead, he sent me to the US for higher studies, trying to put me as far away as he could from the mountains.'

Being the obedient son he was, Jamling did not pursue mountaineering until his father's death in 1986. After losing him, Jamling felt more and more restless. 'After my father died, there was a huge void in the family. For some reason, I started developing the need to hold his legacy until my last breath. I wanted to know my father more, and the best way to do that was to pursue his soul in the mountains.'

As he started pursuing his chances in mountaineering, Jamling also started exploring more about his father, his character and his priorities. For Tenzing, his fame had come along with two major controversies. The first was about his nationality. In the immediate years after 1953, both Nepal and India wanted to own him in his entirety. On the one hand, the government of Nepal declared Tenzing a national hero. Songs and stories started coming out glorifying how a Nepali son had become the first to reach the roof of the world.

On the other hand, the then-prime minister of India Jawaharlal Nehru had made it his personal interest to own Tenzing as an Indian, for he had permanently settled in Darjeeling and all his mountaineering quests had commenced from Indian soil. After 1953, when Tenzing went to the Indian capital of New Delhi, Nehru himself went to the airport to receive him. In subsequent years, Nehru travelled to Darjeeling several times, in a bid to be friends with Tenzing and initiate a national-scale mountaineering school – the HMI.

'The debate over his nationality had always bothered my father,' Jamling said. 'He was born and grew up in Nepal and sought his fortune in mountaineering in India. He regarded both countries as his own. He had taken the flags of both Nepal and India to the top of the world and, when he travelled to the UK, he carried both his Nepali as well as Indian passport. Above all these petty debates over his nationality, he always wanted to identify himself as a Sherpa.'

With regard to the flags, initially the plan was to take the flags of the UN and Great Britain to the summit. However, a close friend of Tenzing in Darjeeling handed him an Indian flag to take with him. Then, in Kathmandu, someone gave him the flag of Nepal as well. 'Sure,' Tenzing said and took all four flags along with him, and planted them together at the roof of the world. When Nepal's flag fluttered on top of Everest, the country was not even a member state of the UN.

Another controversy, on an even larger scale, was the debate over who first reached the summit of Everest – Tenzing or Hillary. By the time the pair arrived in Kathmandu after summiting Everest, the debate was already widespread. While some of the western stakeholders of the expedition claimed it was Hillary who first set foot on the summit of Everest, others wanted Tenzing to hold this achievement. However, the two climbers, throughout their lifetime, never commented on this debate, and kept telling the story of how they had together made it to the top of the world. 'It was pure-spirited teamwork, and not a competition between my father and Hillary,' Jamling said. 'Knowing my father, I can tell you for sure that this must have been the ugliest aspect of his success.'

Jamling takes this controversy very personally and gets riled whenever someone brings it up. 'Hillary and my father knew that this was going to be an unending distress for the rest of their lives. So, they even signed an agreement, clearly stating that the success was equally owned by both of them.' Jamling showed us the original document, written by Hillary in the first person, and signed by both men. The agreement reads:

On May the 29th, Tenzing Sherpa and I left our high camp on Mount Everest for our attempt on the summit. As we climbed upwards to the south summit first one and then the other would take a turn at leading. We crossed over the south summit and moved along the summit ridge. We reached the summit almost together. We embraced each other, over-joyed at our success; then I took photographs of Tenzing holding aloft the flags of Great Britain, Nepal, the United Nations and India.

'No matter how explicitly my father and Hillary proclaimed that it was their teamwork, and not the question of who was first, this controversy kept troubling him,' Jamling said. 'I remember how my father used to tell us: ". . . if I had known people would be this discourteous to our hard work and achievement, I swear, I would never have gone there". When I started unfolding my father's character after his death, I realized how badly hurt he was with all the trivial questions he had to live with until his last breath.'

No matter how hard Jamling tried to understand Tenzing, 'touching his father's soul', which is also the title of his 2001 bestseller, it would not be possible without following his father's footsteps on Everest all the way to the top. In 1996, Jamling finally broke the silence, which he had left behind in his father's office over one and a half decades previously. 'My summit of Everest was a homage to my father and a quest to truly understand his spiritual connection with the mountain,' Jamling told us, explaining how hard he tried as he climbed up to locate the landscapes in the backgrounds of his father's popular Everest photographs. 'Every single step that I took on my way to the top brought me closer to my father. As I set my foot on the summit, I could literally feel the touch of his soul. That touch is going to stay with me forever.'

*

Sniffing around Tenzing's living legacies in the streets of Darjeeling, we finally arrived at the HMI. The HMI, established in 1954, under the direct interest of then-prime minister Jawaharlal Nehru, shares an extended compound with a massive zoo in Darjeeling. At the main gate, which is the entrance to both the zoo as well as the HMI, a guard stopped us, saying, 'The zoo is closed due to the COVID-19 pandemic.'

Following Jamling's advice, we told the guard that we were there to visit the principal of the HMI. After making a few phone calls, the guard let us in and showed us the way to the HMI's premises inside the zoo. 'Take the left lane, and go straight for about 300m (984ft). Please be mindful that you are not allowed to see the other areas of the zoo as it is closed.'

'Okay,' we said, and kept going. Right after we entered by the main gate, we were welcomed by a calming silence, only occasionally broken by the sweet chirping of birds in the zoo's forest.

When we arrived at the HMI, we asked someone the way to the principal's office. He escorted us through the training facilities, a hallway and a climbing wall to the office of the HMI's sitting principal, Group Captain Jai Kishan of the Indian Air Force. Gp Capt. Jai Kishan is himself a noted skydiver and mountaineer with several world records to his name and a Tenzing Norgay Lifetime Achievement Award from the president of India. When we arrived in his office, he was just concluding his conversation with another group of people. We deduced that the HMI was about to expand some of its training infrastructure and Gp Capt. Jai Kishan was discussing naming it after Tenzing Norgay Sherpa. On the wall to the right of the principal's desk, there hung a huge black-and-white framed portrait of Tenzing.

When the other men left, the principal swiftly turned his attention towards us and called his helper for a round of tea. 'Jamling is a very good friend of mine,' the principal started the conversation. 'He said you came from Nepal and wanted to visit the HMI and our museum here. It's all closed now, but I will make sure you get a good tour.'

Over tea, we explained to him our quest to discover more about Tenzing's legacies in Darjeeling. As soon as that name came up, a spark lit in his eyes and a broad, indulgent smile spread across his face. 'It's all his legacies that we are living up to,' he said.

The HMI trains the best adventurers from all over India and even abroad. According to Gp Capt. Jai Kishan, the adventure training is also being adapted for use in daily life, especially in relief and rescue operations. 'Everything that we do here is in the name of Tenzing Norgay, as he is the godfather of this place,' the principle told us.

When Prime Minister Nehru collaborated with Tenzing in establishing the HMI, he had encouraged mountaineering as a movement, stating how he wanted Tenzing to 'create a thousand Tenzings'. To this, Gp Capt. Jai Kishan had the following response: 'I am myself an alumnus of this institute. The HMI has produced several mountaineers till this date. All of them are Tenzings in a sense that we all carry his legacy. However, there was only one Tenzing who scaled Mount Everest for the first time, and no one can replace him, ever.'

The HMI also maintains one of the most precious mountaineering museums in the world. The museum documents the history of mountaineering and evolution of gear and equipment. It tells the story of how ice axes evolved from simple tools made of wood and iron to the present day's lightweight aluminium alloy. The crampons that used to be tremendously heavy and complicated are now simple and easy to use. The oxygen cylinders have become considerably lighter, making the life of climbers easier than ever before. The museum also celebrates the personal histories of remarkable climbers including Tenzing and Hillary, and several other climbers before and after them.

Outside the museum, in an expansive courtyard, there is a massive larger-than-life statue of Tenzing, standing on top of Everest. In the statue, Tenzing is smiling as ever in his full climbing suit, holding up the flags of Nepal, India, Great Britain and the UN, with his sunglasses placed on his forehead and an oxygen mask hanging by his neck. Facing his statue is a memorial platform, built on the exact location where he was cremated. As we gazed at this memorial, standing under the statue, it felt as if we were being controlled by the aura and energy of Tenzing. It was a strange feeling, but it turns out that it's not just us who have felt that connection. Gp Capt. Jai Kishan comes here first thing every morning, and starts his day by touching the feet of Tenzing's statue, in submission and respect.

Chapter 5

'YOU WILL BE THE KING ONE DAY'

'You will be the king one day,' a shaman in the village of Chimakoti in Bhutan told Kushang Dorjee Sherpa. This was sometime in the late 1970s, about 100km (62 miles) south of Bhutan's capital, Thimphu. Teenager Kushang Dorjee, desperate to explore what his future looked like, had arrived in the room of this shaman in the evening. Shamans in the region, covering areas of Nepal, India, Bhutan and Tibet, are locally referred to as *Jhakri*. They are known for their unique ways of worshipping Hindu and Buddhist deities, by playing their *dhyangro*, a frame drum made of animal hide, dancing vigorously and loudly chanting hymns and prayers, rather aggressively. The *Jhakris* are believed to be capable of controlling possessed spirits, curing people's illnesses by possessing the spirit of the sick person, communicating with both gods and demons, and seeing into people's futures.

Kushang Dorjee was quietly seated in a corner of the *Jhakri's* dark room that had a mysterious ambience. Strong smells wafted towards him – a mix of kerosene (used for lighting lamps), a strong local liquor that the visitors offered to the *Jhakri*, and different kinds of aromatic incense lamps continuously burning in every corner of the room. Visitors, like Kushang Dorjee, were seated on the floor waiting patiently. By the wall facing the main door, there was the *Jhakri's* seat, cushions stacked together and decorated with a number of sacred props, which included posters and statues of different gods and goddesses, buffalo horns, bushy yak tails, a long-handled *dhyangro* and peacock feathers, among many other special items.

At about 8pm, the *Jhakri* entered the room, wearing his typical dress – a white turban worn upon his head, a white shirt covered by shawls and

123

ornaments hanging from his neck, and a long white skirt covering his lower body, down to his toes. Kushang Dorjee still recalls how the tiny prayer bells tied around his waist as a belt tinkled together in a mystifying rhythm as he walked through the doorway and into the room. The *Jhakri* didn't greet or acknowledge any of the visitors. He quietly sat on his cushion and started his evening prayers, which everyone observed respectfully.

The *Jhakri* began chanting hymns and mantras very loudly, which young Kushang Dorjee hardly understood. Then he started beating the *dhyangro*, gradually increasing the tempo. The sound soon became so overpowering that Kushang Dorjee could feel its deep bass notes pumping in his heart. After a few minutes, the *Jhakri* started frantically shivering from head to toe, which showed that he was now possessed by the spirits of the gods, and was ready to attend his visitors. It was about midnight when Kushang Dorjee's turn finally came. He approached the *Jhakri*, greeted him and placed his offering of 10 rupees on the ground. The *Jhakri* carefully looked at the rice grains which he scattered on the floor in Kushang Dorjee's name. Then the *Jhakri* announced, 'You will be the king one day.'

Kushang Dorjee's daily realities, however, were far from royal. To him, the *Jhakri's* fortune-telling was just an invention, a blatant joke that did not make any sense at all. The 10 rupees that he had just given as an offering of respect to the *Jhakri*, was what he had accumulated by saving every penny of his earnings over the last two months!

However, after this first encounter with the *Jhakri*, Kushang Dorjee would go back every year, meeting with different shamans from different religions, to cross-check what he had been told. The prediction was the same every time: 'You will be the king one day.'

*

Over two decades later, in 1999, 35-year-old Kushang Dorjee, a Sherpa who, as a teenager, struggled to see his fortune, became the first man on the planet to summit Everest from three points of the compass, a record that still remains unbroken.

Everest has three sides, or faces: the South-West Face and the North Face leading from Nepal and Tibet respectively, and the third one – the East Face, popularly known as Kangshung Face – also on the Tibet side. While most of the summits on Everest have been achieved from the northern and southern faces, there have been only thirteen summits from the mountain's most remote Kangshung Face so far – six in 1983, one in 1988 and three each in 1992 and 1999.

In 1999, Kushang Dorjee and two other climbers of their eleven-member team, which also consisted of his younger brother Sange Sherpa, climbed Everest from its rarely pursued face. The expedition was commissioned with high ambition by the Indian government, selecting the best men from all over the country. The mission was coordinated by the defence ministry of India and had members representing the Indo-Tibetan Border Police, Indian Army, HMI, Nehru Institute of Mountaineering (NIM) and Indian Mountaineering Foundation (IMF).

Since then, there have not been any attempts on Kangshung Face, as this longest and most technical route to the top of the world is considered significantly riskier than the others because of steep rock buttresses and couloirs on its lower section, and lofty glaciers hanging towards the top, like the sword of Damocles.

Kushang Dorjee's Kangshung Face ascent of Everest was extraordinarily long, compared to the climbs attempted from regular routes on the north and south faces. 'Our climb was spread across nearly three months, from April to June,' he recalled. 'It took us one and a half months to figure out the route and fix the ropes. On average, we could only fix about 45m [148ft] of rope in one day. After every two days of work, we would take a rest day.' While Kushang Dorjee led the task of rope-fixing, his brother Sange and some other members of the team constantly supported him. 'It was such a tiresome and slow process,' Kushang Dorjee recalled.

The base of Everest's eastern route sits on the Kangshung Glacier at around 5,500m (18,000ft). From the base, the first camp is reached after four hours of climbing along a narrow, steep passage called the Scottish Gully, plus an additional hour of 'technical rope climbing' on a notoriously steep ice wall. A crevasse with a hanging glacier looms like an umbrella over the first camp, which, for this particular characteristic, is also known as the 'cauliflower'. Navigating through this treacherous crevasse was the first major headache for Kushang Dorjee and his team as they had to fix a bridge of rope to cross the crevasse, and then fix several anchors to be able to climb steadily on the 90-degree cliff. 'Each camp on this route is a longer approach with extremely limited areas for rest,' Kushang Dorjee said. 'We climbed up mostly hanging by the rope and spent the night the same way, leaning back on our harnesses attached to the anchors fixed on the wall. Our team members hardly slept as there was a constant threat of avalanche.'

Indeed, there *was* an avalanche during Kushang Dorjee's expedition, which he and his team members only just survived. It happened soon after they left Camp 2 on the Kangshung route, which has a relatively flat surface covered in deep snow. The avalanche thundered down, sweeping away every tent that the climbers had left behind. According to The Himalayan Database, a digital archive of mountaineering since the early 1900s, eleven people would have died if they had left the camp just a little later.[1]

'Our team leader had actually planned to summit on 29 May, to mark the day when the first successful ascent was made by Tenzing and Hillary,' Kushang Dorjee said. 'According to our original plan, we had a spare day to rest at Camp 2. However, I insisted that we cut short our rest at Camp 2 and keep moving up, as my sixth sense told me that the weather might change and then we might not be able to reach the summit. This hunch saved our lives.'

The eastern route along the Kangshung Face meets with the southern route at nearly 8,000m (26,000ft) at the South Col, which is the location

---

1   The Himalayan Database: The expedition archives of Elizabeth Hawley. Available at https://www.himalayandatabase.com/.

of Camp 4 of the regular southern route and Camp 3 for those climbing up the Kangshung Face. 'For those climbing the regular route, the final summit push starts at Camp 4, which is the South Col,' Kushang Dorjee told us. 'On the Kangshung Face, our summit push had started right at the bottom. When we arrived at the South Col, we were all exhausted beyond belief, and most of our team members were already on the verge of collapse.'

Out of eleven climbers in Kushang Dorjee's team, only seven had made it to the South Col. However, as the oxygen regulators of some climbers at the South Col had stopped working, only three – Kushang, Sange and Amar Prakash – headed for the summit. They finally made it on 28 May 1999.

'Climbing Everest from Kangshung Face was not my choice,' Kushang Dorjee told us. He said he thought it was just another route on Everest. 'In fact, I didn't even know what it would be like or how difficult it was, until I saw the route myself and started working on it.'

Long after his return from this successful Kangshung Face summit, someone told Kushang Dorjee how George Mallory had subtly ruled out the possibility of an eastern route ascent of Everest. During his early reconnaissance of Everest in 1921, Mallory had said, 'Other men less wise, might attempt this way if they could, but emphatically, it was not for us.'[2]

When the Kangshung opportunity came knocking for Kushang Dorjee, he was already associated with the HMI in Darjeeling. The HMI had recommended his name to the defence ministry of India as one of their finest climbers. When Kushang Dorjee knew his name was on the list, he felt honoured. 'It was like an order to me, and I was proud of that,' he recalled. 'That was what took me along. Even though I panicked at the first look of this route, I convinced myself to believe that we could actually make it.' With his record, Kushang Dorjee's name started appearing in the media all over the world. In recognition of his achievements, the government of

2   Venables, S., 2000. *Everest: Alone at the Summit*. Thunder's Mouth Press.

India awarded him with the Tenzing Norgay National Adventure Award, in 2003.

At Kushang Dorjee's home in a small village on the outskirts of Darjeeling, he took us inside a room and talked us through a wall full of his accolades and honours. It is a short downhill trek to arrive at his beautiful home, painted in blue, resonating nothing but satisfaction and peacefulness. There is also a welcoming family dog, who didn't bark at us, but peacefully listened to his owner as he showed us the neighbourhood, pointing with his finger to a plot nearby where a resort is soon going to open. Now in his late 50s, he is living a happy and proud retired life with his wife and children, who are settled with a good education and employment. As he took us on a walk around the neighbourhood, there were many people who saluted him in military style with smiles on their faces, knowing that he is simply a legend.

When it was time for us to return to Darjeeling, Kushang Dorjee found us a taxi, bargained a little on our behalf and bade us a warm farewell. On our way back, our chubby, young driver who represented a section of popular youth in present-day Darjeeling, with stickers of 'punk not dead' pasted on the dashboard of his taxi, seemed interested in talking about Kushang Dorjee with us. 'You know that old man who brought you to my taxi? Young chaps like you should make more friends like him. That will take you further in life. Otherwise, you will also end up in the streets, taking drugs, like some youngsters in our city these days,' he enlightened us with his words of wisdom.

Kushang Dorjee's rise from where he started to where he is today is one of a kind, not any less than that of monarchs...'You will be the king one day!'

*

Kushang Dorjee was born in 1965 in a Sherpa village in the Makalu region of Nepal's Sankhuwasabha District. The Makalu region, which is situated by the Arun River basin, is one of the three major hubs of climbing Sherpas, along with Khumbu and Rolwaling. Kushang Dorjee's village

Nurbuchaur, is set in a green landscape with lush pine and rhododendron forests. Towards its north, the village offers a clear and majestic view of a mountain range that includes Mount Makalu (8,485m, 27,838ft) and Everest, among others. As in other Sherpa villages of Nepal, geographic remoteness and limited connectivity to roads and infrastructure are the common problems. In the 1960s, when Kushang Dorjee was growing up in his village, these problems were several times harsher than they are now.

When we stepped into Kushang's home in Nurbuchaur in 2022, we met his elderly mother in her late 80s. She lives there alone, but is accompanied most of the time by villagers. Kushang has asked her several times to come with him to Darjeeling and live there with his family, but the old woman finds peace in her own village. 'I have gone to Darjeeling two or three times, but I don't think I can stay there permanently,' she told us, in broken Nepali that was difficult to understand. She is aware that her son is a celebrated mountaineer, but does not know of his feats in any detail. The villagers, too, know Kushang's name as a mountaineer who lives in Darjeeling, but very few are aware of his grand achievements.

Born the eldest in the family, Kushang Dorjee had the responsibility of looking after his younger siblings from an early age. He dropped out of school even before completing primary level, and started helping his father in the potato field and looking after the family's yaks and the female naks. From a very early age, he learned how to milk the naks. He still remembers milking a dozen naks all by himself, with his tiny hands.

'It was a great struggle to feed such a huge family like ours,' Kushang Dorjee told us. 'Who would help my father if I had continued with my schooling?' Traditional Nepali society places an extraordinary importance on sons, especially the eldest son of the family, who is required to take up responsibilities as early as possible, and contribute to making ends meet. At that time, health services were poor and no means of family planning existed in the villages. As the number of children in a family increased, more pressures and expectations would build on the eldest son. Just like the eldest son in a royal family gets prepared to take up the throne at any moment after his birth, Kushang Dorjee's training in hardship had also started early on in his life, even before he entered his teenage years.

'After I started working with my father, I hardly had any free time. I actually never had a childhood.' Kushang Dorjee can still clearly visualize the struggles in his village, five decades down the line. 'Life seemed so fast and the struggles we were going through together were far beyond the imagination or the understanding of a seven-year-old child. Yet, we never had enough. There was a constant realization of extreme poverty.'

Kushang Dorjee's journey uphill to the higher altitudes began as a new phase of life, soon after the door into education permanently closed. Among his many responsibilities was to take the yaks and naks to high-altitude grazing fields at 4,000–5,000m (13,000–16,500ft) during the summer and monsoon. 'We had a tiny hut in our high-altitude pasture. Sometimes I used to go and live there with my father and, sometimes, when my father was busy with other work, I had to go and live there alone for several months.'

Dropping out of school did not come with much guilt for Kushang Dorjee and his family. Poor Nepali villages didn't have any reference for how important education was. Nor were the schools in the villages any more useful than just to teach kids the alphabet and numbers. For everyone else, and for Kushang Dorjee himself, at that time, education was the least important of all possible priorities. In front of them was the huge obstacle of poverty that was persistently restricting their vision of life. The only mission of youngsters was to get out of the village any way they could, find a job in Nepali cities towards the southern plains, if not in India or beyond, and make some money to make life a little better.

Kushang Dorjee must have been around ten years old when, after returning home to Nurbuchaur from one of his high-altitude pasture trips, he got his first opportunity to step out of the village. An acquaintance in the village offered him an opportunity to go to the city of Dharan to fetch salt. 'I grew up hearing about cities, the roads, vehicles and good houses in Dharan. I used to envy others who went to Dharan, while I climbed uphill with the animals,' Kushang Dorjee said. 'The opportunity had finally come, and I said to myself – well, let's see what Dharan is all about.'

As autumn came to an end every year, people in the high-altitude villages of the region used to gather together to collect all the harvests, which mostly included potato, millet, wheat and barley, and then go to Dharan. Once there, they would sell their goods and, with the money they made, would buy the precious salt, and head back home. From what Kushang Dorjee recalls, the round-trip to Dharan from the Makalu region would take exactly sixteen days – seven days to climb down, one day to trade and another eight days to climb back up.

One morning, young Kushang Dorjee and some others left Nurbuchaur with loads of millet and potato on their backs. All Kushang Dorjee had in mind was an excitement that he could not describe in words. There were several tiny villages on the way, where they would stop to spend the night. In every hamlet they stayed, they would cache some food for their use on the return journey. 'We used to drop our food on the way to reduce the amount of load while returning from Dharan,' Kushang Dorjee said. 'At first, I was hesitant about this, as I was not sure how we were going to figure out the exact same houses in those villages. Moreover, what if the house owners ate it all themselves before our return or didn't give it back to us? As it was my first time on a completely alien journey, I was so conscious of all the little things. But I came to know that this has been the same forever, and the houses we stayed in were of the friends or relatives of our own villagers. That relieved me a little.'

As the convoy approached lower altitudes, he experienced a magical transformation of the remote mountain life beyond which he had never thought any other world existed. First, as the terrain got easier downwards, the walking got effortless. The houses and villages were getting bigger and nicer. There were tiny shops on the way. The kinds of animals he had grown up with also changed; there were no more yaks and naks, but only cows, buffaloes, goats and chickens. The roads started getting wider and, finally, in Dharan, he saw a motor vehicle. The night he arrived in Dharan, he also experienced for the first time the magic of a light bulb.

By the 1970s, Dharan had already become one of the major hubs in the region. The city was vibrant with people from the eastern hilly areas of Nepal thronging there, training for several months and then applying for the recruitment tests of the British Army. Therefore, the city also had a considerable number of British recruiters, a major attraction for new arrivals in Dharan. The British Army jobs were one of the best opportunities available for young Nepalis back then. However, it required years of preparation and passing difficult physical tests. People from Mongolian ethnicities of Nepal, including Rai, Limbu, Magar and Gurung, among others, were the preferred choices in the British Army recruitments. The recruitment camp in Dharan, therefore, aptly leveraged a thick settlement of Mongol-ethnicity in the eastern hilly areas of Nepal. Although Sherpas are also one of the Mongolian ethnicities of Nepal, for their geographic remoteness and detachment with the world outside their mountain villages, they were never explored as potential recruits in the British Army, compared to other ethnicities from the mid-hills.

Dharan also had other attractions. The first generation of Nepali-British armies who had fought in the world wars had settled in Dharan in their new beautiful houses. This new settlement had made Dharan a fast-progressing city with modern facilities. Around the 1970s, when Kushang Dorjee stepped in Dharan for the first time, a mega road construction project, funded by the British, was about to start. The 51-km (31.5-mile) Dharan–Dhankuta highway now connects Dharan with several other mid-hilly districts of the region.

There is another major city – Biratnagar – which borders India, some 40km (25 miles) away from Dharan. Biratnagar, located in the lowland plains, is a much older city. It's hotter compared to Dharan, which is located in the cooler foothills. Besides that, the city has a cultural mix from India, a factor that arguably led to the formation of the new city of Dharan, especially for the settlement of ex-Gurkhas and their families.

On their way back from Dharan, Kushang Dorjee impressed the members of his team by carrying nearly 20kg (44lb) of salt on his back. 'We moved up with loads of salt,' Kushang Dorjee said. 'As we stopped in the houses on the way where we had left our food while coming to Dharan, I felt like going back to Dharan again and again. By pushing myself beyond limits, I impressed the seniors in the team. This opened my way forever, and I started travelling to Dharan every year, two to three times.'

No matter how many times Kushang Dorjee undertook the journey in the years to come, each time he was in Dharan brought back to him the dreams of a better life. 'There was a time when I really wanted to stay back in Dharan and never go up to the village. But I was very young, and had no idea how I was going to survive in Dharan on my own.'

Moreover, back in his village, Kushang Dorjee's parents had different plans for him. Before he was born, his mother and her friend had sworn between themselves to marry their children to each other. As the friend of Kushang Dorjee's mother gave birth to a girl two years after Kushang Dorjee was born, the vow that the two women had made years ago was finally set in stone. When Kushang was 12 and his by-default fiancée 10, the parents married them.

'We lived in the same neighbourhood, and the girl I was supposed to marry was my friend. We grew up playing together with other kids in our village,' Kushang Dorjee recalled. 'I was told we were about to get married, but I didn't understand any of that very well. There were several rituals that went on for over a month. Finally, on the wedding day, someone gave me new clothes and told me they had brought them from Dharan. I was fascinated.'

In Nepalese wedding culture, the groom has to smear vermilion powder on the bride's forehead, a significant tradition authenticating the sacredness of a marriage. After marriage, the vermilion becomes a key asset of the women, and they use it as an identical make-up for the rest of their life, until the death of the husband.

Kushang Dorjee does not remember too many rituals that he was part of during his wedding. However, he has a clear memory of the vermilion ritual. 'I was too little to do that correctly, so somebody held my hand with a pinch of vermilion and directed it on my bride's forehead,' he said.

Kushang Dorjee's distress started soon after his marriage. 'The girl used to cry a lot. Clearly, she wanted to return to her home with her parents,' he said. 'It was a similar feeling for me as well. I was not at the age to develop feelings of love with a woman. Yet, they made us sleep together in the same room. We both used to panic a lot and it was no less than torture.' Three years passed by and Kushang Dorjee started feeling happier only when he was in Dharan to carry salt and other goods. During the rest of the time at home, he was mostly uncomfortable.

At the age of 15, on one of his trips to Dharan, Kushang Dorjee was joined by his wife's elder brother, who was also his close friend. On the first night of this trip, his friend woke Kushang Dorjee up at 3am.

He whispered, 'Kushang...Kushang...Wake up! Wake up quickly!'

Kushang Dorjee yawned in his half sleep, 'Why? What's wrong? It's still dark. Sleep. We have time until morning.'

'Just wake up, fast! Let's run away, before anyone sees us,' the whispering continued.

The very next second, Kushang Dorjee's eyes were wide open. 'Where to?' he whispered back.

'Let's go to Darjeeling. Let's run away fast, while everyone is sleeping.'

The boys left their beds in Dharan and moved out in the dark, eastbound, towards Darjeeling.

The boys were young, strong and determined to seek a life better than the one they had back in their village. Their only problem, after they sneaked out while everyone was sleeping, was that they had no money at all. After one day's walk from the plains of Dharan, the boys arrived at a small town. There, they were employed as porters at a rice mill, with a daily wage of 2 rupees. After seven days of working, they were able to collect only 28 rupees, which was clearly not enough to take them to their destination. They also did not have the luxury of staying there and working until they had collected enough, as if anybody from the village found them, they would have to return without realizing their Darjeeling dreams.

On the eighth day, Kushang Dorjee had an idea. He had a rare nine-faced Rudraksha, with a green ruby on its top, tied around his neck. Rudraksha is an Elaeocarpus seed used as prayer beads in Hinduism and Buddhism. Rudraksha seeds are believed to be the teardrops of Lord Rudra, another name for Lord Shiva. These seeds are said to have one to twenty-one faces, and those with fewer faces are rare and valuable. For instance, a three-faced Rudraksha is believed to signify the trinity of Lord Shiva, Lord Brahma and Lord Vishnu. A Rudraksha with only one face is believed to grow only once on its tree in several years.

Kushang Dorjee's nine-faced Rudraksha was also highly valuable, not just because it was rare or had a green ruby attached to it, but because he had got it from his father, and the father from the grandfather. It was a family tradition to pass the prayer bead to the eldest son, one generation after another.

Desperate to leave that place as soon as he could and reach his destination, Kushang Dorjee took out the Rudraksha and offered to sell it to the owner of the rice mill he was working in.

'How much do you want for this?' the rice mill owner asked.

'I don't know. How much will you give?' Kushang Dorjee replied, not knowing the real worth of his valuable asset.

'I will give you 80 rupees.'

'Fine,' Kushang Dorjee said, took the 80 rupees and marched on, crossing Nepal's eastern border of Kakarbhitta to the adjacent Indian city of Siliguri.

Kushang Dorjee and his friend met a man in Siliguri, who asked them where they were going. The boys told him they were headed for Darjeeling, in search of work. The man told them that there were no jobs in Darjeeling, and instead offered to find them work in Bhutan.

'It's very hard to find a job in Darjeeling. If you guys agree, I will find you work at a construction site in Bhutan. You will be paid 5 rupees a day.'

'Can we work there for a couple of months and return home?' Kushang Dorjee asked, knowing that he had to go back as he had a family and wife at home.

'Of course!' the man said. 'It's up to you how long you want to work there.'

In the next couple of days, the boys were in Chimakoti in Bhutan, ready to explore what life had to offer them. 'I was excited about the daily wage of 5 rupees that the man had promised,' he recalled. 'I thought I would collect some money and go back home after a few months.'

Kushang Dorjee still remembers his first day at the construction site of the Chukha hydropower project in Chimakoti. The hydropower plant was in the country's Wang Chu River, a major tributary to the Brahmaputra, one of the world's longest rivers, connecting Tibet, China, India and Bangladesh. There were dozens of boys just like him, who were queued up for medical tests. Some were Nepalis, some Bhutanese and some Indians. When his turn came, someone asked him to take off all his clothes. Kushang Dorjee did as he was told and turned 360 degrees, naked, confirming that he did not have any physical issues. He was then sent to another queue, where a person pricked a needle into him, extracting blood. 'That must have been our blood test,' Kushang Dorjee told us. 'I did not know what was going on, but I was still very excited and nervous about everything.'

Kushang Dorjee passed all the medical examinations and was finally sent to his living quarters. His friend was sent to another location and

Kushang Dorjee was all on his own. The very next day, he was sent to a stone mining location with a heavy hammer. In the 1970s, the project was still in its preliminary phase and demanded a lot of physical labour. Cashing in on this opportunity, the agents and contractors had brought in young boys from Nepal, India and even Bhutan, to work. Without a second thought, Kushang Dorjee started mining stones, imagining that he would be holding the 5 rupees at the end of the day, his highest salary so far.

After hammering the stones for the whole day, Kushang Dorjee was sent back to his shelter, with no money in hand. 'I asked someone there and he told me that the wages would be distributed at the end of the month. I thought that was fine and just kept working.' Kushang Dorjee would see his friend occasionally during the day when they were working, but the workers were not allowed to talk. 'We would just exchange smiles and keep working,' he said.

A few days later, just as he was getting accustomed to mining the stones, Kushang Dorjee was transferred to another location within the same site, this time to carry construction materials from one point to another. Within another couple of weeks, when he got transferred to several other locations demanding different kinds of labour, Kushang Dorjee realized it was not one particular job that was expected of him. 'But that was fine, as I was getting to learn different aspects of the work there,' he said.

At the end of his first month, the boys were lined up again. Someone told Kushang Dorjee that it was the day of salary distribution. He hadn't felt so happy since he had left home. He looked around to find his friend, but could not see him. 'He must be in another queue,' Kushang Dorjee thought, and kept waiting in his line. When his turn came, he gave his thumbprint sign on a piece of paper and gestured his hands forward, excited to finally touch his month's hard-earned money. The moment he looked at the money in his hand, Kushang Dorjee felt dizzy. All he had in his hand was 5 rupees. 'This must be a mistake,' Kushang Dorjee told himself, but before he could enquire, he got pushed out of the line. Confused and devastated, he discovered that it was his full salary. The contractor had kept his own cut and paid for the living costs of the workers out of their salaries.

Like Kushang Dorjee, there were others who were not happy with the remuneration. Somebody shouted, 'This is too little. I will leave this place right now.' Just as a revolt was about to ensue among the workers, the guards came running and started thrashing the workers to the ground. The moment Kushang Dorjee saw his fellow workers being beaten, he soon realized that leaving the place was not an option. Only 15 years old when he was sold to the contractor, Kushang Dorjee did not have the courage to run away from his employer's constant watch. 'We have been sold here,' Kushang Dorjee told himself, his head spinning with dizziness and his vision blurred with tears. All of his dreams for a life better than the one he had back in his village crumbled into pieces. 'All the work that I had enjoyed during my first month there with the expectation of a good income suddenly started getting heavy. I felt all the pain at once,' he said.

The living conditions at the construction site were unbelievably harsh. For his food, all Kushang Dorjee received from the contractor every month was 2.5kg (5.5lb) each of wheat flour and rice, a little bit of salt and some cooking oil. 'To make sure that my food rations lasted for the month, I used to boil the flour in water with some cooking oil to make a thick solution. I ate that twice a day,' Kushang Dorjee recalled.

Further, sleeping was an absolute nightmare. The living quarters provided to the labourers were makeshift shelters made of polythene and cardboard, wrapped around a four-cornered bamboo frame. There were no proper blankets or jackets, and Kushang Dorjee had only a sweater he had brought from Nepal for warmth, all day and night. 'The shelter would leak during monsoon. During the winter, it used to be extremely cold,' he added. 'I found a jute sack used to carry wheat flour. That became my sleeping bag for all the years I was in Chimakoti.' Chimakoti village, situated in a hilly area by the river, is usually cold in every season of the year. Back then, the village was just a small settlement of fewer than 100 houses.

Kushang Dorjee spent another four or five years of his life as a bonded labourer in the same construction site in Chimakoti. He never saw his friend who he'd arrived with again and believes he was transferred elsewhere. At some point, Kushang had started to believe that it was his fate to grow old there and that he would be crushed to death one day by the load on his own back.

For that reason, the *Jhakri*'s prophecy about Kushang Dorjee's future – 'You will be the king one day!' – no matter how unlikely it was, sparked hope in what was for Kushang Dorjee otherwise a battle lost in unreserved hopelessness.

'It must have been around 1979 or 1980, when a fellow Bengali worker from India came to me and proposed to plan an escape,' Kushang Dorjee said. 'I got back my purpose in life – to escape the hell we were in and just see if there was still a possibility for a life slightly better than the one we had there.'

The boys had two options – either go downhill from Chimakoti towards Bhutan's border with India, or uphill from Chimakoti, towards the city of Paro, host to Bhutan's only international airport. 'We thought it would be easier for our employers to come searching for us downhill towards the border than in the direction of Paro,' Kushang Dorjee said. 'One morning, we gathered our courage and left towards Paro on a public jeep.'

There were several police checkpoints on the way. 'Thinking of it now, it was very unlikely that our employers in Chimakoti could stop us at the checkpoints as they neither had our photographs nor any reference about our identities. On top of that, we were just cheap bonded labourers and I don't think our running away was any major loss for them,' Kushang Dorjee said. 'However, at the time, we were scared to the bone, and did not want to take any chances.'

The two boys would get off the jeep a little before each checkpoint. Kushang Dorjee would crouch and hide himself behind the vehicle, taking slow steps along with the jeep as it crawled towards the checkpoint, finally crossing it on foot. The Bengali boy, similarly, kneeled down by the front tyre to check if there was a puncture, and crawled past the checkpoint, hiding his face. 'There is no way the guards at the checkpoints would not have noticed us doing all that,' Kushang Dorjee giggled. 'They did not stop us only because there was nothing suspicious about us. They must have been wondering why we were doing all that.'

The boys got off the jeep before entering Paro and took shelter at a carpenter's workshop. Fortunately, the carpenter was looking for helping hands when the boys arrived and they were instantly employed. Their job was to cut down trees at a nearby forest and saw the logs. The job was several times easier than what they had been doing at Chimakoti. On top of that, the living conditions and the remuneration were also beyond decent. 'We had not eaten rice in over four years. The food we got there was royal by our standards. Each time I ate, I recalled how the shamans had predicted back in Chimakoti – "You will be the king one day!" ' Kushang Dorjee said.

*

All this time, Kushang Dorjee had been missing home badly. After working for about one year at the carpenter's workshop, he had saved nearly 1,200 rupees. He finally started planning his return. One morning, he said farewell to his employer and his Bengali friend and left Bhutan to go to his village in Nepal. However, soon after crossing Bhutan's border with India, he started having second thoughts. *There will be so many questions. What will I tell my father and mother? Oh…There is my wife as well. She must be waiting for me. What will I tell her? How will I face her? That will all be so awkward, and if I return home now, they might never let me go again.*

Having faced so many atrocities and finally free to explore the world on his own, committing to a mundane village life was simply not an option good enough for Kushang Dorjee. From India's Siliguri, he turned his feet towards Sikkim in the north, instead of Nepal's bordering town of Kakarbhitta to the west. As he went north, back in his village in Nepal, after seven years of waiting, his childhood wife got married to one of his cousins.

Kushang Dorjee went to Lachung in northeast Sikkim and found himself work in road construction. Apart from hired labourers like Kushang Dorjee, one person from each family in the nearby villages was required to contribute their labour in the construction of the road. That's where Kushang Dorjee saw Pinky. For the first time in his life, Kushang Dorjee felt butterflies in his stomach, and started stealing moments during work to look into the eyes of his beloved. The exchanges started with smiles and gradually came to the offering of a daytime meal. 'We hardly talked and only threw smiles at each other. Then she started sharing her food with me. I had come to believe that we were in love, but we didn't express this,' he said.

That's when Kushang Dorjee's modest education of just a few years came in handy. 'I could scribble a few words. With lots of struggle, I started writing letters expressing how beautiful I found her, along with proposals for meeting in private,' he said. 'Guess what, my letters worked. Pinky came to meet me. After a couple of such meetings, I asked her to marry me. Without accepting or rejecting, she just shied away. This made me anxious as I took that as a rejection.'

Kushang Dorjee's hopes of love were resurrected during a football match between the labour workers in Lachung. As the boys played, the girls from nearby villages came to the ground to watch the match. On one occasion, when Kushang Dorjee got the ball and started dribbling it towards the opponents' goal, he happened to see Pinky vigorously cheering him on in the crowd. 'This convinced me that I still had my chances in love,' Kushang Dorjee recalled. 'That's when I decided I should marry her before anyone else did.'

Kushang Dorjee wrote another confident letter, asking, for one final time, about marriage. Pinky sent a messenger this time – her cousin sister – to talk to Kushang Dorjee and confirm if he was really in love. 'She asked me if I was not planning to sell her elsewhere,' Kushang Dorjee said. 'As it had come to this, I became surer that we were going to get married soon.'

However, it was not possible for Kushang Dorjee to convince Pinky's parents. First, he was an outsider in Lachung, a poor labourer. Besides that, he belonged to a different caste. Knowing that he would never get the consent of her parents, Kushang Dorjee started planning for a capture marriage, a tradition in Sikkim and some parts of eastern Nepal, where a boy selects a bride who may not consent easily, or when he wants to avoid the long procedure involving the family's consent and the expenditure of an arranged marriage. In Sikkim, after capture, if a girl refuses to get married for three days, she is allowed to return to her parents. If she agrees, the wedding can take place in the presence of parents, relatives and friends from both sides. Festival fairs are considered the perfect occasion to capture brides of their choice for boys, and Kushang Dorjee started preparing for the same, during the Lhosar festival in February 1982.

The day finally came. Pinky had agreed to meet Kushang Dorjee at the festival. As soon as they met, he held her hands and forced her into a van that he had hired. 'I told her I was going to capture her for marriage, but, as I had expected, she was reluctant. I put her in a van and slipped into Bhutan, once again,' he said.

After the capture, Kushang Dorjee had three days to convince Pinky to marry him, but he feared that even if she agreed, her parents might create problems later, as Kushang Dorjee was poor and did not have a family or a pool of friends to support him in Sikkim. 'As we were both in love already, I was sure she would agree to marry me,' he said. 'So, I brought her to Bhutan, to the same carpentry workshop I had worked in after escaping from Chimakoti. She cried a lot on the first day, but soon agreed to marry me.'

During his work in Sikkim, Kushang Dorjee had saved 4,000 rupees, which he used for the wedding. Then he started working again at the same workshop, this time with a companion standing by him. Life slowly started getting more comfortable than it had been previously. There, the couple also had their first two children, a boy and a girl.

*

Kushang Dorjee was part of the wider Nepali-speaking community in Bhutan. The first reports of people of Nepali origin in Bhutan were around 1620, when the Bhutanese ruler commissioned a few craftsmen from the Kathmandu Valley in Nepal to construct a silver stupa. After that, people of Nepali origin started to settle in uninhabited areas of southern Bhutan, and the south soon became the country's main supplier of food. Bhutanese of Nepali origin, known as *Lhotshampas* locally, were flourishing along with the economy of Bhutan. By the 1930s, much of the south was under cultivation by a population of Nepali origin, which was constantly on the rise.

By the 1980s, the government of Bhutan had started perceiving the growing Nepali dichotomy as a threat to their national unity, and consequently enacted a new citizenship law under their 'one nation, one people' policy, forcing the use of Driglam Namzha, the Bhutanese national dress and etiquette code. This policy required citizens to wear the attire of the northern Bhutanese in public places under penalty of fines, and reinforced the status of Dzongkha as the national language. A decade later, after a rather violent inter-ethnic conflict in Bhutan, hundreds of thousands of Nepali-speaking Bhutanese fled to Nepal and became refugees.

After Bhutan adopted these new policies, Kushang Dorjee recalls the start of an uprising among the Nepali-speaking community there. While many started protesting against government regulations, some had started fleeing the country already in the late 1980s. Kushang Dorjee was one of them. Although he did not have any deep roots in Bhutan, he sensed a threat to the well-being of his family and silently moved out in 1987. This time, with his wife and two children, Kushang Dorjee went straight to Darjeeling, finally arriving at the destination that he had left for from Dharan one day with a friend, over a decade ago.

*

When Kushang Dorjee came to Darjeeling, mountaineering was already in full swing. The HMI had been conducting extensive mountaineering training for climbers from all over the country, and a number of expeditions around the mountains of India as well as Nepal were being commissioned one after another. Sherpas travelling to Darjeeling from different mountain villages of Nepal, including from the Khumbu region, were also increasing and, with the legacy of Tenzing Norgay (see Chapter 4), Sherpas had gained maximum trust at the HMI as competent climbers.

Just like Tenzing Norgay, Kushang Dorjee settled with his family in the small village of Alubari, and started working in potato farms and as a labourer at a nearby train station in Ghoom. Two years before he arrived in Darjeeling, Kushang Dorjee's younger brother, Sange, had already come there from their home in Nepal's Sankhuwasabha District. Kushang Dorjee sought the help of his brother to assimilate with the Sherpa community in Darjeeling, and gradually started exploring his chances at the HMI.

'I used to envy the Sherpas carrying colourful rucksacks around Darjeeling,' he said. 'To me as a Sherpa, it was clear that my life would be all about carrying loads here and there. I just wanted to upgrade a little, and be a better porter with rucksacks, with all those colourful strings and clips.'

With so many ups and downs in life thus far, and with all the drifting away from his mountain life to the construction sites and carpentry workshops of Bhutan and Sikkim, Kushang Dorjee had been completely cut off from mountains for over a decade. Yet, he was a Sherpa and, at the HMI, he sneaked into the training courses with other Sherpas of Darjeeling and quickly learned the ways of climbing. He developed an understanding about ropes used for climbing, the suits and the gear, and soon became ready to join the climbers as a porter.

In 1989, the HMI sent Kushang Dorjee on a Kanchenjunga expedition as a porter. 'I was with a team of American climbers, and, for the first time in Kanchenjunga, I realized that my life was changing,' he said.

For Kushang Dorjee, the mountain was difficult to climb, but he had met so many more demanding challenges in life that it all felt easy to him. 'Back in Chimakoti, I had grown up working with an empty stomach. Here,

I was getting good and timely food,' he said. 'In Chimakoti, I used to have sleepless nights as I did not have anything to keep myself warm. In the mountain, I had layers of warm clothes, including quality down jackets. As we worked on Kanchenjunga, I had a team with me that I could depend on, and with whom I could crack jokes and share things. The team had full faith in me and I could trust them fully. On top of everything, the pay was decent.'

The following year, Kushang Dorjee was included in a route-opening team in a Makalu expedition with the Japanese. 'We opened the route up to 8,000m (26,247ft),' he said, recalling his first experience at that altitude. 'It was mostly smooth, and I don't remember struggling too much while climbing up to that height,' he said. Although only the clients went over 8,000m (26,247ft) and scaled the summit, for Kushang Dorjee, it was a huge achievement and a check of his own high-altitude capacity.

Having passed his first two tests in Kanchenjunga and Makalu with flying colours, Kushang Dorjee got his first summit opportunity in 1991, on Nanda Devi 'East' in India's Uttarakhand region, also considered one of the most technical mountains in the world to climb.

The director at the HMI asked Kushang Dorjee, 'Do you think you can go to Nanda Devi? It's very technical and difficult to climb.'

Without a hint of doubt, and excited about his first summit opportunity, Kushang Dorjee responded in a rather assertive tone, '... *ahhh...kina nasaknu hau? Sakihalchha ni*' ('What are you talking about? Of course. I can definitely do that.')

As he told us this story at his home in Darjeeling, leaning against a wall that spoke out loud of his achievements in life, Kushang Dorjee was equally assertive. We could see the same spark in his eyes, and the tone in which he relayed this story made us feel as if he was speaking with the HMI director, and not us. His assertiveness spoke clearly of his determination and his belief in his own capability, as if he had been climbing the mountains all his life.

'I was excited and determined about scaling Nanda Devi, as it would be my first ever summit on any mountain,' Kushang Dorjee said. 'The mountain was very difficult, but my excitement won over all the challenges. I stood on top of the mountain and told myself, no matter how challenging it was – well, this was a piece of cake.'

The following year, in 1992, Kushang Dorjee went to Everest for the first time. Only two Sherpas accompanying the clients were going to get a chance to go to the summit, and Kushang Dorjee did all he could to be one of them. In a bid to impress the team leader, Kushang Dorjee did five rotations up to Camp 4 at 8,000m (26,247ft), carrying goods and supplies. Yet, alas, he did not get the opportunity. Rather, his younger brother Sange, who was also a member of the team, got the summit chance. 'I was an assertive Sherpa, always ready to question the decisions of the team leader,' Kushang Dorjee giggled. 'But my brother was naïve and wouldn't question anything. They wanted a "Yes Man" as a Sherpa, and therefore he got selected and not me.'

Although he did not get a chance to go to the summit on his first time on Everest, the next year, he got another opportunity. This time, he went all the way to the top. During his mountaineering career, Kushang Dorjee scaled the summit of Everest 5 times – add to that over 30 summits of different mountains across India and Nepal. As summits kept adding to his profile, back in the HMI, Kushang Dorjee was taking a rather thoughtful leap in mountaineering.

One of the senior instructors at the HMI, Dorje Latu, appointed Kushang Dorjee as his personal assistant. There used to be several batches of trainees at the HMI every year. The best of the climbers from all over India, including from the army and police, used to come to the HMI for an extensive mountaineering course. As the helper of instructor Dorje Latu, Kushang Dorjee got direct exposure to all aspects of the training and further honed his climbing skills. 'My main responsibility was to help the instructor to arrange logistics for the training, carry training equipment here and there, and take care of the trainees' timetable, food and accommodation,' he said. 'Beyond my job description, I also went as far as serving the food in the mess, sometimes cooking and even cleaning plates.'

As the instructor's helper, Kushang Dorjee got direct access to the course classes and learned technicalities around climbing first-hand, together with the students. 'It was hard for me to understand theoretical aspects in the beginning,' Kushang Dorjee said. 'Still, I used to sit in a corner and listen carefully, trying to understand as much as I could. Even if I didn't understand a few things, I always had another chance to clear my doubts, during the training of the next batch.'

Reinforcing his knowledge and skills one group after another, Kushang Dorjee himself became an expert and one of the most dependable climbers at the HMI. After his Kangshung Face feat in 1999, he earned unquestionable recognition and got a permanent government job as an instructor at the HMI. He was even promoted gradually to become the chief instructor of the institute. Today, the government-run museum at the HMI has dedicated a premium space to Kushang Dorjee's stature, exhibiting his personal climbing suit, gear and photographs. As the government of India preserves his prominence, for this retired Sherpa the moment of pride is when his neighbours salute him in the street. He cherishes the companionship of his wife and the guardianship he is able to offer to his children. 'This is all that I had once lost in my life, but I have gained all of it back again,' he contemplated, recalling the shamans' prophecies back in Bhutan.

If Kushang Dorjee's rise 'from rags to riches' does not align with the traits of a king, what does?

Chapter 6

THE MOUNTAINS OF THE
SHERPA WOMEN

7 March 1993.

Members of Nepal's first women's Everest expedition team are about to leave Kathmandu for Lukla. Dozens of people, including relatives, well-wishers and journalists, have gathered at the home of Pasang Lhamu Sherpa, the expedition team leader.

For the families, this is a moment full of emotion – these women are daughters, wives, sisters, mothers, friends…and this is the final goodbye before what is going to be a historical mission. For some, the Nepali women's aspiration to step on top of the world is surprising, while others wonder: 'Can they really make it?'

For the women themselves, though, their thoughts are not on whether the expedition will be successful. In these last minutes before they leave, they have not been thinking about the journey or the adventure, but about the children they are leaving back home. Beyond these feelings, emotions and personal motivations, this expedition has already become a matter of significant national and public interest.

Members of the expedition – Pasang Lhamu, Lhakpa Futi Sherpa and Nanda Rai – are seated on a sofa in Pasang Lhamu's living room, while people approach them one by one to offer *khaada*, a Buddhist way of bidding best wishes. There are hugs and continuous exchanges of smiles. The room is full of energy, and a positive aura emanates from everyone's best wishes and prayers. Someone enters the living room with a tray carrying Chinese clay teacups, making their way through the crowd to the sofa where the showstoppers are seated. Pasang Lhamu picks up a cup. Just as she is about to take her first sip, team member Lhakpa Futi notices a small crack on one side of the cup. Everybody in the room sees the same, as does Pasang Lhamu herself.

Lhakpa Futi notices a flash of concern pass over Pasang Lhamu's face and the energy and positive vibes in the room wane a little, quickly lowering into a heavy silence. Lhakpa Futi tries to convince herself that the broken teacup is just a coincidence, but the nagging doubt won't subside.

The teacup is immediately replaced, and the atmosphere in the room apprehensively returns to the optimism and enjoyment of just moments before. However, it is now tainted, as superstition has it that broken teacups bring ominous signs in a journey. Despite this, nobody in this room today will dare to challenge the fate of this expedition. It has already come too far, especially as no other Nepali expedition has ever garnered as much attention before the summit. From here, there is no going back.

As they step out of the house, Pasang Lhamu's children wave goodbye to their mother and the other team members. This reminds Lhakpa Futi of her child, and she receives the goodbyes from Pasang Lhamu's children with an unusual intensity. 'What if this becomes the final goodbye and we never make it back?'

For Lhakpa Futi, the expedition of 1993 had started to turn ugly even before the broken teacup incident.

A few days previously, Lhakpa Futi had gone to Boudhanath Stupa, a major Buddhist shrine in Kathmandu (see page 55), to offer her prayers and ask for blessings for the upcoming expedition. She wanted to hang prayer flags on the stupa from top to bottom as an offering to the gods. Buddhists offer colourful prayer flags with printed mantras and hymns from Tibetan scriptures in stupas and monasteries. Lhakpa Futi was told four bundles of prayer flags would be more than enough to cover the entire length of the stupa, with its 36-m (118-ft) dome. However, that day, the bundles fell a little short and didn't cover the whole length of the stupa from top to bottom.

'This was a bad sign, but I did not think of it too much at the time,' Lhakpa

Futi said. 'It was only when other events started unfolding, including the broken teacup incident, that I started connecting the dots.' Lhakpa Futi has documented her unfulfilled quest and memories from 1993 expedition in her autobiography *Forty Years in the Mountains*.

*

The spring of 1993 was a vibrant time at Everest Base Camp. Alongside Pasang Lhamu's unit, there was another climbing team, which consisted of Nepali and Indian women climbers.

Pasang Lhamu was actually supposed to be the deputy team leader of this Indo–Nepali group. However, when she was later denied that position, she decided to form a separate group and pursue climbing on her own, possibly even summiting before the group she had left. The Indo–Nepali expedition group included Nimi Sherpa, who was also aspiring to become the first Nepali woman to climb Everest.

Apart from these two teams, Koreans, Americans, Europeans and Russians were on the mountain that year. There were also other well-known Sherpas of that time, including Ang Rita Sherpa, who had already climbed Everest without oxygen seven times (see page 256). By the end of this busy season, a total of 90 people had reached the summit of Everest.

As Lhakpa Futi recalls, her unit of women climbers was constantly trying to stand out at Base Camp and proudly identify themselves as the first women from Nepal to disrupt the status quo. A banner hanging outside their tent would attract foreigners, who would invite the women climbers for lunch or dinner. The team also got along very well with the Indo–Nepali group and they would regularly hop into each other's tents to see how their friends were doing.

Back then, helicopters were not as common in Base Camp as they are now. Therefore, any messages had to come or go via a mail-runner, a person designated to deliver letters and notes from Lukla to Base Camp and vice versa, literally by running. In the first few weeks, as the climbers were busy acclimatizing to Base Camp, a mail-runner dropped a letter from Pasang

Lhamu's daughter in her tent. In the letter, Pasang Lhamu's daughter had scribbled a picture of her mother on top of the world. Pasang Lhamu and Lhakpa Futi read the letter together and were overcome with emotion. The two mothers hugged each other and cried a lot that day.

Just as everything seemed under control, another disturbing incident brought back the gloomy augurs of the broken teacup and the prayer flags at Boudhanath Stupa for Lhakpa Futi.

A few days before they started their ascent, a *puja* (prayer) was organized at Base Camp to pray for safety and ask for forgiveness from the mountain mother goddess for stepping on her body. As is customary, a wooden structure called a *lingo* was erected to tie prayer flags to. As a Buddhist Lama priest conducted the *puja*, someone approached the *lingo* to tie on a prayer flag. The person stumbled upon a string tied on the *lingo* and almost pulled the structure to the ground.

'This incident sent chills down my spine,' Lhakpa Futi recalled. 'For the first time, I feared for the fate of our expedition. I immediately turned towards the top of Everest and whirled some enchanted rice grains.'

However, the series of incidents did not stop there.

One morning, Pasang Lhamu woke up and shared a bad dream she had had with Lhakpa Futi. ' "I had a dream where I saw myself praying at an unknown monastery. I heard that a prayer said at an unknown monastery is a bad sign. I don't feel so well today",' Lhakpa Futi recalls Pasang Lhamu telling her.

As they moved up to the higher camps, the expedition slowly started getting uglier and more desolate for Lhakpa Futi. To her surprise, Pasang Lhamu proposed to split the expedition into two. She was willing to go alone first, with a few guides, and send Lhakpa Futi and Nanda Rai together later after her return.

When Lhakpa Futi objected – 'Both of us have left our little children at home. We have been together in this all the way. Let's complete this mission together' – she still remembers how Pasang Lhamu reacted: 'Do you think I will steal the top of Everest by going there before you?'

Despite all the uncertainties, as this was a decision of the team leader, Lhakpa Futi and Nanda Rai decided to let Pasang Lhamu go ahead and scale the summit without them.

The day the team arrived at Camp 2, Nanda Rai started showing symptoms of high-altitude sickness. She had been vomiting a lot, and her lips and the skin around her eyes were turning blue. The team consulted with a doctor in an American camp and immediately took Nanda Rai back to Base Camp. Lhakpa Futi accompanied her ailing partner while Pasang Lhamu and the other team members stayed at Camp 2.

At Base Camp that night, it was Lhakpa Futi's turn to have a bad dream. In her dream, Pasang Lhamu had apparently scaled the summit and was being brought down in an inverted umbrella, in which she sat silently, dressed unusually in black attire. The dream also had Pasang Lhamu celebrating her success, dancing and singing on a summit that was not actually Everest.

When Lhakpa Futi returned to Camp 2 the following day, Pasang Lhamu had already left for the summit along with her Sherpa guides, determined to win against her close competitors in the Indo–Nepali team. Lhakpa Futi was shocked that Pasang Lhamu had not waited even for a last exchange of good wishes before heading up. Added to this, Pasang Lhamu had made her summit push from Camp 2 on a Thursday, believed by some to be an 'unlucky' day.

With a heavy heart, Lhakpa Futi could only wait for Pasang Lhamu to come back down so that she could also go to the summit. Lhakpa Futi started preparing for a pre-summit rotation to the higher camp to prepare herself for the final push in the following days. On 22 April, she walked up to Camp 3 alone, where she met a group of Korean climbers. One of the Korean climbers read Lhakpa Futi's palm and declared that she would not be able to scale the summit of Everest that year. That same night in Camp 3,

Lhakpa Futi heard Pasang Lhamu calling out her name from a distance. She crept out of the tent but did not see anything. This repeated several times throughout the night and only added to Lhakpa Futi's unease.

The following day, she climbed down to Camp 2 and shared the previous night's hallucination with the other team members. To everyone's surprise, a Sherpa in the team said he had also had a similar vision of Pasang Lhamu calling out his name for help all night.

*

On 22 April 1993, Pasang Lhamu made it to the summit of Everest along with Sherpa guides Sonam Tsering and Pemba Norbu. The country found a national hero in this 32-year-old woman; however, what many recall as a smooth ascent to the top of the world, turned rather ugly during the descent and the celebration was to be short-lived.

While descending, Sonam Tsering fell sick somewhere near the South Summit, and the three had to wait there overnight, expending all the oxygen they had. The next morning, Pasang Lhamu sent Pemba Norbu to fetch oxygen from the lower camps, while she stayed with the ailing guide.

A few hours later, Pemba Norbu arrived at Camp 2, panting heavily. He informed everyone that the three of them had scaled the summit the previous day but that it had taken five hours to cover the distance from the top of Everest to the South Summit on the way down, which usually takes about an hour. He also told them that Sonam Tsering was sick and stuck between life and death. When Lhakpa Futi heard this, she recalled her conversation with him on their way up from Base Camp. 'Of all the Sherpas in the team, I was particularly close with Sonam *dai* [a Nepali term for elder brother]. He had told me that he had also been having bad dreams – drinking blood from a cup,' she said. 'He had told me several times to take care of myself if anything happened in the mountain that year.'

Soon after Pemba Norbu left the South Summit to get oxygen, the weather conditions started deteriorating rapidly. In those days, weather prediction systems were not as accurate and accessible as they are now, and there would not have been any real-time monitoring of the changing wind patterns. There was a heavy storm and massive snowfall several feet deep on the surface of Everest up in the death zone, which prevented Pemba Norbu or anyone else from rescuing Pasang Lhamu and Sonam Tsering from the South Summit.

'The storm stayed for over two weeks,' recalled Lhakpa Futi. 'By the end of the day that Pemba Norbu climbed down to our station in Camp 2 to get oxygen, we had already figured out that Pasang *didi* [a Nepali term for elder sister] and Sonam Tsering were no more.

'Before joining the expedition team, I had been actively skiing in Switzerland and other parts of Europe, so I was super fit. Pasang *didi* had been on Everest already in her earlier attempts, so she knew the route well. If we were in it together, I wonder if our stories might have been different,' Lhakpa Futi contemplated.

A team of climbers who summited Everest 18 days later when the storm had passed recovered the body of Pasang Lhamu at 8,750m (28,700ft), but couldn't locate Sonam Tsering. The recovery of her body from deep into the death zone and all the efforts made to bring her down was a rarity; many consider carrying a dead body down from above 8,000m (26,247ft) in elevation a task that is not worth all the risks and, even today, people who die in the death zone are usually left there (see page 284). On top of that, bringing a body down from Everest is several times costlier than climbing itself.

As the first Nepali woman to climb Everest, Pasang Lhamu received posthumous recognition as a national hero and her funeral in Kathmandu was attended by thousands. Her biography was later included in the school curriculum. Many also regard her as an icon equally as significant as Tenzing Norgay, if not more. A postage stamp has been issued in her name and a life-size statue of her stands today in Kathmandu's Boudha neighbourhood (also known as Boudhnath). The government has also named Mount Jasamba (7,315m, 23,999ft) as Pasang Lhamu Peak and a 117-km (73-mile) road as Pasang Lhamu Highway.

The legacy of the 1993 expedition will be remembered as long as people go to the mountains. Some like to view it only in terms of its glory and heroism. For many, it is a story of desperation, while for others it is just another mountain tragedy. For Lhakpa Futi, there are no black-and-white answers either. 'Sometimes, I think I could have saved Pasang *didi* if she had taken me with her,' she said. 'Sometimes, I think Pasang *didi* saved my life by not taking me.'

Torn between conflicting thoughts, Pasang Lhamu's death brought an end to Lhakpa Futi's Everest dreams. She decided never to climb mountains again, but rather to contribute to climbing in any capacity she could. To date, she has supported the mountain-climbing industry of Nepal by helping with mountaineering curriculum development and social work in mountain communities, as well as ground monitoring of mountain expeditions through real-time weather forecasts and communication.

*

Pasang Lhamu's summit of Everest was a significant breakthrough in the long-standing deprivation and sociocultural constraints on women across Nepal. In a society where women were, and still are, mostly restricted within households, a woman spending several nights outside the home and reaching the top of Everest was far beyond anyone's imagination.

The historical, cultural and religious norms of Nepali society rarely accepted the independent existence of a woman and when Pasang Lhamu stepped up to her mission, the country had abolished the Sati system – an act or custom of a Hindu widow burning herself to death or being burned to death on the funeral pyre of her husband – only about 70 years previously.

The story of Pasang Lhamu, Lhakpa Futi and a few other women who were gradually becoming icons in the early 1990s, therefore, holds substantial value in terms of how they had already defied several social restrictions on them, even before the 1993 expedition. At a time when there were limited teahouses, safe lodges and means of communication in the trekking routes high up in the mountain villages, a handful of Sherpa women, including Pasang Lhamu and Lhakpa Futi, had already taken a massive leap by planting a step in mountaineering adventure. The challenges they faced in the mountains were several times bigger than those encountered by their male counterparts.

'Throughout the day, we would struggle to keep ourselves alive in the mountains,' Lhakpa Futi recalled. 'In the night, as we slept in the tents, the threat was over the safety of our bodies. Add to that the rumours, gossip and questions about our character that we had to face after returning home from a mountain or a trekking trip, spending several weeks with known and unknown people.'

After her Everest summit, even though it ended tragically, Pasang Lhamu rose to become a national hero. As a result, 30 years down the line, she is still a household name.

Of course, things have changed a lot since the time of Pasang Lhamu. According to official data from the early 1990s, only 17 per cent of Nepali women were literate. Today, the women's literacy rate stands at over 57 per cent. After Pasang Lhamu, scores of Nepali women have summited Everest and a number of women today are trekking guides. Despite everything, however, Nepali women still struggle to find their place against deep-rooted cultural norms that have existed for hundreds of years. It is a slightly different form of mountain that Nepali women climb every day. Even within the Sherpa community, it's men who dominate mountaineering adventure and trekking. Sherpa women, in the meantime, have found their niche in the operation of the tourism industry in the mountain villages by running teahouses, hotels and lodges.

*

Not very far from Everest Base Camp, at an altitude of 4,400m (14,450ft), stands the village of Dingboche. In Dingboche, sometime in the late 1990s, the mundane village life of 22-year-old Furdiki Sherpa was about to take an exciting turn with the new-found love of her life – Mingma Sherpa, a carpenter who had just arrived there from a lower altitude village in the Solukhumbu District. The eldest daughter of veteran Icefall doctor Ang Nima Sherpa, Furdiki would be busy most of the time looking after her younger siblings and cattle, and helping her mother with household chores. Her encounter with the carpenter gave her a much-needed break from this mundane routine. After some initial exchanges of smiles and greetings with Mingma, she had already started feeling butterflies in her stomach. Mingma, on the other hand, was very shy and would steal moments from his carpentry work to fall in love with Furdiki, but found it hard to express his feelings.

In this small village of about two hundred individuals, hiding a transpiring love story from the villagers was simply not possible. While some started gossiping about the affair, others began lobbying for the wedding of Furdiki and Mingma. Some men from Mingma's village married women from Dingboche and lived as *gharjwaai*, with their wives' families, a common practice in the region. Furdiki's father himself had married her mother and stayed with her family in Dingboche as a *gharjwaai*.

The men from Mingma's village convinced Mingma to marry Furdiki and live with her family as a *gharjwaai*. This was the perfect proposal for Furdiki as she did not want to leave her family yet, especially her father, with whom she shared a special bond. As this relationship would fulfil the missing elements of love and excitement in both of their somewhat lonely lives, their three months of attraction quickly transformed into a marriage for life.

It was only after they were married that Furdiki and Mingma got to know each other more. Mingma turned out to be far shyer and more reserved than Furdiki had imagined. 'Most of the time, he would only be working. He would hardly talk to me, let alone hang out with friends,' Furdiki giggled.

After the marriage, Mingma continued with his carpentry. For his extraordinary strength carrying heavy loads, helpfulness, unquestioning honesty and diligence at work, Mingma became dear to all the villagers in no time. Livelihood opportunities were limited in this lonely village, mostly active only during the spring and autumn seasons. For the rest of the year, the village would be engulfed in snow, without much to do. Furdiki rented a house and started running a small tourist lodge, also known as a teahouse. But the business would be limited to only two to three months throughout the year, and the combined income of both Mingma and Furdiki was hardly enough to make ends meet.

After two years of marriage, the couple gave birth to a child. After this, they moved to Chhukhung, a temporary lodge habitation at 4,700m (15,400ft), in a trail west of Dingboche leading to Island Peak, a trekking peak for beginner mountaineers. Furdiki and Mingma started a lodge there. As the income from the lodge was not quite enough to sustain living throughout the year, they bought four yaks. They would rent the yaks to transport goods from Namche Bazaar to the village and sometimes Everest Base Camp and other areas in the region. Furdiki would mostly send Mingma with the yaks while she kept busy looking after the lodge and their child. 'For someone so quiet, probably that was the best profession,' Furdiki laughed. 'You don't have to talk with the yaks, do you?'

As men are busy trekking and mountaineering during spring and autumn, young mothers cooking and serving tourists at their lodge, carrying a baby on their back in a basket hanging by their forehead, is a common sight even today all across the region. In Chhukhung, when Mingma was away with the yaks, Furdiki would do precisely this.

During busy seasons, operating a lodge at that altitude, especially with a baby, is similar to fighting a battle in the mountains. As water takes no time to freeze, the women have to keep boiling it every minute. Tourists and trekkers entering the lodge are out of breath most of the time, and it is a tough job catering to their needs for warm water and juice. With no more than one or two staff in the lodge, cooking and serving is equally demanding; needless to say, there is also the need to keep the lodge and rooms clean and sanitized at all times. On top of everything, Furdiki was illiterate and could hardly count on her fingers up to ten. Therefore, keeping up with the accounts and record-keeping at the lodge was equally tormenting for her.

For a break sometimes, Mingma would stay home and look after the lodge while Furdiki accompanied the yaks. Once, when Furdiki was on her way to Chhukhung from Namche Bazaar with the yaks, carrying the baby on her back, she encountered her father, Ang Nima. Ang Nima melted when he witnessed the hardship his beloved daughter had been going through all this time. He quickly came up with a proposal to get his son-in-law employed as an Icefall doctor, just like him. Mingma had what it took to excel in the mountains and the opportunity to train with his veteran father-in-law was the cherry on top. Mingma's routine life was about to take a dramatic turn. He was about to go to the mountains.

*

As an Icefall doctor, Mingma's job was limited to the areas near Base Camp, precisely from the Khumbu Icefall region to Camp 2. Yet, his job was one of the most demanding ones, dealing with the extremely dangerous Khumbu Icefall (see page 22)

As we've seen, the risks in this region primarily come with the highly dynamic movement of the trail, which is sometimes even likely to capsize the route upside down. Then there are deep crevasses created by the friction of chunks of fast- and slow-moving ice. Add to that the several ice seracs (blocks or pillars of ice that are formed where crevasses intersect) on the way, increasing the risk of avalanche for the climbers passing by.

For the Icefall doctors, identification of the best route is often based on experience and predictions. To ensure these predictions won't fail, the Icefall doctors put their own lives in danger, test the routes and verify them for other climbers.

Let's picture a group of Icefall doctors working to bridge a deep crevasse in the Icefall with a ladder. The Icefall doctors at one side of the crevasse calculate the length of their ladder against the width of the crevasse. Then they throw the ladder to rest one end on the other side, creating a bridge over the crevasse. They fix this bridge on their side with screws and ropes, but the ladder is still untethered on the other side. The ice is slippery, and the untethered end of the ladder glides left and right as one of the Icefall doctors, with the weight of ropes and screws on his back, carefully crawls over to get to the other side so that he can fix it.

'Every summit of Everest owes all the glory to the Icefall doctors like my father and husband,' Furdiki said. 'While they are committed to ensuring a safe route for all the climbers coming behind them, the Icefall doctors are all on their own, risking their lives every minute identifying, fixing and testing the route.'

Beyond any technical skills with ice and equipment, Icefall doctors are also known as people with a sixth sense, who can figure out and predict the volatile behaviour of the movement of ice and identify the safest passages for climbers to follow. For their ability to dynamically interact with the ice, rocks and snow, the Icefall doctors can predict the glacier's movement, probably better than any other technology in the world.

'People say that my father could actually have a conversation with the ice,' Furdiki said. 'He would carefully stick his ear against the ice, listen to the sounds coming from the inner core and tell how likely that particular bulk of ice was to stay stable, melt or shift.'

Under the shadow of his father-in-law, Mingma slowly got accustomed to these skills of dealing with ice on Everest. However, no matter how experienced an Icefall doctor is or how well backed up with a team and equipment, predictions and judgements sometimes fail. Nine years into this profession, in 2013, Mingma got caught in such a misjudgement at a crevasse between Camps 1 and 2. He fell off the ladder while trying to fix it and perished. A day before this incident, he had a phone conversation with his wife in Chhukhung from Everest Base Camp. Like always, he said, 'People say that the route is easier this year.'

'Every time I talked with him about his work, he never said how difficult and risky it was. Rather, he kept on stressing how easy it was getting every year with new skills, experience and equipment,' Furdiki told us.

It was only later, when she went to the mountain following her husband's footsteps, that Furdiki realized how toxic this profession had been all those years Mingma was there. 'Had I seen it earlier, I would have kept sending my husband with the yaks, no matter what.'

*

The first few years after the death of her husband were all about mourning for Furdiki. Only about a month before Mingma's incident in the mountain, Furdiki had also lost her father in Dingboche. After losing the two most important men in her life, Furdiki decided to leave Khumbu and stay in Kathmandu with some of her relatives. 'The first two years, I did nothing,' she said. 'When my financial needs started squeezing me, I began exploring options in trekking.'

In Kathmandu one evening, during her daily prayers at Boudhanath Stupa, Furdiki met with Nima Doma Sherpa, an acquaintance from the Khumbu region. Nima Doma was a widow like herself, who had lost her husband in the 2014 avalanche at Khumbu Icefall (see Chapter 2). As the plights of the two women were similar, they quickly became good friends and started meeting each other every day in Boudha, making plans for the weekend and visiting restaurants together.

One Saturday, the women went to a wall-climbing recreation centre in Kathmandu. Afterwards, when they sat down for a coffee, Furdiki unexpectedly suggested that they summit Everest.

They both had a special connection with the mountain and, more than an adventure, an Everest summit would be a tribute to their deceased partners and an opportunity to share spiritually the things that their husbands had never told them about the mountains. In more simple terms, the women wanted to walk in the footsteps left on the Everest trail by their husbands and seek some solace for their heavy hearts. But the women had never been on a mountain before, nor did they have any relevant skills or training. However, determined to achieve what they dreamed of together, Furdiki and Nima Doma started basic mountaineering training in 2017.

The training alone would not be enough. Climbing Everest requires hefty financial back-up, enough to cover all the training, permit charges and equipment, as well as the guide, among other things. Furdiki and Nima Doma started an informal fundraising campaign in 2018. They travelled in the Khumbu region, village-to-village, and asked for any help anyone could extend. This involved pitching their idea about the Everest mission, repeating their story time and again from one household to another, and convincing people about the cause they were upholding.

Barring a few households here and there, the Khumbu region did not disappoint these women determined to go to the roof of the world. 'We heard good words of encouragement from most of the people in the Everest region. This motivated us a lot as we had the confidence that we were not in it alone,' Furdiki said. 'But there were piercing comments as well, when some people told us to stop begging for money and go back to the village and seek a livelihood by farming.' Despite these negative comments, after a two-week fundraising trip across the region, they had accumulated decent savings for their mission.

Back in Kathmandu, Furdiki and Nima Doma sought help from the wider Sherpa community, the expedition companies, Sherpa-led businesses and government offices. While some supported in cash, others provided equipment and training fees. The amount they collected from all these sources was finally enough to fund their expedition. After topping up their basic mountaineering training of 2017 with advanced ice-climbing training at Phortse in 2018, Furdiki and Nima Doma finally headed north, aiming for the expedition in 2019.

As they were still collecting funds until the very last minute, their stay at Everest Base Camp was only for two weeks. Usually, climbers spend at least a month at Base Camp, acclimatizing, preparing and training. 'Although shorter, our two-week stay at Base Camp was just enough for us,' Furdiki said. 'Driven by our cause to follow the footsteps of our beloveds, we were already quite strong, physically and mentally.'

As the women headed up from Base Camp for pre-summit acclimatization rotations to higher camps, all the mental strength they had accumulated started slowly falling apart – not because the mountain was too difficult, but because of the memories that came dancing before their eyes on the trail. From Khumbu Icefall until Camp 2, whenever Furdiki saw old, abandoned and broken pieces of ropes, it would remind her of her husband and father. 'I kept on thinking that these remains must have been left by my father and husband years ago,' she said. 'My eyes were constantly wet.'

Then she came across a crevasse bridged by a ladder. As she gazed downwards, each crevasse seemed to tell the story of how her husband might have fallen, leaving insurmountable pain deep in Furdiki's heart and instantly reducing her to tears.

It was a similar story for Nima Doma. Whenever they passed by an avalanche or a serac, she would burst into tears, imagining how an avalanche just like that had crushed her husband to death. 'Our entire journey up Everest was like a tear-trail. From bottom to top and top to bottom, our eyes were hardly dry,' Furdiki said. Throughout the journey, the two women kept hugging each other, crying together and consoling each other in any way they could.

'At Camp I, we thought together that our husbands might have married for the second time if we had died in their place, and that there was no point crying so much after all these years,' she said. 'These words of consolation, however, made us cry even more. The next day, whenever we came across a crevasse or an avalanche looming overhead, the story would repeat itself.'

The Sherpa guide who was with Furdiki and Nima Doma had also been constantly trying to console the women. Furdiki recalls his words: 'It is not just your husbands who have died in this place. This place is like this, and there is no getting away from it. I might die tomorrow in an accident. Even you two may die. Who will come here and cry after you if you perish in the mountain?'

While the acclimatization rotations to different camps on Everest are meant to prepare the climbers for the altitude and weather, for Furdiki and Nima Doma, the rotation trip was rather a process of emotional acclimatization. Furdiki and Nima Doma were now ready for the final push whenever the summit window opened. During their time of rest at Base Camp, they chose to go to nearby Lobuche Peak, a lower altitude mountain that climbers use for practice and acclimatization (see page 88). As per government rules, a permit to climb a major mountain like Everest comes with a bonus permit to climb smaller peaks like Lobuche. By the time the women returned from Lobuche to Base Camp, the summit window had still not opened, so they travelled to Furdiki's village in Dingboche, at a distance of about one day for them, spent three days there then returned to Base Camp for the final summit push.

A little more consoled and stable than their first time, the tear-trail continued for both of them. On 23 May 2019, at dawn, the women finally made it to the top and lived the mountain life that their husbands had perished in. At the summit, they quickly donned Sherpa attire and clicked pictures. The feeling of standing at the highest point on earth stirred up their emotions once again. This time, though, it was about having done something that they never would have thought of until a few years back.

Only when she got accustomed to trekking at high altitudes did Furdiki appreciate how naïve she had been about the job of a Sherpa all her life. Previously, when her husband and father were on the mountain, she used to think of them whenever there was a storm or the weather was gloomy. 'Whenever the weather was not so good, I thought of my father and husband having a hard time there. On bright sunny days, I thought they were safe,' she said. 'When I started trekking myself, I realized that people usually don't trek or climb in bad weather. Actually, they are safe inside the tents on gloomy days. Rather, the bright days are riskier because they are out in the mountains facing all sorts of challenges.'

*

Furdiki is now a full-time trekking guide. In her experience, people are often initially hesitant about having a woman as their guide. 'I don't know why this is so,' Furdiki said. 'I think they assume we are not as strong and resourceful as men. But when they learn about my Everest summit, they are keen on travelling with me.'

Both of Furdiki's daughters are at university in the USA. They have video chats almost every day, and often her daughters tell her how their friends are amazed to learn that their mother is a mountaineer with Everest in her résumé.

In Kathmandu, Furdiki keeps getting phone calls from journalists for interviews and features. Her stories have appeared in the national media, and she has also been covered by the BBC. With all these accolades and attention on her, Furdiki has higher aims now. Together with her companion Nima Doma, she plans to go to the summit of the highest peaks in all seven continents. Furdiki and Nima Doma are currently working hard to achieve this dream, raising funds and training.

'I have learned that people move on, no matter what,' Furdiki said. 'But I still have a major grudge from that ascent of Everest. I had expected it to somehow make my heart a little lighter. Just the opposite – each time I think about the journey on Everest, my heart feels heavier and I tend to miss my husband more.'

Chapter 7

AN ODD LEGEND

On 23 May 2013, the day before his 42nd birthday, Phurba Tashi Sherpa came to the world's attention with his 21st Everest summit, equalling the then-record of Apa Sherpa, popularly known as 'Super Sherpa'. Thereafter, Phurba Tashi – nicknamed 'Everest Yak' for his superior strength in dealing with altitude and climbing logistics – would never go to the mountains again. Young, fit and a highly demanded guide, when he decided to quit, Phurba Tashi still had a promising career ahead of him.

To date, most of the Sherpas who have been on top of the world as many times as Phurba Tashi have had a climbing career of over two decades. For Phurba Tashi, it had taken less than one and a half.

Throughout his career, even when he made back-to-back summits in a single season, sometimes even thrice a year, he 'never sustained a scratch' on his body.

'My experience and courage always backed me and, above all, luck,' he told us.

So, what was it that stopped him from going to the mountains after his 21st summit?

*

The village of Khumjung, where Phurba Tashi lives with his family, stands 4,000m (13,000ft) in elevation away from the famous Namche Bazaar, next to one of the world's highest airfields in Syangboche.

While these days Namche Bazaar is a commercial hub of the region's tourism, where most people are always in a hurry and almost all the houses are tourist hotels, Khumjung is a relatively quiet home to the Sherpas. A thick settlement of over 500 households, Khumjung, and its adjoining twin village of Khunde, offer a particular treat for the eyes.

All of the houses here follow a similar pattern of construction with green tin roofs and white walls. Unlike other mountain settlements, these two villages sit on extensive plain land, surrounded by mountains. Towards the northern end of the villages, there are two trails – one leading from Namche Bazaar to Mong La and the villages of Phortse, Dole, Machhermo and Gokyo. The other leads towards Everest Base Camp, passing through Tengboche, Dingboche and other higher altitude villages. Observing Khumjung from a distance, the village looks like a patch of several houses, perched safely in the crouched belly of the holy Mount Khumbila (5,761m, 18,900ft). As we approached and entered the valley at its northern end, the village zoomed in, but still offered us a complete view up to the belly of Khumbila.

We had arrived in Khumjung on a relatively warm February afternoon, on our way back from the village of Phortse. Walking by the shops and houses on both sides of a small walking trail lined with stones, we penetrated the thick settlement. Khumjung, with its kitchen gardens and greenhouse tunnels for growing vegetables, appeared to us like a peaceful homely settlement. From the very first sight, it seemed that we had arrived at a happy place, enjoying the abundance bestowed upon it by nature. Before Namche Bazaar's commercial rise, for many years Khumjung served as the base for several mountain expedition teams, including the 1953 successful Everest expedition of Tenzing Norgay Sherpa and Sir Edmund Hillary (see Chapter 4). Later, Sir Edmund Hillary invested much of his time and money into developing this place and contributed to constructing a school, a hospital and the airfield in Syangboche.

The quiet village of Khumjung was even quieter when we arrived there in the middle of the COVID-19 pandemic, asking for Phurba Tashi's home. The villagers showed us the way, and we finally arrived at a football ground by the school built by Hillary.

At one end of the ground is Phurba Tashi's Tashi Friendship Lodge, huddled together with other similar houses in the area. Across from it, past the ground, is a route to the Syangboche airfield and Thame village. Although the Syangboche airport is not in operation for passenger flights, helicopters regularly use it to drop off supplies and airlift the sick.

We entered the premises of the Tashi Friendship Lodge and, inside, were welcomed by a Tibetan mastiff that was, thankfully, tied to a pole. Initially, when we opened the gate, the dog just gave us a steady look, as if confused how to react. The village had rarely seen an outsider throughout the pandemic, so our sudden appearance may have taken the canine by surprise. 'Such a gentleman' we said to ourselves about the mastiff, and entered, not too worried about whether the dog would be offended. However, as soon as we started to walk, the mastiff roared from the bottom of his throat, then started barking at full pelt. It scared us, but as he was tied to a pole, we came to enjoy the booming bark, as if a singer with a deep bass voice was performing.

The dog's barking attracted Phurba Tashi's wife, who instantly came outside to welcome us. She escorted us to the lodge's dining hall, where we sat by a stove used to heat the room and sipped the tea she had brought us. We asked her if Phurba Tashi was around.

'He is in the backyard, working on some broken water pipes,' she replied. While we waited for him to return, we befriended their talkative, five-year-old daughter.

Over dinner that evening, our conversation with Phurba Tashi began with the one question that had been at the forefront of our minds: 'Do you miss the mountains?' Phurba Tashi did not have a black-and-white answer. Instead, he shared with us his incredible story.

*

For several years when he was climbing the mountains, Phurba Tashi's parents did not have any idea what he was actually doing. When he first told his parents he wanted to go to the mountains, they had agreed on one condition – that Phurba Tashi would limit his activities only up to Base Camp.

Upon the recommendation of his parents, Phurba Tashi got the job of a kitchen helper in 1995. However, the Base Camp kitchen was never enough for him. 'The people returning from the summit got so much attention,' he said. 'As my job was only to wash dishes and serve food to the climbers, I always felt ashamed and sometimes angered over my limitations.'

In autumn 1996, Phurba Tashi was a kitchen boy in a Manaslu expedition. He was supposed to be stationed at the base camp and had no chances of going any further. However, one of the other Sherpa guides fell down while climbing near the mountain's first camp and injured his back.

'That year when we were in Manaslu, it had snowed for over a week already. It was impossible for a helicopter to fly to Camp 1 for rescue,' Phurba Tashi said. 'I was the only one who was available to go to rescue the team member. This was my first chance ever to go above the base camp on a mountain, so I took this very seriously. I carried the injured back to the base camp on my back. As a helicopter could not even come up to the base camp, I had to carry him again to a helipad in Samagaun, the nearest village settlement.'

Recognizing Phurba Tashi's extraordinary strength, the foreign members of the team gifted him some climbing gear and equipment including skis. 'This made me believe in myself,' he told us. 'That was when I realized I was made to be in the mountains, not the kitchen.'

The following year, Phurba Tashi decided to claim what he thought he rightfully deserved. He gathered his nerves and told the expedition company that he would join them only if he got to go higher in the mountain. The expedition companies are always looking for strong Sherpas to lead their clients up in the mountains. As they had seen Phurba Tashi's strength at Manaslu a year earlier, they agreed. This landed him his first mountaineering gig on Everest, from the northern side in Tibet. As a porter guide, Phurba Tashi had a chance to reach the summit. However, the expedition was abandoned at 8,600m (28,200ft) as members of the climbing team fell sick.

In 1998, Phurba Tashi was hired again by the same company to go to Mount Cho Oyu (8,188m, 26,864ft). This time, without any obstacles or hindrances, Phurba Tashi made it – this was his first significant achievement in mountain climbing. The following year, he was asked to join another Everest expedition, again from the northern route. This time, the conditions favoured Phurba Tashi and, without any major hurdles, he stood atop Everest.

'I had finally lived my long-standing dream and I was sure that was just the beginning,' Phurba Tashi said. 'The only thing that was bothering me, as I stood on top of Everest in 1999, was that my parents were still in the dark about my ventures. Even after returning from that trip, I did not dare tell them that I had started climbing. I never had that courage. My parents figured out that I had started climbing a few years later, but I never told them myself.'

Soon after he marked his first Everest summit, Phurba Tashi started getting employed as a mountain guide and as a member of the rope-fixing team that takes on the crucial tough task of fixing ropes for the climbers before every season. For several years throughout his career, he went to the top twice every season – first fixing the ropes and then taking his clients to the summit.

Climbing Everest had become such a normal routine for him that he never took the numbers and records too seriously. Once in 2006, Phurba Tashi's client fell sick, and they had to return from just a few metres below the top. There was a new Tibetan guide in the team who had never been on the top of Everest. Phurba Tashi offered the first-timer a chance to go to the top as he himself took full responsibility of guiding the client down.

'The boy went to the top and joined us on the way back in a matter of minutes,' he said. He knew what it meant for this young man to be on the summit. 'When I put myself in his shoes, I realized how much the summit of

Everest must have meant to him. I had been there several times, as a result of which, it did not mean as much to me as it meant to that young boy,' Phurba Tashi added.

As long as he had been climbing from Tibet, keeping his parents in the dark about his stint in mountain climbing was not too difficult. However, when his climbing started from the southern side of Nepal in 2007, Phurba Tashi had to be extra careful to make sure his parents did not discover his secret through word of mouth.

'The amount of effort I made while climbing the mountains was not any less than keeping this fact from my parents,' he said.

In the subsequent years, throughout his three months of stay at Base Camp on the Nepal side every climbing season, Phurba Tashi would show up at home every other weekend as if to mark his attendance before his parents. From Base Camp, Khumjung is about a four-day walk for normal trekkers. Phurba Tashi would literally run and tread this journey in less than eight hours.

'I wanted to give the impression that I had not been climbing like other Sherpas from the village,' he recalled, as this revered Sherpa served us more soup for dinner.

Phurba Tashi was gradually recognized as one of the most competent Sherpas of contemporary times and started making round trips of Everest two or three times in a single year.

Phurba Tashi knows his parents were never happy about him climbing the mountains. Yet, though his game of hide-and-seek with his parents eventually subsided, he never confronted them, and nor did his parents confront him; over the years, this created a profound emotional deadlock between them.

*

Long before he embarked on his mountaineering journey, Phurba Tashi was a shepherd. As a young teenager, during school breaks, especially in the winter, he would join his brother in the family's pasture lands on the Gokyo trail at 4,000–4,500m (13,000–14,800ft) – the altitudes of Africa's fourth highest peak Mount Meru and Europe's tenth highest peak Mount Dom.

The brothers would look after over one hundred cattle taken there from Khumjung for grazing and spend their time in the family's isolated makeshift shelter at the pasture. The cattle consisted of yaks and naks, which are used for transporting goods at altitudes over 3,000m (9,800ft), as well as zopkioks – a cross-breed of naks and cows or oxen that survive lower altitudes and carry goods from as low as 2,000m (6,600ft). The breeding of zopkioks is a unique and rare indigenous expertise found among the people of the Himalayas.

Phurba Tashi's holidays as a child were unusual compared to those of kids his age in most other parts of the world. These breaks would take him away from his parents for several months. In this era, without mobile phones or portable solar panels, he had to spend cold nights in the makeshift shelter with no electricity, little fire for heat, limited warm clothes and only potatoes to eat.

The mornings would begin with releasing the animals into the field. Afternoons would be all about collecting the dung, which they would dry and use for fire and roasting potatoes. The leftover dung and ashes were, and still are, used as manure in the potato farms of Sherpa families, usually near their grazing pasture.

Whenever the animals drifted from their herd and didn't return in the evening, hardships would double for Phurba Tashi and his brother, as they had to go out in the extreme cold, look for the animals and guide them back to the safety of the shed.

Looking for the lost animals required extraordinary navigation skills. Shepherds had to follow the trail left on the grass by the grazing animals and carefully listen to the howling of the winds and the barking of the dogs. On top of everything, there would be the fear of wolves.

'There used to be a lot of wolves in those days. They rarely attacked humans, but other animals were under constant threat of the wolves,'

Phurba Tashi recalled. 'Even if they did not attack us, we used to be so frightened of them, especially while going out to look for animals in the night. Such a horror that was!'

The life that Phurba Tashi had as a child was common for many in the Himalayas. The families living at an altitude of 3,500m (11,500ft) or below usually own a pasture at the higher altitudes, where animals are taken for grazing, potatoes are grown and members of the family seasonally migrate to.

Phurba Tashi remembers clearly one particular incident when he was at the pasture during one of his school winter breaks. A team of tourists trekking in the region had camped near their pasture. The cook of their trekking unit was someone from Khumjung, whom Phurba Tashi and his brother knew very well. Throughout their stay there, Phurba Tashi was fascinated by the look of the foreigners. Even more fascinating was the foreign food that the cook gave him and his brother.

'Such a taste that was,' Phurba Tashi recollected, with a smile on his face. He does not quite remember what exactly he ate, but he remembers it was something resembling noodles. 'That must have been spaghetti, but I am not quite sure.'

Back then, most of the time, Phurba Tashi used to eat *dhindo*, a traditional staple Nepali meal prepared by mixing flour with boiling water. As rice was scarce and very expensive in the high-altitude villages of the Khumbu region, even a simple meal of rice, lentils and vegetables would have been a luxury to him back then. Whatever it was that he ate in the foreign camp – noodles or spaghetti – the food was simply beyond his wildest imagination.

Phurba Tashi considers the care of grazing animals as years of high-altitude training that the Sherpas go through. Therefore, when somebody asks him the secret behind his strength in the mountains, he first dismisses the question claiming that he is not the only strong one. After that, referring to the difficulties that all Sherpa kids have been through in order to survive on the mountains, he said to us, 'I don't know. It must be the genes.'

He added, 'I would still get to return home after the holidays were over. For my brother who was not in school, and many others like him, there was no option but to look after the animals throughout the year.'

As if to emphasize the point, Phurba Tashi suddenly broke from his storytelling during one of our interview sessions one evening. It was getting foggy outside. He looked out of the window and quickly rushed out of the room to fetch in some of his yaks that were grazing outside.

*

8 September 2002.

Marco Siffredi, a celebrated French snowboarder and mountaineer, disappeared, never to be found again, while making a snowboard descent from Hornbein Couloir, a narrow and steep passage on the north face of Everest on the Tibetan side.

After an arduous 12.5 hours in the death zone, at around 2.15pm, Marco finally stepped on the top of Everest. There, he was welcomed by Phurba Tashi with a gentle smile, followed by some humorous dance moves. A man of few words, usually shy and reticent with his smiles, Phurba Tashi still remembers how he felt like celebrating that day, dancing and cheering.

In his modest English, he shouted as he danced, 'Summit, summit! Where are we? At the summit!'

While Phurba Tashi was the first in the team to reach the summit that day, other fellow Sherpas of the group – Panuru and Dawa Tenzing – arrived together with Marco and joined in the celebration.

He still recalls how exhausted Marco was that day: 'He celebrated with us, but hesitantly, as he had repeatedly been saying he was too tired.'

The team had a solid reason to celebrate. In a rare achievement, this was the only autumn expedition happening that year and there was nobody else on the mountain apart from the team of four. Their ascent had been gruelling, as their approach to Everest was stricken by heavy snowfall, a narrow summit window and a delayed push in the death zone. The conditions were such that their pace was reduced to a strength-sapping crawl and they were moving at a third of the speed they normally would. But they had finally made it, against all odds, and this summit was even regarded as 'one of its kind' by the alpine community.

'Notwithstanding the prior hurdles, the weather on the day of the summit was pleasant,' Phurba Tashi recalled. 'It was enough to make us forget about all that we had gone through on this journey.'

Despite all the glory, the adventure was only about to begin, as Marco was aiming to plunge down the north face on his snowboard while the Sherpas returned via the regular route.

By the time they had arrived at the top, the phone they were carrying was already out of battery, and the exhausted climbers could not make any last weather checks before descending. Less than an hour after summiting, as they prepared to descend, the otherwise pleasant weather was turning bad and it was getting cloudy.

In light of the deteriorating weather, Phurba Tashi and the fellow Sherpas started having doubts about Marco's snowboard descent. 'At the same time, however, we also knew how competent a climber and sportsman Marco was,' he said.

A year before, Marco had achieved an outstanding feat, descending from the top of the world via the Norton Couloir on a snowboard. He was back this year to do it again, this time on the Hornbein Couloir.

'We were not worried about Marco as he was better known for his descending skills. Moreover, snowboarding was his thing, and with thick snow that had piled on the surface that day, we thought it was not going to be as hard as we were imagining,' Phurba Tashi recalled.

What's more, the Sherpas were fully aware of Marco's months of dedication, hard work, investment and training. Marco had dreamed of this moment – a dream that he might not get to achieve if this attempt wasn't successful. Suddenly calling an end to all of it was a rather tricky decision for the Sherpas to make.

Despite all these positive thoughts about the mission, the Sherpas finally requested Marco not to go. However, by now, he was determined to carry on his mission and had sported all his gear.

From the top, the four descended to the point where they would part ways.

A few metres below the summit, on the way to a point called the 'Second Step' on this northern route while descending, Marco went left and the other climbers went right, bidding goodbye with a vow to meet the next day.

'We descended the Second Step extra carefully as there was a lot of snow that day,' Phurba Tashi recalled.

The Second Step is a 40-m (131-ft) vertical plunge that begins at 8,610m (28,250ft). Climbers sometimes even use ladders to negotiate it.

When the Sherpas were descending that day, many obstacles came their way. As they started their descent late in the afternoon, they were soon caught in the darkness of night. It started snowing heavily, blurring the walking line. Even the ropes fixed in the route got buried beneath the snow. As there was no other expedition happening at that time of year, no camps had been set on the way.

'At some point, we thought we were going to die,' Phurba Tashi said as he recalled the horror. 'We even envied Marco and his snowboard. We were sure he had already arrived at ABC, sipping warm soup inside the tent, while we struggled to find our way in the dark.'

Around midnight, the Sherpas arrived at ABC, quickly entered their tent, drank some soup and slept.

Early the next morning, a Sherpa supposed to receive Marco on his snowboard at ABC showed up in Phurba Tashi's tent, looking for Marco. As Marco had never arrived the previous day, the Sherpa thought the team might have abandoned the snowboard stunt and returned via the regular route together.

Phurba Tashi and his fellow Sherpas were taken by surprise. All their speculations about how easily Marco might have arrived at ABC had turned out to be seriously wrong. The fearless sportsman had died doing what he probably loved the most. As Hornbein Couloir is not a regular climbing route, and no one knew at what point Marco had fallen, his body was never found.

The vacuum of his absence tore apart both his loved ones back home and the three Sherpas who had danced with him on top of the world only the day before.

When Marco's family arrived, they met Phurba Tashi soon after, but all he had to share with them was a story and a few photos he had taken during Marco's last moments in Everest.

'I still have sleepless nights when I think about Marco and our journey in the mountain,' Phurba Tashi said.

For Phurba Tashi, the disappearance of Marco sparked a realization: 'No matter how competent someone is and how solid a person's reasons are for taking up challenges in the mountains, nature is superior, and it is always going to remain the same forever,' he contemplated. 'Sometimes, when I think too hard about the realities of the mountains, I begin to understand why my parents were so much against climbing.'

*

15 May 2007.

The early-morning sunrise welcomed British climber David Tait and Phurba Tashi on top of the world. As the duo made the summit from the northern route, the world got only a quarter of the story it was waiting for. There was a lot more to come.

The mission was a double traverse, something that had never been tried before on Everest. The climbers would start their expedition from Tibet, descend the southern route in Nepal and, after three days of rest at the southern base camp, would repeat the route and complete the cycle by finally arriving where they had started – the Tibetan base camp of Everest.

On the morning of 15 May, when David and Phurba Tashi stepped on top of the world, there was a whole new set of challenges ahead. That year, the window for summiting the southern side had not yet opened, and the ropes had been fixed only up to the South Col. This meant that David and Phurba Tashi were not going to have the support of pre-fixed ropes while descending from the top of Everest to the South Col. On top of that, it was going to be the first time on the southern route for both of them. Thus, they would have to find their way through the knife-edge ridges and puzzling conundrum of rocks and snow, which they knew only theoretically.

Several other members of the team, who had climbed Everest from the northern route together with David and Phurba Tashi, returned that way, while the duo was looking to descend the whole new route. 'I was somewhat worried when we started to descend,' Phurba Tashi recalled.

Just before David and Phurba Tashi started preparing for their challenging descent down the southern route, Phurba Tashi was caught on a Discovery Channel camera saying, 'I have never done anything crazy like this.'

Exhausted and under immense mental pressure, Phurba Tashi unfolded the ropes and took out his axe and hammer. 'By 2007, I was a fairly good mountain climber. I also had prior experience in rope fixing. However, that was the first time I was fixing ropes while descending – that, too, on an unknown route. This is a practice that is rare even today. Ropes are meant to be fixed on the way up, not down.'

Deep into the death zone, in most cases, climbers put all their energy into ascending, while the descent is mostly about keeping themselves standing on their feet. For Phurba Tashi, all the effort in navigating down the unknown route and hammering holes in the mountain with his axe, while at the same time continuously supporting David, was incredibly demanding.

The narrow Everest summit window may not be the same for the climbers approaching the mountain from the north and south sides every season. 'As the window from the southern side was not yet open, we were completely on our own while descending,' he recalled. 'It was far more challenging than during any other descent. When I finally saw a couple of people at Camp 4 on the southern side, I was so relieved.'

After a demanding 24 hours in the death zone – first on the northern route while ascending and then on the southern side during descent – Phurba Tashi and David arrived at Camp 2 to spend the night.

The next morning, just as the duo were about to head towards the base camp completing their Tibet-to-Nepal traverse, David spoke to his teammates on the radio and suddenly called off the return Nepal-to-Tibet traverse. This was a shock to the world of mountaineering as everything about that expedition was on track.

Both David and Phurba Tashi were exhausted, and the remaining leg of that mission was definitely going to be difficult. Still, the mission was on time, and the climbers had three days to rest at the base camp on the Nepal side, all as planned, before they headed back to the mountain again. Despite all the hardship they had gone through, especially while descending, neither of them had sustained any injury.

The team members on both the Nepal and Tibet side, including Phurba Tashi himself, were shocked over David's decision to quit the mission halfway through. Everyone tried to convince David that it was still worth giving it a shot and sticking to the plan. However, as David was adamant about his decision, the first-ever double traverse of Everest was abandoned.

All this time, Phurba Tashi was naïve and acting upon what he was instructed. 'I told him that we could easily do the double traverse as both of us were fit and all situations were under control,' he told us. 'But he had already made up his mind. Instead, he offered me to continue with the double traverse alone.'

While he had an opportunity to set a record by completing the traverse alone, Phurba Tashi thought it would not be appropriate to leave his client and set the record all by himself. 'If you are not going, why would I? I think the single traverse all the way from north to south is an achievement in itself,' he told David.

Phurba Tashi was surprised, but he did not push David any further in trying to convince him to resume their curtailed feat. Little did he know that he was at the centre of David's decision.

David had seen how Phurba Tashi was far superior to himself in every aspect of mountain climbing and yet would easily give up the record for David just because he was getting paid.

David's reading of Phurba Tashi had begun right at the base camp on the Tibetan side. That year before they started their mission, Phurba Tashi had already scaled the summit to fix the ropes on the northern route. It had taken him only six hours to arrive at the base camp from the top of Everest, while the same had taken thirteen hours for David in 2005.

Later, speaking publicly, David said, 'I was fully aware that I would be accompanied by this man (Phurba) on my double traverse, and I had these reservations in my mind. I was thinking: "Who am I kidding? I can do the equivalent of him, but I can't do it anywhere near as fast".'[1]

On the southern route, David was again awestruck by Phurba Tashi's efforts and speed in navigating, fixing the ropes and descending. It had taken Phurba Tashi only six hours to find his way through the unknown route down to the safety of Camp 4, which is faster than for most climbers who have the support of pre-fixed ropes.

This realization bothered David very much, and he stood down believing that he was not the rightful owner of the record that year. David revealed his moral dilemma in continuing with the double traverse and claiming a record: 'I could have hung in there long enough to do it, but when it comes to a world's-first, you generally assume it's a meritocracy – that the person with the greatest stamina and speed is the person who has the record.'

During our first interview with Phurba Tashi at his home in Khumjung, he never mentioned this extraordinary story of the double traverse attempt. When we tried to reach him to talk further during the monsoon of 2021,

---

1   Bryant, C., 20 Jul. 2007. 'Conquering the Everest within'. Available at https://www.yourlocalguardian.co.uk/news/1560399.conquering-the-everest-within/.

he was uncontactable, even by phone. His wife told us he had gone to the family pasture in the highlands near Gokyo Lake to look after his grazing yaks. As the schools were closed due to COVID-19, he had also taken his five-year-old daughter with him. Phurba Tashi's wife told us that he would be away for several weeks.

When we finally got to hear the story of the double traverse attempt from Phurba Tashi, we asked him if he feels honoured by all the values and respect David gave him in that expedition. Surprisingly, Phurba Tashi did not seem to know in great detail the reasons why David had cancelled the double traverse that year. When we told him how David had honoured him all over the world, he said, with his particular modesty, 'Well, David must be right. But I think he was also very talented and strong. Not just me, I think any other Sherpa can do the double traverse even today.'

*

In 2014, Phurba Tashi was all set to add two more Everest summits to his résumé, fixing the ropes and guiding a client, when the avalanche disaster that year cancelled all expeditions. He was set to climb again the following year when the earthquake led to a further suspension of climbing.

It was then that he took a sudden retirement.

The earthquake of 2015 wasn't the only disaster in his life. That year, both his parents passed away, causing him to ask a number of questions. 'Even though my parents were never happy about my climbing, I always felt I had their blessings in the mountains,' he said. 'Now that they have left me forever, I have lost all my courage, no matter how fierce I once was.'

Today, Phurba Tashi seeks the love of his parents in all the little expectations they had of him. He has taken a vow to fulfil their wishes by not climbing the mountain ever again. Apart from that, he wishes to offer his respect to his parents and ask for their forgiveness by caring for the yaks, naks and zopkioks they left behind. The family still rears sixty animals.

'I have not sold a single animal after the death of my parents. I don't even intend to sell them in the future,' he said, adding that he feels the animals are members of his family. 'This is the reality that I have come to, and I wish to hold on to it for the rest of my life.'

Contrary to all the limelight related to mountain climbing, Phurba Tashi today lives a quiet life with his family. He helps his wife run the family lodge in Khumjung, his eldest son is studying to become a Buddhist monk in the Tengboche monastery and he also has twin sons who are studying in Kathmandu. One of them wishes to become a footballer in the future.

And then there is his mischievous daughter, for whom Phurba Tashi has set up a small tent in the courtyard of his house to play in. He brought this tent home from one of his Everest expeditions. Sometimes, he sneaks into the tent and plays with his daughter for hours.

After a life of high drama, Phurba Tashi is a man of few ambitions.

Chapter 8

A FAMILY FROM ROLWALING

In spring 1996, Pemba Gyalze Sherpa got an odd job on Everest. As a cook at the last camp at nearly 8,000m (26,247ft), also known as Camp 4, Pemba Gyalze was in charge of feeding people with no appetite. His task was to make sure climbers ate well and enough while heading towards the summit. 'However, while heading up, climbers are generally so exhausted that eating is often the least of their priorities,' Pemba Gyalze said.

Standing at the last camp, the summit of Everest is so near, but the journey through the death zone is going to be so tormenting that no one likes to think about eating anything. All they have in mind is a tight timeline – waking up and leaving Camp 4 for the final summit push, standing at the summit as early in the morning as possible, and returning to Camp 4 by noon the following day. In such circumstances, the job of high-altitude cooks like Pemba Gyalze is crucial for the success of expeditions, as hungry climbers can collapse at any moment in the death zone.

'We constantly nag the climbers, reminding them to eat. Nine out of ten climbers will say they are not hungry, but as cooking staff, we have to make sure they have eaten well before heading for the summit,' Pemba Gyalze told us.

Cooking at Camp 4 is a whole new dimension of an expedition in Everest. The cooks have an informal kitchen set-up, equipped with tiny gas stoves and use-and-throw plastic and paper utensils. The menu only has four or five items – noodles, soup, hot water, tea and coffee – and the kitchen staff are constantly struggling to serve food warm at that altitude. 'It is so difficult to manage as a cook. First, people are so unwilling to eat anything. Second, hardly anyone is content with the food we serve,' Pemba Gyalze giggled.

After the climbers have left Camp 4 with full stomachs, the cooks start preparing food for those returning from the summit. And so the story repeats. The climbers heading down will say they don't want to eat anything, but as Base Camp is still too far, cooks like Pemba Gyalze will insist that they are hungry and exhausted, even though some climbers may not feel it, and encourage them to eat.

However, in 1996, the main reason for climbers collapsing wasn't to do with lack of nutrition, but a furious blizzard which struck deep in the death zone, and led to a completely unprecedented turn of events.

On the afternoon of 10 May, when Pemba Gyalze was preparing to receive the climbers of his group who had left Camp 4 for the summit the previous night, a strong wind started raging over the death zone. Even on good days during the summit window, the death zone of Everest gets windy during late afternoon, which increases the risk for slow climbers who sometimes take as long as 24 hours to make the round trip to the top from Camp 4. Nevertheless, despite the wind, all the risks and the slower climbers, it is not always that bad, and does not necessarily result in any fatal accidents.

However, the wind was unusually strong that day – it quickly took the form of a blizzard measuring as much as 112kmph (70mph). As the wind mixed with pallets of thick snow, it started damaging one of the world's toughest trails and highest resting camps, and obscured the visibility. A number of climbers, including the American veteran Scott Fischer and New Zealander veteran Rob Hall and their clients, got stuck in the death zone.

'We were already in a state of panic at Camp 4. The wind had destroyed most of the tents. All the supplies we had in our stock, including food and oxygen, were buried under broken tents and scattered all over the snow due to the blizzard,' Pemba Gyalze said as he recalled the chaos of that day.

'There were several people stuck in the death zone, and there we were, clueless about our next moves.'

The blizzard of 1996 claimed eight lives in the death zone of Everest, including Fischer and Hall. Pemba Gyalze still vividly recalls eavesdropping on the last radio conversation of Rob Hall with his wife at Camp 4: 'His wife was in tears and was constantly cheering her man to get a little further. It all felt like a film to me. But everything was for real.'

Relating to us the disaster of 1996 some 25 years later at his hometown in Rolwaling Valley, Pemba Gyalze served us an omelette. His residential lodge today stands at an elevation of 3,700m (12,139ft) in the lap of the Himalayas, which is the elevation of some of the highest mountains in Europe. After COVID-19, Rolwaling Valley received more than 5,000 domestic visitors in 2021 alone. As the president of a local association of hoteliers, Pemba Gyalze is deeply concerned about the tourist facilities and the quality of services they can offer these visitors.

Pemba Gyalze has always been a true welcomer, constantly thinking about how best he can take care of the needs and requirements of people whom he is catering for. That night at Camp 4, he was also struggling to put together whatever food supplies he could get his hands on, and a vacuum flask with warm tea, so that he could welcome anyone returning from above, after surviving the blizzard.

'Survivors that night were in a bizarre state. Many were descending without glasses, caps or helmets. Some had even lost their oxygen regulators and tanks in the blizzard,' he said. 'They were arriving at the camp like zombies walking in the dark. Many had gone snow-blind and could hardly see anything,' he recalled. 'Additionally, there was so much noise from panicked people and the continuous wind that it was hard for anybody to hear us shouting. So, we showed them the direction towards a few standing tents by drumming steel plates.'

As oxygen supplies were also sparse that night, Pemba Gyalze and his friends pulled out oxygen tanks from the rubble of tents destroyed by the unending blizzard and sprayed it into the tents where everybody was huddled together. Pemba Gyalze thinks people would have died if there was no oxygen inside the tent. Tents that usually accommodate only two or three people had up to a dozen people crammed inside that night.

Pemba Gyalze had an ice axe in his hand while he struggled to put together supplies at the camp. The blizzard was still ongoing and there were frequent thunderstorms. Only after he got pricking electric shocks several times in his hands, did he realize it was because the iron ice axe had been attracting the current. He quickly got rid of it.

Pemba Gyalze wanted to do more. He wanted to step out of his kitchen job and go up to rescue the stranded climbers. However, he neither had the authority, nor the proper climbing suit or gear. 'As I was not supposed to go higher than Camp 4, I did not have a proper down jacket. I was wearing shoes, technically not fit for climbing,' he said. We showed Pemba Gyalze our normal trekking shoes that cost less than US$100 and asked if his were any better in 1996, at an altitude of 8,000m (26,247ft). He burst into laughter and told us, 'No way! If I was wearing anything like that, I would have probably gone further to rescue people that night.'

Back in 1996, most of the Sherpas in expeditions were still not recognized as equal climbing partners by westerners. A very few experienced Sherpas would make it into the expedition teams as Sirdars and guides, while the majority were only treated as climbing porters, cooks and support staff. Therefore, apart from a few 'privileged' ones, who could go to the summit of Everest, most Sherpas, even those like Pemba Gyalze who went all the way up to the last camp at 8,000m (26,247ft), would have to do without professional gear and equipment. When the blizzard hit, Pemba Gyalze was wearing a pair of 'woollen' shoes, which he had bought in Kathmandu for less than US$25. The Sherpas believed the shoes got warmer and bulkier after each wash. From what he can recall, attaching the heavy crampons that were used in those days to these shoes took an unusually long time.

According to Pemba Gyalze, a number of Sherpas like himself at Camp 4 that night had to remain useless at a time of dire need. 'Most of us were thought of as people born in high altitude who could carry loads in the mountains that high. If we'd had better gear, equipment, training and authority, I am sure we could have saved some people,' he said. 'We pulled ourselves together and went a little above the camp, around the South Col, the following morning, but a lot of damage had already been done by then.'

Near South Col, Pemba Gyalze noticed a semi-conscious Japanese woman struggling to keep herself alive against hypothermia in the chilling cold by faintly waving her hands. She was on her way back after summiting Everest a day earlier. Pemba Gyalze approached and tried to pull her up to carry her. However, her body had already given up and couldn't make any effort for survival. Pemba Gyalze tried to pull her up again, but she had already collapsed and died.

For Pemba Gyalze, the disaster of 1996 was a huge setback. For a while, he thought he would not be able to go back to the mountains again, for all the ugliness of the climbing world he had experienced first-hand. However, he had his own priorities of earning a living, getting more jobs on the mountains and securing his career for his family's future.

'Even when I was struggling to do my bit at Camp 4 that night, deep down somewhere, I was trying to catch the attention of potential employers. I have to be honest about it,' he reflected.

*

Pemba Gyalze kept going to the mountains in the subsequent years. After 1996, his younger brother, Pemba Dorje Sherpa, had also started accompanying him as an assistant kitchen helper in trekking trips or on smaller mountains. In the family of 11 siblings, there were two brothers with the first name 'Pemba' and three with the first name 'Phurba'. (In the Sherpa community, the first name of a child is given according to the day he is born. For instance, 'Pemba' for those born on a Saturday, 'Mingma' for those born on a Tuesday and 'Phurba' for those born on a Thursday.)

As Pemba Gyalze gained more experience, he started getting jobs more easily and established himself as a trusted Sherpa in the high-altitude kitchens. At the same time, Pemba Dorje gained experience under the direct supervision of his elder brother.

Although Pemba Gyalze made it to the last camp kitchen almost every season, he never expressed any keen interest in going to the top of Everest. He wanted to play it safe and thought that standing on the summit of Everest was not worth all the risks involved in the death zone. Moreover, adding Everest summits to a résumé was not as financially lucrative then as it later became in the years to come. During that time, Sherpas accompanying their clients to the top used to get an unattractive summit bonus of only about US$250, and Pemba Gyalze did not want to sell his safety for that meagre amount.

'The amount that Sherpas were making for risking their lives up to the summit was less than what porters rotating up to Camp 4 with climbers' goods several times throughout the season were making,' Pemba Gyalze shared. 'For this reason, I never really pushed myself.'

In 2000, Pemba Gyalze took Pemba Dorje to Everest for the first time in a well-organized and well-funded Japanese expedition from the northern side. The group of over a dozen aspiring Japanese summiteers had a Sherpa guide each, and had also taken at least half a dozen Sherpas more as back-up. There was enough oxygen and gear for each of them to comfortably go to the summit. This was a luxurious arrangement even by present-day standards.

Pemba Dorje had already caught the attention of the Japanese team as he had proven himself as the strongest Sherpa with them by carrying up to 36kg (79lb) of weight to the last camp in one go. Impressed by the abilities of this first-timer, the Japanese had trusted him with guiding the eldest member of the team to the summit. Pemba Dorje was going to the summit of Everest for his very first time, yet his elder brother, Pemba Gyalze, who was far more familiar and skilled in the mountain, was still reluctant.

'Let's go up together this time. The weather is good. We have a good team and there are good enough supplies,' Pemba Dorje said, trying to convince his elder brother.

'Well, our going or staying back at the camp won't really make any difference. Let's just stay here,' Pemba Gyalze replied.

'There is no point staying back in fear. I am going anyway. If we are together, we can take care of each other if anything goes wrong,' the younger one stressed.

'Well, if you say so, I am ready. But you will have to agree to return from any point above if the conditions are not favourable,' Pemba Gyalze reluctantly agreed.

Two decades down the line, Pemba Dorje reflects on why his elder brother so easily agreed to his stubbornness that year.

'It is simple,' he said to us at a rooftop jazz restaurant on the outskirts of Kathmandu. Pemba Dorje looked away, down the terrace, gazing at the vehicles that were passing on the road below, as if trying to hide his emotions that were easily visible in his wet eyes. 'My brother was not the kind who would compromise his safety for what was a trivial achievement for him – the summit of Everest. That year, for the first time in his life, he sold his safety for mine.'

Without any hint of trouble in the death zone, the two brothers stood atop Everest in 2000 and returned to safety quite easily. The feat that the two siblings achieved together that year was going to hold a whole other significance to their nine siblings in line under them, back in Rolwaling Valley.

*

November 2021.

On a chilly Kathmandu morning, we found ourselves on the back seat of a passenger jeep, headed northeast to the district of Dolakha, home to Rolwaling Valley. Sitting in the front seat was Pemba Gyalze's younger sister Dawa Diki Sherpa, fifth of the eleven siblings.

Unlike the Khumbu region, there are no airports in Rolwaling Valley, and the entire journey has to be on wheels and on foot. The district headquarters of Dolakha – Charikot – is about a five-hour ride along a narrow hilly highway broken in many places. From Charikot, after another four-hour ride in the same jeep, we arrived in Chhyotchhyot, the gateway to Rolwaling Valley. After this last stop connected by road, we would be trekking upwards to the high-altitude villages and mountains.

From Chhyotchhyot, we crossed a suspension bridge over the Tamakoshi River and headed uphill for Simigaun, our destination for the day. Dawa Diki, a fit young woman in her mid-30s, who was guiding us to Rolwaling, is herself an Everest summiteer. Bringing up her Everest feat, we told her how lucky we were to be guided by her. To this, she simply replied, 'You would have made this trek even without me, so no problem.'

We had been trying to encourage her to speak of her Everest achievement, but she wasn't as excited about it as we were. To every Everest question we asked, she had a one- or two-word answer. First, we thought she was being modest or was an introvert, but later we realized that her silence about Everest was the result of her loss; her husband passed away at Everest Base Camp in 2015, when the earthquake triggered an avalanche. To Dawa Diki today, other things in day-to-day life are simply more interesting than her Everest summit. She is several times more forthcoming about other things in life, such as her family and her village.

The stair trail to Simigaun was so uphill that we had to stop and take long breaths after every ten or twenty steps. While our hearts would be fiercely palpitating, from several steps ahead Dawa Diki would look back on us with a sceptical smile at our slow pace and encourage us to keep walking. 'Please don't panic. Just keep moving your feet carefully.'

We felt that it was the right time to throw at our guide our trekking résumé. We told her how we had trekked in the Everest region several times. But we knew very well that while our reference of elevation was about 5,400m (17,700ft), for Dawa Diki it was Everest itself. She airily acknowledged what we were proud of, and just kept walking.

From Chhyotchhyot, we had already entered the Gaurishankar Conservation Area, named after Rolwaling's resident mountain, Mount Gaurishankar (7,134m, 23,406ft), which is now not climbed out of respect for its religious value. The mountain consists of two peaks – Gauri and Shankar – named after Hindu deities Lord Shiva (Shankar) and his partner Parwati (Gauri). Before Everest was measured for the first time in the mid-19th century, Gaurishankar was believed to be the highest peak in the world. One unique aspect of this mountain is that it seems to take a completely different shape, depending on the viewer's angle of sight. Nepal's standard time zone was also determined by the meridian of Gaurishankar.

The Gaurishankar Conservation Area is particularly unique as it is the natural habitat for the snow leopard and red panda. More than 36 red pandas are believed to live in the region today, along with 235 different species of birds. The region is also popular for its flora and fauna – rich vegetation including several medicinal herbs, for which extensive ethnobotanical research was conducted in the 1930s.

Rolwaling Valley is home to 16 different types of forests and about 300 different plants and flowers that blossom during monsoon every year. 'The number of tourists visiting Rolwaling to observe these flowers during monsoon is on an increasing trend lately,' Dawa Diki told us on the trek. 'Purists find Rolwaling predominantly serene, especially as it is not yet as commercialized as the Everest region or other mountain trails of Nepal.'

The major attraction in the Rolwaling trail is Tsho Rolpa glacial lake, which is an embodiment of the impact of climate change and global warming. Tsho Rolpa, which was a small pond until 70 years ago, has expanded to become a huge lake, which we could not see in its entirety from one place. The lake has expanded from 0.23km^2 (0.09 square miles) in the late 1950s to 16km^2 (6.18 square miles) in the present day. Tsho Rolpa, which is also the major source to the Tamakoshi River, is considered to be at high risk of a glacial lake outburst flood (GLOF).

Nepal's largest hydroelectricity project – Upper Tamakoshi – is sited on the Tamakoshi River, and receives water from Tsho Rolpa. Ironically, when we visited Rolwaling in 2021, the three villages of Na (4,200m, 13,780ft), Beding (3,700m, 12,140ft) and Thangdingma (3,300m, 10,830ft), through which the water from Tsho Rolpa passes down to Tamakoshi, were still in complete darkness, yet to be connected to the national grid.

These villages are three human settlements in Rolwaling Valley, which emerged as one of the key Sherpa hubs of Nepal after the Khumbu region. As in the Khumbu villages of Phortse, Thame and Khumjung, almost every house in Rolwaling has an Everest summiteer. However, there are very few houses – the entire Rolwaling Valley is inhabited by the same set of just over 50 households that own a house and an animal shed in all three villages.

The families migrate, along with their yaks and naks, to their high-altitude abodes in Na from spring to autumn, as there is enough fresh grass at the higher altitude during this time. The highest yak camps are set up to 5,000m (16,400ft). During these same seasons, there is a high influx of trekkers to Tsho Rolpa and Dudh Pokhari, a holy pond a little above Tsho Rolpa. As Na is the last stop for trekkers, villagers also get to do some tourism business during this time. When winter starts, the families migrate to their lower-altitude homes in Beding and Thangdingma. A number of families also have a home in Kathmandu. Villagers who do not own yaks or naks, or have someone else to look after their cattle, come down to Kathmandu during winter and reunite with their children and relatives.

*

After three days of continuous trekking in the tricky trails from Chhyotchhyot, we were finally about to arrive in Beding. The morning we left our night shelter in Donggang, Dawa Diki explained to us the way to Beding, which was a steady, uncompromising uphill journey. She was finding it hard to match her pace with ours, so she pressed on ahead of us, while we trekked on at our own sluggish speed.

As it was the start of winter, families living in Na had already migrated to their homes in Beding. That was where we were supposed to meet and interview Pemba Gyalze and his family. On the way to Beding, we enjoyed the view of high-altitude terrain. As we moved up, the trees and vegetation grew shorter and shorter; even the pine trees looked like short hedges scattered across the ground. It was a sunny day, but the entire trail was not in direct sunlight and so even a short encounter with a ray of sun in the tricky twists and turns made us feel royal.

After six hours of trekking – the exact amount of time that was written on an information board we had passed on the way – we arrived at a suspension bridge, across which was the village of Beding. On the other side, we saw a young boy wearing a surf hat, who was playing with sheep grazing nearby. The boy was carrying a vacuum flask and a bag on his back. After we crossed the bridge, the boy welcomed us and said that Dawa Diki, who had arrived in the village three hours previously, had sent him there to greet us. The boy was Norbu, the son of Pemba Gyalze.

We were elated. The boy surprised us further by treating us to warm coffee from his flask, an apple and biscuits. After a short break, we followed him and, in a matter of minutes, we were finally inside Pemba Gyalze's house in Beding, where he, his wife Yanjung, mother Kinjum and Dawa Diki welcomed us together.

The stone-built house was fairly new and also served as a lodge for trekkers. Across a trail by the house's main entrance was a stream that flowed from Tsho Rolpa Lake, on its way to joining the Tamakoshi River. Behind the house is a rocky mountain, above which there is a majestic view of Gaurishankar at the Nepal–Tibet border. There is a kitchen, a dining hall and the mother's room on the upper floor. The ground floor has other bedrooms, including ones used by the family and trekkers for lodging.

Life was pretty hectic inside the house. All the members were busy in the kitchen and everyone was trying to make us feel comfortable and warm, as we were totally exhausted. While Yanjung offered us back-to-back tea, Pemba Gyalze's 70-year-old mother set herself on a mission to help us rejuvenate our dead mobile phones. She brought us her personal charging power bank with a tiny solar panel, placed it in the sun and offered it for our use.

Pemba Gyalze seemed a little unwell. 'My stomach is somewhat upset,' he said. 'I happened to eat meat at a friend's place a few days ago. I think it brought me bad energies.' We figured it must be minor gastritis or acidity and offered him a pack of antacids. They seemed to work and he soon became conversational...

We started with COVID-19.

Pemba Gyalze explained to us how the region was not much affected by the pandemic, as the village is remote and not as populated as the cities. However, Sherpas did not get any jobs for nearly two years and so their income was affected, but it was not as bad as in the cities, as the village still survives on its own produce and informal economies. Potatoes grow well in the region and the villagers have also learned new ways to cultivate seasonal and non-seasonal crops in plastic greenhouse tunnels. 'But it is really strange how everybody was stuck inside home for so many months in a row,' Pemba Gyalze said.

Yanjung suddenly brought up COVID-19 vaccines. She asked us if we were vaccinated, to which we responded 'yes', and asked back if she and her family were vaccinated too. 'Yes,' she said, with an unusual sourness to her expression. 'I went to the vaccination camp as I was told there were American and Indian vaccines. But it turned out they had Chinese vaccines, and I had to have that.'

Yanjung, who is of Tibetan origin, came to Nepal in her early teens as a Tibetan refugee with her maternal uncle after the death of her mother in Tibet. Now, the Chinese government does not allow her to go to Tibet, while her family and relatives in Tibet also can't visit Nepal. 'She has a grudge in her heart and gets agitated with anything related to China. She can't digest that she has Chinese medicine in her body,' Pemba Gyalze teased.

Pemba Gyalze had summited Everest twice from the Tibetan side. When in Tibet, he was well-received by his in-laws in the town of Tingri. 'I have a very special bond with them,' he said, adding how sorry he feels for his wife and that it is uncertain if she will ever be able to see her family there. Pemba Gyalze met and married Yanjung in Kathmandu.

Pemba Gyalze, Yanjung and Norbu were supposed to travel to Kathmandu the day before we arrived in Beding. However, they had decided to stay back and show us around, at the request of Pemba Gyalze's other siblings in Kathmandu, whom we had first approached and met. Kinjum, however, was adamant about not leaving the village. No matter how cold it gets she likes it there, so her children had made arrangements in Beding so she would not have to worry about anything throughout winter. The villagers are primarily dependent on dried yak dung and wood for fuel, and the siblings had hired three people to collect enough to last Kinjum throughout the winter, so that she wouldn't have to go outside much in the extreme cold. They had also stocked food in the house to last throughout the season.

The following day, while the rest of the family left Beding for Kathmandu, we were supposed to head upward to Tsho Rolpa, a journey that isn't ideal at that time of year. The last stop on the way to Tsho Rolpa, the village of Na, had already been closed as all the families had migrated to Beding and lower villages for winter. Dawa Diki again became our guide, along with one more person – Dorje Sherpa, a cook in his mid-20s, hired by Pemba Gyalze's siblings in Kathmandu to help their mother during winter. To the rear, Dorje carried food and supplies in a bamboo basket hanging by his forehead, while Dawa Diki led the trek and we followed on.

The journey to Na was unusually quiet.

We could only hear a constant howling of wind mixed with the downwards flow of the stream from Tsho Rolpa Lake. As we gained altitude, trees started disappearing and all we could see were dwarf shrubs, sedges, grasses, mosses and lichens. Even the unusual-looking birds, which we could hardly identify, seemed to be struggling to take off, merely making short-distance jumps from one shrub to another. We saw sheep grazing on the tiny shrubs emerging out of the rocky trail. Showing us those sheep, Dorje told us, 'The sheep are now headed to lower altitudes. This means that it may snow anytime soon.'

When we finally arrived in Na at around noon, only one house had smoke coming out of its chimney, while the rest of the village was as unoccupied as the trail we had just been treading. This was the first time we were standing in a village literally shut down, without any human hustle and bustle. For a moment, we felt as though we had arrived in one of those deserted villages you see in Westerns.

We were warm as we walked, but soon after stopping to rest at Na, it started getting colder. Even the midday sun was unable to fend off the cold, especially as the frequent movement of clouds would cloak the sun every now and then. Na sits in the lap of Mount Chobuje, a 6,685-m (21,932-ft) peak, which, when we observed it right from the bottom, our heads tilted at a 90-degree angle, seemed as if it were higher than Everest itself.

With smoke coming out of only one of the chimneys in the village, we quickly figured out that Dawa Diki had, once again, arrived there far ahead of us. We followed the direction of the smoke and arrived at the doorstep of the family's lodge. We could see something cooking in the kitchen, but there was nobody inside. The door was open and Dawa Diki's mobile phone was just lying there. After a while, she returned with an armful of dried yak dung. When we tried to casually alert her not to be so careless, leaving the door open like that with her mobile phone inside, Dawa Diki laughed, 'There is nobody in the village right now and leaving the door open or closed makes no difference at all,' reminding us again of where we were.

That evening, we struggled to keep ourselves warm in bed. With all our clothes on, including down jackets and socks, we buried ourselves under three blankets, but our feet were still freezing. Dawa Diki sneaked inside our room, asked us to stay warm and then went outside to collect the dung herself, as if all that cold meant nothing to her.

The following day was going to be even more challenging. All the way up to Tsho Rolpa from Na, we were set to gain the elevation of more than 400m (1,300ft), then return all the way down to Na, and then to Beding to spend the night. Before going to bed that night, we imagined how much worse the situation could be if anything bad happened in Na – say, the constantly feared outburst flood from Tsho Rolpa Lake. It was only us in the entire village and there was no phone connection. We kept recalling Pemba Gyalze's words back in Beding the day before: 'People in Rolwaling are living in constant threat from Tsho Rolpa Lake. Imagine living in a house with a huge water tank in the terrace, which you know will burst one day.'

*

It was already dark when we arrived in Beding, after making the trip to Tsho Rolpa from Na. The lodge that was earlier populated with Pemba Gyalze's family, now only housed his mother, Kinjum. This time, knowing that we would be exhausted from an extraordinarily long trip, she offered us warm *Jhwaikhatte*, a strong local liquor made by fermenting millet, and served sizzling with some grains of rice deep-fried in a spoonful of hot ghee.

After dinner, we sat with Kinjum over another round of *Jhwaikhatte*. She had a smartphone, recently sent by one of her daughters in the USA. Someone had downloaded a video of her youngest daughter, Nima Lhamu Sherpa, on to the phone which tells the story of how she summited Everest. Kinjum knew little about smartphones and could hardly dial numbers, but she had learned by heart the location of the video on her phone, and was able to quickly load and watch it over and over again, several times a day. She fondly showed us the video, which, in one of its sequences, has Nima Lhamu explaining how she trekked from a place called Phakding near Lukla to Pangboche in Khumbu in a single day. For average trekkers, it is a one-day trek from Phakding to Namche Bazaar. From Namche Bazaar, it would take another two days for a lowlander to arrive in Pangboche. Locals generally make it from Phakding to Pangboche in one to two days. Dorje was also watching the video with us. He objected, 'It is impossible to walk all the way from Phakding to Pangboche in a day. I don't believe her.' Kinjum got agitated and light-heartedly countered Dorje, 'Why would they report this in the news like this if it were not true? I think you are simply jealous.' The room burst into laughter.

That night after dinner, we had a long conversation with Kinjum. She explained that she feels that she has had an ordinary life, full of love and compassion, with her husband Chhiring Norbu Sherpa and her children. In just a few words, she described Chhiring Norbu as a big man, extraordinarily strong and foolhardy in nature.

Chhiring Norbu was also a trekking porter and had worked in Sir Edmund Hillary's team. When he heard Hillary was building a school in Khumjung, he carried 20l (35pt) of locally-brewed millet liquor, and crossed the 5,750-m (18,865-ft) Tashi Lapcha Pass over to the Khumbu region, to meet Hillary and ensure his own village in Rolwaling Valley was not left out. Chhiring Norbu impressed Hillary with his dedication and encouraged him to contribute towards building a school in Beding as well.

Tashi Lapcha is a technically demanding pass that separates Rolwaling Valley from Khumbu's Thame village. The trail leading through the Trakarding Glacier from above the Tsho Rolpa Lake demands highly organized skills of the trekkers, and takes three days to cross over to Thame. However, for local Sherpas, who are already acclimatized to the elevation, it only takes a day to cross Tashi Lapcha with trekkers' goods and supplies, and drop them in Thame. Kinjum herself had done this trail with loads on her back several times before marrying Chhiring Norbu.

Kinjum also talked about how impulsive and foolhardy her husband was: 'He would hardly think twice before committing to any work and accomplishing it no matter what,' she recalled. 'Sometimes, he also used to get into brawls with people for small reasons. I have heard there are people in Thame who still remember my husband for his craziness.'

Kinjum recalled two particular occasions when her husband took his impetuosity to the next level. One of their naks had given birth to a baby. Their third son, Pemba Dorje, who had climbed Everest with their eldest son Pemba Gyalze in 2000 (see page 190), tried to play with the nak's baby, agitating its mother. He got hit right in the face and the blow from the nak's pointed horns ripped his upper lip up to his cheek. Everyone in the family panicked and were considering taking Pemba Dorje to Kathmandu for treatment. However, Chhiring Norbu thought it could be too late. He quickly grabbed the boy and sewed his wound closed with a needle and thread as if he was stitching a piece of cloth. To this day, Pemba Dorje has a faint scar on his face from that incident.

The other incident also involved Pemba Dorje. While playing at their home in Na, he happened to dislocate his elbow. Chhiring Norbu sat his crying son on a bench and went inside the kitchen. He grabbed a steel tea mug, cut it in half, forming an arc, and fitted it right above the broken elbow, creating a support for the dislocated bone. He cut a plastic bottle at both ends and inserted his son's broken hand inside to ensure it was kept steady. 'He was definitely not an expert, but in the heat of the moment, he did what he thought was right,' Kinjum said. The child's injury got better in time, but he still cannot bend his hand fully to touch his shoulder with the tip of his finger.

'His siblings sometimes casually make fun of that, even today,' Kinjum giggled. 'Initially, I thought he might not be able to work in the fields or carry loads. I was worried his life would be difficult. But beyond all my doubts, my son, with a ripped lip sewn like a cloth and a limb injured for life, changed the family's fortunes,' Kinjum added, referring to the two brothers' summit of Everest.

Kinjum's life has been full of adventure – quite literally, with all her children and the struggles of day-to-day life in Rolwaling. At the figurative level, the deeds and the companionship of a partner like Chhiring Norbu made her life even more adventurous and fun. Chhiring Norbu passed away in 2005, leaving behind a deep pool of fond memories.

*

The family's Everest legacy, which began in 2000 with Pemba Gyalze and Pemba Dorje, was carried forward by their other siblings. In the years following 2000, two other brothers of the family, Phurba Thundu Sherpa and Nima Gyalzen Sherpa, scaled Everest.

In 2003, Pemba Dorje was part of an Everest cleaning expedition on the southern side from Nepal, led by the Japanese. Pemba Dorje again caught the attention of the Japanese team members by demonstrating an extraordinary speed in climbing the mountain. After the cleaning mission was over, at Everest Base Camp, the Japanese team members encouraged him to pursue a speed climbing of Everest. They offered him sponsorship for a solo speed-trip if he was willing to take up the challenge. Pemba Dorje swiftly agreed.

On 22 May 2003, Pemba Dorje left Base Camp at around 5pm. His only mission was to walk continuously without taking any rest on the way. In order to ensure a smooth journey without breaks in between, the Japanese had thoughtfully arranged for enough oxygen, chocolate bars that he could munch while walking, and a water pipe, giving him an unhindered supply of water from a small tank in his backpack. He stood at the summit of Everest in just 12 hours and 45 minutes. The previous speed record was that of veteran Babu Chiri Sherpa, who had taken 16 hours and 56 minutes to reach the summit from Base Camp (see page 10). The same year, three days after Pemba Dorje broke Babu Chiri's previous record, another Sherpa – Lhakpa Gelu – climbed Everest in 10 hours, 56 minutes and 46 seconds.

Pemba Dorje was surprised at himself for having climbed Everest so quickly, without any prior planning. With a little more organized strategy and effort, he was sure he could do even better, breaking Lhakpa Gelu's record. Back in Kathmandu, he shared with his brother, Pemba Gyalze, that he wanted to do another speed ascent with more planning the following year. Being the safe player he has always been, the elder brother told him not to be so absurd, telling him…'Nobody can challenge the mountain.

If it takes three days to climb Everest, it has to be three days and not less.'
However, Pemba Dorje had already made up his mind.

'But I have broken the previous record of Babu Chiri. I am sure I can do better,' he persisted.

'People say that Babu Chiri's strengths are like that of a truck engine. There can be exceptions like him, but taking so much risk is simply not worth it. What if you never come back?' Pemba Gyalze replied.

Pemba Gyalze's efforts to prevent his brother from pursuing a madness on the mountain went in vain, as Pemba Dorje was as stubborn as he had been in 2000. In the spring of 2004, he left for Everest Base Camp, with a single mission: to break any existing records of the fastest ascent of Everest.

At 6pm on 20 May 2004, Pemba Dorje left Everest Base Camp. By starting his ascent in the evening, he wanted to skip any possible disturbance from anyone on the way. In Khumbu Icefall, he crossed the long ladder bridges installed over deep crevasses. 'If anything happens to me here, no one will even know,' he thought to himself, but kept on walking. The 20-year-old Sherpa, trying to stand out as one of the world's best climbers, kept his cool as he walked and, within an hour, arrived at Camp 1.

The moon was up and the sky was clear. He looked up and thought, 'I should reach the top while the moon is still up.' Other climbers at Camp 1 had already retreated to their tents, sipping soup or warm tea. Pemba Dorje just kept walking, passed by all the tents and, in less than 45 minutes, arrived at Nuptse Face (see page 31). At about 9.15pm, he left Camp 2 and, en route at 10.10pm, contacted the support team at Base Camp over the radio. He contacted them again at 10.51pm and said he had arrived at Camp 3. Talking over the radio every half an hour and solemnly walking under the moon as everyone else on the mountain rested, Pemba Dorje arrived at the Hillary Step at around 1.45am. At 2.10am, he finally stood at the summit of Everest, all alone, with a new record of the fastest ascent in 8 hours and 10 minutes. He had set a Guinness World Record by becoming the fastest climber on Everest, a feat for which he is better known as Pemba 'Speed' in the climbing community today. Although this speed ascent of 2004 was later mired in controversy,[1] there is no doubt that Pemba 'Speed' is one of the fastest.

Pemba Dorje's success in breaking Babu Chiri's record in 2003 and his own record in 2004 became massive news globally. On his way back to Kathmandu, a team from the Nepal army that had gone to Everest that year, gave him a lift in their chopper. Dozens of people from the climbing community and people from the media had huddled outside Kathmandu's Tribhuvan International Airport to welcome the new climbing sensation. One of them was his elder brother, Pemba Gyalze. Knowing that he was the star's brother, the army had given him access to their helipad. When the helicopter finally landed and the two brothers met, Pemba Dorje joked, 'Why are you here? You thought I was going to die!'

'I was worried about you,' Pemba Gyalze replied, and instantly burst into tears.

'Even I couldn't stop my tears. I felt really bad that I had somehow hurt my brother's feelings,' Pemba Dorje told us, again looking away to outside the restaurant, trying to hide the tears that were clearly shining in his eyes.

*

The siblings' pursuit of Everest continued in the years to come. While there were glories and pride on one hand, the year 2006 brought the family a whole new reality of climbing, which the eldest of the brothers, Pemba Gyalze, had always feared.

In autumn 2006, another brother in the family – Phurba Tenzing Sherpa – who was only 17 years old at the time, was about to make his debut in the world of climbing. On the recommendation of his eldest brother

---

1   Later, in 2013, Lhakpa Gelu challenged the 2004 speed-ascent claim of Pemba 'Speed' at Nepal's Supreme Court, citing insufficient evidence. In 2017, the court upheld the claim, stating that the evidence provided by Pemba 'Speed' was not sufficient.

Pemba Gyalze, who was already well-known as a guide, Phurba Tenzing took his first steps, accompanying another elder brother, Phurba Thundu, on a Pumori expedition.

Pumori stands 8km (5 miles) apart from Everest on the same Mahalangur Range. From Everest Base Camp, Pumori can be seen facing Everest from the opposite side. Used by some climbers to practise their skills of mountaineering before climbing Everest, Pumori has a significant death record of nearly 10 per cent due to its vulnerability to avalanches and technicalities. Pumori also offers climbers standing on its top a magnificent 360-degree view of the surrounding mountains, particularly Everest and Mount Lhotse (8,516m, 27,940ft). For its proximity to Everest, Pumori is also believed to be the daughter of Everest. In Sherpa language, 'Pu' means 'the daughter'.

The two brothers – Phurba Tenzing and Phurba Thundu – accompanied by three other Sherpas, were guiding a group of Austrian climbers on Pumori. Since it was his first time, Phurba Tenzing was excited and nervous in equal parts. Phurba Thundu, on the other hand, was on constant watch, ensuring that his younger brother was coping with his debut mountain-climbing gig.

'Throughout our journey to the base camp, my brother was continuously reminding me of the to-dos and not-to-dos,' Phurba Tenzing recalled. 'He would tell me not to stay idle for a long time on the mountain, not to keep my hands in my pockets while walking or climbing, and to keep myself closely attached to the rope no matter what. I was obviously aware of these things. I could sense my brother was a little extra-conscious about my safety.'

On 13 October, the Sherpas headed up to fix the ropes, while their clients were acclimatizing at Camp 1. 'We were together until Camp 2. From Camp 2, one of us had to return to Camp 1 and take care of the clients, while the others would go up to the last camp (Camp 3) and fix the rope all the way to the summit. As I was the youngest and with no prior experience, they asked me to go to Camp 1 and attend to the clients. They stayed at Camp 2 and prepared to go to the higher camp the following day.'

Phurba Tenzing was so far enjoying the adventure. The following morning, he went down to Gorakshep to buy camera batteries for one of the clients. Gorakshep is the last settlement at 5,164m (16,942ft), before arriving at Everest Base Camp, Pumori and other neighbouring mountains, and is only open during expedition and trekking seasons.

Phurba Tenzing popped into one of the shops and asked for the batteries. He didn't wait too long, as he had to be with the clients at Camp 1, which was about two hours away. He stuffed the batteries inside his jacket pocket and got himself moving again. Soon after, he left Gorakshep and walked towards Pumori at his own pace.

'Suddenly, there was a huge, deafening thud and, before my eyes, I saw an avalanche dropping down from one of the higher camps in Pumori,' he said, showing us the picture of Pumori on his MacBook, pointing to the exact location where the avalanche had fallen in 2006. 'It was my first time, for God's sake, and I didn't expect anything like that. I had never seen an avalanche in my life. It was so fast that, for a moment, I thought a massive crow had flown past Pumori and disappeared.'

Phurba Tenzing started panicking. He knew his brother and the other three Sherpas were somewhere near the avalanche. From the look of it, Phurba Tenzing had already figured out they must have been hit. And if they were hit by such an avalanche, there wasn't any chance of survival. However, his brotherly instinct didn't want to believe anything negative. He ran as fast as he could, as if he could blow away all the rubble of the avalanche and rescue his brother and the other Sherpas.

'I didn't even take a moment to cry. I genuinely believed that my brother was alive and needed me badly,' he said. 'I ran so fast that the distance of two hours from Gorakshep to Pumori took me only about half an hour.'

At the Pumori base camp, there was absolute chaos. The Austrian clients, who had run down from Camp 1 to the base camp, were in a panic, not knowing what to do. When Phurba Tenzing arrived there panting, what he saw was beyond human control. The avalanche that had dropped from somewhere between Camps 2 and 3 had come all the way down to base camp and even as low as the bottom of the mountain. The mass of snow and rocks had swept absolutely everything away at the higher camps. Phurba Tenzing figured out that the four Sherpas had also been swept away by it. However, he still believed they were alive and started pricking through the cold ice with whatever he could – bare hands, ice axes, crampons…all manner of things. Phurba Tenzing does not recall how many hours he went on like that for, but, finally, he saw a hand. From the watch on the hand, he recognised it was his brother. He shovelled the snow and pulled his brother out of the rubble, checking for any signs of life.

'His body was broken in so many places,' he said, taking a long pause, as if he was returning to the scene for a moment. 'His neck was broken, his ribs were broken, and his hands and legs… Nothing was in one piece.'

Phurba Tenzing suddenly stopped. The light-hearted conversation had arrived at a point of unbearable heaviness. He stood up silently, left the restaurant and lit a cigarette.

For several minutes, Phurba Tenzing had looked for other bodies as well, but all in vain. The bodies of the three Sherpas who were caught in the avalanche along with Phurba Thundu, were never found and are still missing. Phurba Tenzing called his eldest brother Pemba Gyalze and gave him the devastating news. He then arranged for a helicopter to airlift Phurba Thundu's body to Kathmandu for final rites.

Back then, as mobile phones and reliable networks were limited to only a handful of people in the cities, the spread of the news back home in Rolwaling Valley took a completely different form. People knew that there had been an avalanche at Pumori, killing four Sherpas. 'As two Sherpas in that team were us brothers, people in the village thought both of us had died in the accident,' Phurba Tenzing told us.

When Phurba Tenzing made it home, the family was incredibly relieved to see him alive. For Pemba Gyalze, however, who'd sought to catch the attention of employers by working hard in the rescue of the 1996 disaster, the death of his own brother was both a climax and a calling. Soon after that incident, he retired from climbing, returned to his village and took a vow to never go to the mountains again. Phurba Tenzing, too, promised to abandon the 'futility' of mountain climbing and went back to Rolwaling.

*

After 2006, although he was enjoying the everyday village life, Phurba Tenzing was already starting to feel an odd restlessness, with a longing to make something meaningful out of his life. The country had just emerged out of a decade-long armed Maoist conflict. The peace process had just started, and a greater number of people from all over the world had started thronging the mountains. The demand for Sherpas was gradually increasing.

It was not too difficult for Phurba Tenzing to get a break, as his brother Pemba 'Speed', was already a big name in the climbing industry. As pressures of earning money and making life more comfortable had started building on young Phurba Tenzing, the only possibility he could see before him was mountain climbing, and he did not think too hard about breaking his promise to himself.

In the spring of 2008, Phurba Tenzing was taking slow and steady steps deep into the death zone of Everest, this time with his brother Pemba 'Speed'. The brothers had left their clients at Camp 4 and headed towards the summit with several sponsorship flags that they were supposed to take to the top of the world. They would come back to the summit later with their clients as the load was too heavy to do it all in one ascent. However, this time, with the flags, it was as if they were simply taking a casual hike in the death zone, where usually every little bit of energy is priceless. After standing at the summit of Everest, the two brothers returned to Camp 4, and soon headed back again, safely guiding their clients to the summit.

'It may not have been a world record, as summits are counted only from the bottom to the top, but that sure was a record for myself. On my very first time, I stood on top of Everest twice,' said Phurba Tenzing, who currently has 15 Everest summits in his résumé, at the age of just 33. (At the age of 24, Phurba had already made nine Everest summits, becoming the youngest person to climb Mount Everest for the greatest number of times.)

With two successful summits, Phurba Tenzing had now secured a lifelong mountaineering career for himself. However, the summit of Everest left him with nothing but surprises. 'There was absolutely nothing at the peak. The view is great only when the weather is good, but that's not always,' he said. 'I wondered why people were so foolish to put their lives at risk for the mountains.'

Only after summiting Everest for two or three consecutive years, Phurba Tenzing came to realize what prestige it had on the world stage. 'I realized that it was associated with people's dreams and the psyche of adventure. Even more than that, for him it was the market value and the business of Everest climbing. It was several times greater than the little money we had been happily making at Everest.' With this realization, Phurba Tenzing now owns a mountaineering company and trades in millions. The company was a quick success owing to Phurba Tenzing's proven climbing abilities, the legacy of his family and a wide network of mountaineers he had been able to secure throughout his climbing career. In 2021 he guided a Chinese woman's speed climbing on Everest. She became the fastest woman to scale Everest with a world record of 25 hours and 50 minutes. Phurba Tenzing's company also takes people with disabilities to the top of the world. After him, several other siblings from the family followed the trails to the mountains.

*

In 2021, Nima Lhamu stood on top of the world at the age of 21, becoming the eighth of the siblings to follow her brothers' and sisters' footprints on Everest. With her on this expedition were brothers Pemba 'Speed' and Nima Gyalzen. The siblings had reached the top of the world without any pre-rotations (see page 165). Therefore, for the young Nima Lhamu, her first step on Everest was headed straight for the final summit push itself. Nima Lhamu's summit broke the earlier world record of seven siblings to stand atop Everest. (In 2018, when Pemba 'Speed', Phurba Tenzing, Phurba Thiley Sherpa and Dawa Diki together climbed Everest, they had equalled the record of the highest number of siblings from one family reaching the summit. The 2018 feat also made another unique record, of the highest number of siblings arriving at any 8,000-m (26,247-ft) peak at the same time.)

Back in Rolwaling Valley, over another round of *Jhwaikhatte*, we asked Kinjum how it feels to be the only woman on earth to have given birth to the highest number of Everest summiteers. This is a question that she gets from curious people all over the world, to which she cannot give a simple answer. 'I don't know. Whenever people talk about records and mountains, I miss my son Thundu and my son-in-law [Dawa Diki's husband],' she said.

A woman of few words, Kinjum tends to weigh all the glories against the cost that her family has paid in the mountains. She can't figure out which is heavier.

Chapter 9

PLAYING THE LONG GAME

In 1993, two brand-new Russian Mi-17 helicopters en route to Nepal via Iran landed in Karachi in Pakistan. Flying over the Caspian Sea and vast Iranian territories, the Russian beasts had arrived in South Asia, not so far from their new home, Nepal. But the final leg for these choppers was not going to be easy. The American, European and Indian helicopters already flying in the Nepali sky would do what they could to avoid sharing the airspace with the Russian-bred choppers. After all, it was the post-Cold War era, the Soviet Union had collapsed and the solid king-sized Russian choppers were reportedly a threat to existing businesses. As several western embassies in Kathmandu, India and overseas flexed their muscles, the Russian choppers' maiden voyage didn't go according to plan. They got stuck in Karachi.

*

At this time, Ang Tshering Sherpa, then 40 years old, was trying to stretch his family's vibrant mountaineering business in Kathmandu into aviation. This was a time when foreign climbing companies attracted much business in the area and only sought local help to gather up Sherpas and arrange logistics in Nepal. Amid international competition, Ang Tshering's company – a first-generation mountaineering facility entirely run by a Sherpa – was a lone wolf in the industry.

In Nepal, the early 1990s was just the right time to take a giant leap for businesses like Ang Tshering's. After more than three decades of autocratic monarch rule, the country had transitioned into a new multiparty democracy, offering bright prospects for overall economic development. Ang Tshering also wanted to cash in on this opportunity and make it big.

When the helicopters got stuck in Karachi, Ang Tshering had already cleared the full payment of US$1 million (the contemporary exchange rate of US$1 was equal to 50–60 Nepali rupees) for them to the Russian company. His company was one of the first in Nepal to get an aviation licence after the country adopted a liberal sky policy in 1992. For Ang Tshering, bringing the Russian helicopters to Nepal was critical as he had already made the payment. On top of that, a deal that he had earlier tried with the French had already been cancelled.

Desperate to clear the way for his helicopters, Ang Tshering knocked on doors at all ministries and offices. The government officials were supportive, but could do nothing to convince India to allow the choppers to use their sky on the way to Nepal.

One month quickly passed by, and it was getting more and more expensive to keep the helicopters at Karachi. For all that time, Ang Tshering had been paying the airport in Karachi its parking fees. Not only that, he was paying the living costs of the 11 foreign crew members stuck together with the helicopters.

Just when Ang Tshering was starting to think about selling the choppers back to the Russians at a lower price, he had an idea.

The idea was to approach the Chinese to let the Russian helicopters use their sky to fly to Nepal. As Ang Tshering saw this alternative as his only remaining option, and even a tiny mistake or a loophole could shut down his aviation dreams forever, he wanted to be sure not to miss this opportunity. While Nepal's then-prime minister Girija Prasad Koirala, who also headed the foreign ministry, was attending a UN General Assembly, one of Ang Tshering's friends, who was the tourism minister at that time, had some independent leverage, allowing his stuck choppers a glimmer of hope.

Ang Tshering made his way to the Chinese embassy in Kathmandu with the request. As this matter involved India, China had an opportunity to make a statement and readily accepted Ang Tshering's request. The two giant neighbours – India and China – had undergone war over border disputes twice, in 1962 and 1967. Moreover, there is also a huge ideological clash between the two countries, as India has always been closer to western interests.

The choppers took off from the airport in Karachi without making too much noise, taking an unusual route via Chinese air, crossing over the Himalayan gorges and landing in Kathmandu's Tribhuvan International Airport. Ang Tshering successfully tricked his choppers into Nepal against the will of his mighty opposers. A man who grew up witnessing yaks transport goods in his hometown was now about to fly his own aircraft.

*

Ang Tshering was born to an affluent family (though their economic affluence was nothing more than owning a little more livestock than others in the village) from Khumjung in the same year that Sir Edmund Hillary and Tenzing Norgay stepped on top of the world for the first time.

Ang Tshering's family was also considerably influential in the village for three reasons. Firstly, in the 19th century, Ang Tshering's great-grandfather became one of the three local administrators of the Khumbu region, appointed by the then-Rana rulers of Kathmandu. Before then, when the several tiny kingdoms all over present-day Nepal were being annexed together in the 18th century, rulers from lower regions had attempted an attack on Khumbu, but all in vain due to the high altitude and unfavourable fighting conditions. Before the Rana rulers appointed administrators in Khumbu representing Nepal as a country, the entire region was isolated and was not bound to any national rules and taxes.

Secondly, his great grandfather was part of the Everest expedition attempts in the early 1920s. In 1924, when veteran British climber George Mallory disappeared in the mountain, Ang Tshering's grandfather was among those who saw him for the last time.

Thirdly, in 1960, Ang Tshering's father, Konjo Chumbi Sherpa, went on a world tour with Sir Edmund Hillary, showing the world the skeletal remains of what they believed belonged to the yeti. Towards the end of the 1950s, Hillary had secured significant funding from the

American publisher World Books to commission an organized search for this mysterious creature in the Himalayan region of Nepal. Following the tracks of earlier evidence – a giant footstep on the snow supposed to be of the yeti – which was captured in Rolwaling Valley by Eric Shipton in 1951, Hillary launched a fierce mission covering a wide range spread across the Khumbu, Rolwaling and Makalu regions of Nepal.

During the same yeti expedition, when the explorers arrived in Khumbu, the region was suffering from an outbreak of smallpox, commonly known as *Bifar*. A number of Sherpas were seriously ill and there was no medical provision. It was impossible to get medical supplies by road and there were no airfields in the entire region for an airplane to land. Sir Edmund Hillary stepped up to the task and gathered young Sherpas to level a ground near Pangboche at the foot of Ama Dablam to create a little airstrip. 'Today, very few people are aware of that airstrip carved at around 4,500m (14,800ft) by Hillary during his yeti expedition. It was used to transport medical supplies and doctors to bring the fast-spreading smallpox in the region under control,' Ang Tshering told us.

The yeti expedition was backed with technology, which involved telescopes, microphones, trip wires, capture guns loaded with tranquillizer, cameras, and all sorts. However, the expedition failed to come up with anything substantial, though Hillary was getting increasingly convinced of the yeti's existence in the mountains. He proposed to take a yeti's skull that was held in the Khumjung monastery on a world tour and raise some money to build a school in Khumjung. The villagers agreed, but on the condition that Konjo Chumbi would be part of the tour, chaperoning the priceless specimen, which was of great religious significance to the entire region.

The following year, when Queen Elizabeth II and Prince Philip visited Nepal, they extended Ang Tshering's father an invitation to Kathmandu. As events in London had prevented Hillary and Konjo Chumbi from meeting the royals as planned, the Queen had personally asked to meet Ang Tshering's parents in Kathmandu.

On their 18-day journey to Kathmandu (Ang Tshering stayed behind in Khumjung), Konjo Chumbi's pregnant wife gave birth to their younger son, Ang Tshering's brother. They showed up in a meeting with the Queen in Kathmandu with the newborn baby. When Prince Philip learned that the five-day-old baby was yet to be named, he gave the young one his name. After Sherpas' naming rituals, later on, the baby was called Thukten Philip Sherpa.

'For all these different reasons, my father was an influential figure in the entire region,' Ang Tshering recalled. 'I still remember how mountaineers and expedition leaders would come to Khumbu asking for my father's favours, mainly in finding porters.'

*

Ang Tshering got his first taste of trekking and tourism in 1963, at the age of ten. His father and an uncle were coordinating the logistics and management of Sherpas and porters in the first American Everest expedition of that year.

Coordinating an expedition at that time meant travelling down to Kathmandu Valley with hundreds of porters, receiving the foreign guests and coming back to Khumbu, walking for at least three weeks. Although a child, Ang Tshering, who was enrolled in the primary school built by Hillary, was one of the very few educated members of the village, who knew a few English words to communicate with the foreigners. The practical skills of this ten-year-old were an asset for his father and uncle, so he went with them on the trip, at the age of ten, walking most of the way, only occasionally carried by porters.

It took over two weeks for the team to arrive in Banepa, a small town towards the east of Kathmandu Valley. From Banepa, Ang Tshering had his first ever motor ride. The Sherpas boarded a lorry and entered Kathmandu, where they received the American team of 19 climbers and some scientists.

The American mission was much more than just the world power's bid to step on top of the world. Less than a year before the team came to Everest,

President John F Kennedy had announced, 'We choose to go to the moon in this decade and do the other things, not because they are easy, but because they are hard.'

The Cold War was at its peak and, around the same time, America had been investing heavily in science and technology. A tiny bit of that heavy investment made its way into the Sherpa trail in the form of the first American Everest expedition. Among the sponsors of that mission were the US State Department, the US Air Force and the National Aeronautics and Space Administration (NASA).

This was the first time Ang Tshering had seen so many people all at the same time; as well as the number of people, there was an enormous amount of equipment, gear and food. From what Ang Tshering can recall, throughout their stay in Kathmandu, he never saw his father and uncle in a peaceful state of mind. 'As they were coordinating over 900 porters and Sherpas in the team, my father and uncle did not have a single moment to rest,' Ang Tshering recalled. 'Then there I was. A ten-year-old, bridging the responsibilities of my father and uncle with such a huge American mission.'

Ang Tshering has hazy memories of Kathmandu in 1963. From what he recalls, there were only two hotels in the city, in one of which the Americans had stayed. In the third week of February, the team embarked on their journey from Kathmandu to the Khumbu region. As nearly one thousand people walked together, little Ang Tshering made sure he was not out of the sight of his father and uncle.

The caravan stopped to rest at a place called Thosey by a river, several days before arriving in Lukla. The Americans jumped into the water to swim as the queue of porters was slowly approaching. 'There was a suspension bridge over the river, which several loaded porters were trying to cross at the same time,' Ang Tshering told us.

The bridge could not take the entire load. It broke, and several porters fell directly into the river, along with the loads they were carrying. Thankfully, the Americans who were already in the river were quick to rescue the porters and retrieve the loads. The mishap injured eight porters.

That night in Thosey, Ang Tshering's father appeared unusually serious. After the foreigners went to sleep, he did not come to the tent to sleep until late into the night. When he peeked out, little Ang Tshering saw his father and uncle talking with other Sherpas of the team. 'They all appeared very tense,' he said. 'But I had no idea what that was all about.'

The following day, Ang Tshering discovered what the fuss was about. Though the team had been able to retrieve much of what had fallen into the river the previous day, one pack was still missing.

Ang Tshering's father, uncle and some Sherpas went to look for the lost load early that morning. Thankfully, they found it and came back to the campsite with wide smiles. 'I had never seen my father so happy. It made me happy as well,' Ang Tshering said. 'A few hours later, my dad told me that it was not like any other load containing food or clothes. The pack that went missing contained several kilos of money.'

There was a massive party that night and all were happy and relieved. 'To me, this was the best day of that journey,' he said. Before sleeping, Ang Tshering's father told him, 'This could have turned the entire mission chaotic. We would not have had any money to pay the porters and Sherpas.'

As the caravan progressed on its journey, Ang Tshering's father appointed three trusted Sherpas to closely accompany the porter who had been carrying the money. Finally, the camp was set at the base of Everest around the third week of March. The journey from Kathmandu to Khumbu was over three weeks.

As Ang Tshering returned home with a life full of memories, the American team completed their mission on 1 May 1963, when James W Whittaker and Nawang Gombu Sherpa, a nephew of Tenzing Norgay, reached the summit. Four other Americans reached the top later, on 22 May 1963, making that year special for the Americans.

'This journey was like a retreat to me. I was in my father's and uncle's company, and for helping them converse with the foreigners, I would get chocolates as remuneration,' Ang Tshering recalled. 'My real first business was in 1966 when I guided a Japanese climber from our village Khumjung to the base camp of Mount Lhotse Shar [8,383m, 27,503ft] near the Imja Glacier.'

In 1966, a group of Japanese climbers had been preparing to climb Lhotse Shar, a subsidiary peak of Lhotse. The Sirdar of that group was a Sherpa from the same neighbourhood as Ang Tshering. One of the members of the Japanese team was due to arrive a few days after everyone else and, when the Sirdar left with his group from Khumjung to the base camp, he called on Ang Tshering and asked him to guide the other client to the base camp.

For the locals, Khumjung to the base camp of Lhotse Shar is just a day's trek. Ang Tshering had been there many times before. 'There used to be a grazing field near the glacier and, as our cattle grazed, we would play on the glacier, gliding here and there. There was a small pond, the size of a kids' swimming pool in cities these days. The same pond expanded over years to become the huge Imja Tsho [Lake], engulfing the grazing fields as well as lumps of ice on which we used to play.' Imja Tsho, at 5,000m (16,400ft), which was the size of a swimming pool in the early 1960s, as Ang Tshering explained, is bigger than a square kilometre (0.39 square miles) today.

As requested by the Sirdar, Ang Tshering guided the Japanese client to the base camp and, beyond his expectations, was paid 125 rupees. 'That was a huge deal of money back then. In today's money, that would be several hundred thousand rupees,' Ang Tshering giggled, explaining how the Japanese also loaded him with chocolates, dry meat, cookies and noodles. 'My pockets had never been heavier. I came home and handed over all the money to my mother.'

*

Ang Tshering's exposure to the 1963 American Everest expedition and the profitable gig of 1966 with the Japanese had given him a glimpse of what was going to happen in the region over the coming years.

Talking with us nearly 60 years later at his lavish office property with a wall-climbing recreation centre in the downtown Thamel area of Kathmandu, Ang Tshering recalled how, for several years after 1963 and 1966, he kept striving for the same thrill, adventure, excitement and fun. However, times were different back then.

A major expedition like the one in 1963 would happen only once every several years. Commercial mountaineering had not yet started and only the national expeditions initiated and funded by different countries were taking place. Climbing was extremely expensive as the expedition teams would have to bring all the equipment, gear, food and camping tents by themselves. There were not many hotels in Kathmandu itself, let alone the Khumbu region. All that was available to support these expeditions in Nepal were the untrained Sherpas, backed only by indigenous skills in the mountains and ignorant courage. Moreover, only a few handfuls of these Sherpas would get the job in expeditions as there were not many available.

No matter what, Ang Tshering cherished his memories from the American expedition and started weaving a dream of someday repeating such moments. 'At that time, all I could imagine was spending more time with the foreigners, talking with them and enjoying their delicious western food,' Ang Tshering recalled, smiling from ear to ear. 'In that sense, the gradual growth of the climbing industry seems to have been pretty much in synchronization with my transition into teenager, youth and other phases of life. However, before I got another break in the mountains, there were several years of silence and a long tormenting wait. As a teenager, I was limited to living the normal life of a Sherpa kid in Khumjung.'

Ang Tshering was enrolled in the primary school that Hillary built in Khumjung. He was one of the few Sherpa kids from his time to get a formal school education, taught in English. Before Hillary built the school, that still runs today, some Sherpas would join the monasteries to become monks. The education of a monk would also be limited to only one of the sons in a family, while the rest would have to struggle and find a livelihood for themselves and their families.

During holidays, Ang Tshering would join his family members at their pasture near Mong La (over 4,500m, 14,800ft), a pass in a trail connecting the crossroads leading towards Gokyo Lake to the left and Everest Base Camp to the right.

*

One evening, a few years before Hillary built the school in Khumjung, Ang Tshering left the family's makeshift shelter near Mong La to herd a flock of sheep and some yaks. 'I remember taking an uphill trail to a small grassland, about a kilometre [0.6 miles] away from our shelter,' he said. 'I could not have missed the trail and lost my way back since I had gone there several times before. However, I don't have any memory of what happened there; I was not home with my parents until late that night.'

When Ang Tshering woke up, he was dizzy, semi-conscious and it was already dark. He looked around and figured out he was in a cave, several metres above the field where he had taken the sheep for grazing. 'I had no business coming this far into a cave and I was scared to the core,' he recalled. 'I gathered my courage and stepped out of the cave. A thick cloud of mist had gathered all over and I could hardly see anything. I couldn't even figure out the trail downhill towards our shelter. My head was still spinning.'

After several minutes of struggle not knowing where to go, Ang Tshering heard his father, then his mother. They had been continuously shouting his name and he was finally able to recover his sense of direction. He followed the echoing of his name, and took careful, desperate steps downhill. From a little below where he had woken up, he saw flames, the vision of which was blurred due to his spinning head and a thick layer of mist. He continued in the same direction and was finally able to make contact with his family. 'I must have suffered from high-altitude sickness that evening,' Ang Tshering recalled. 'However, I still can't work out how and why I went to that cave.'

For everyone else, this was an episode of witch-hunt by *Banjhakri*. Throughout different parts of hilly and mountainous regions of Nepal, many believe that *Banjhakri*, a blood-thirsty witch of the forest with backward-pointing feet, abducts children with the potential of becoming great shamans and brings them to the cave for shamanic training. As all children abducted by *Banjhakri* cannot pass the shamanic tests, they are at risk of harm, when, according to folklore, *Banjhakri* may even eat them or cast black magic upon them, resulting in harmful consequences in the future.

Ang Tshering fell terribly sick after that incident. As the village didn't have hospitals, his parents sought a spiritual shamanic cure for his ailments, a common practice in remote villages without hospitals, even today. Around the time that Ang Tshering fell sick, a high-ranking Lama from Tibet had come to visit a monastery in Thamo in the Khumbu region. Ang Tshering's father put his ailing son on a horse and took him to see the Lama. From Khumjung, Thamo is a half-day trek on foot.

'I only have a faint memory of that horse ride and the encounter with the Lama,' Ang Tshering said. 'The Lama examined me, went through his own sacred process navigating through a person's body and life, and prescribed some Himalayan herbal medicines. Before we left, he declared that there were chances I might die in another six months. However, if I managed to survive, he said I would become a great person someday.'

Ang Tshering's father took the Lama's prediction about his son rather seriously. He did everything he could to ensure his son didn't die over the next six months and, when Ang Tshering got better, he started hoping that the Lama's words would come true. To him, in order to become a great person someday, a prerequisite was education. He hired five monks from Tibet to educate his son and some other boys from the village at his own home. Before Hillary built the school in Khumjung, this informal facility established by Ang Tshering's father served as an education centre for the children of the village. After Hillary's school came into operation, the boys and girls were enrolled in it, and thus started the wave of formal education in the entire Khumbu region.

As the village school established by Hillary only went up to Grade 5, most of the Sherpa children had no option but to drop out after that. Unlike today, the Sherpas' economy had not yet boomed enough to send their children to Kathmandu for further education. Yet, as Ang Tshering came from an influential family in Khumbu, and especially with the great Lama's prediction that he would make it big someday, his parents decided that he should continue his education.

Ang Tshering and four other boys from the village were enrolled in a government school in Salleri, a village at a lower elevation in Solu, bordering with Okhaldhunga district. About a week's trek down from Khumbu, Okhaldhunga was then the administrative centre of the entire region and all the major government offices were based there. People from surrounding districts had to travel there for any official affairs and the administrators of Khumbu (of which Ang Tshering's father was one) had to trek down to Okhaldhunga every year to register taxes collected from their respective catchment villages. Okhaldhunga also had shops, eateries, roads and schools, and was one of the few districts in the region that held the board exams of Grade 10 – the SLC (see page 67) – every year.

After taking the SLC, Ang Tshering travelled to Kathmandu, where his elder sister had married and settled, took a bridging course in teaching and later an Intermediate in Science (ISC). While waiting for the ISC results, in 1972, Ang Tshering took up a job with a trekking agency called Mountain Travel, and went to Lukla as their eastern region manager. 'The number of mountain expeditions was limited back then, but this company kept me busy in trekking,' he said.

*

One day, Ang Tshering was waiting at the Tenzing-Hillary Airport in Lukla (see page 33) for a chartered flight to land. Back then, Lukla used to have only chartered flights, most of which were operated by the agency Ang Tshering was working for. He was supposed to receive a group of trekkers. The plane landed and, along with the trekkers, Ang Tshering's brother-in-law also disembarked. He was holding a newspaper in his hand. As Ang Tshering was greeting the tourists, his brother-in-law grabbed him by the arm, took him aside and showed him the paper.

'Isn't this your serial ID?' he asked, pointing at a number which he had underlined in the newspaper.

'Oh, yes! What's the result? Have I passed?' Ang Tshering quickly became nervous, knowing that the ISC results were out.

'Yes. You have cleared your ISC. This is huge,' the brother-in-law said.

Ang Tshering had so far been enjoying his work in trekking and tourism, and, deep down somewhere, he wanted to continue with it. However, the family, particularly his father, was determined to see his son making it big, just like the Tibetan Lama had predicted long ago in the monastery in Thame. 'That was the highest anyone had ever been educated in my family,' Ang Tshering said. 'Everybody wanted me to become a doctor.'

Back then, studying medicine was not possible in Nepal as the country did not have any medical schools. Those who came from rich families could afford to pursue medicine abroad. However, for common people like Ang Tshering, the only way was to crack difficult competitive exams for scholarships under the Colombo Plan, a pact reached between 28 countries to build human resources in the impoverished South Asian region. As part of the Colombo Plan, the government would send deserving students abroad for technical studies like medicine and engineering, among others. Even today, being able to afford to study medicine without a scholarship is a big deal for the average Nepali family.

After several months of preparation, when Ang Tshering sat down to write the exam paper, he nailed it, and he knew it. He had taken the exams in

English, which was an added benefit. The results came and, unsurprisingly, Ang Tshering passed. He now had to have an interview. 'My communication skills are not so good. I think this is the furthest I can get,' he said to himself as he entered the interview hall.

It was a nine-member interview panel, which consisted of top educationists of Nepal, ministry secretaries and other high-ranking government officials. Throughout the 35-minute session, Ang Tshering's heart pounded. When it was finally over and he was about to step out of the room, one of the interviewers representing Nepal's Ministry of Education stood up and said, 'Good job, Sherpa!'

These last words made Ang Tshering hopeful and, when the results came out, with the names of 17 successful candidates, his was on top. 'I didn't know if that was because my name started with an 'A' or if I had topped the competitive process,' he said, resonating modesty. 'Whatever it was, I was on the list, and had been selected to study medicine in India.'

A Sherpa from Khumbu was about to become a doctor. Ang Tshering headed south, to the Indian state of Bihar, and enrolled in the famous Darbhanga Medical College.

Upon his arrival in Darbhanga, Ang Tshering immediately faced a rather difficult test. For a man who belonged to the mountains, the hot climate of Darbhanga proved tormenting to him. 'In just a few months of arriving in Darbhanga, I started developing allergies all over my body,' he said. 'The medicines only worked for as long as I was taking them. As soon as I finished a course of medicine, my allergies would flare up again. I also started falling sick more frequently. The most recurring symptom became the swelling of the glands in my throat. Nothing seemed to be helping my body cope with the climate and 52-m (170-ft) altitude of Darbhanga.'

By the time Ang Tshering passed the third year of his five-year medicine course, his gland problem had worsened and he needed an operation. Yet, he clung on, hoping to complete his studies and return to Nepal. 'The fourth year had just started, and I was sick as usual,' he said. 'The doctor who had operated on my glands during my third year was our main professor, and he quickly recognized me. He called me to his chamber.'

'How are you doing, Mr Sherpa?' the professor asked.

'I am fine, professor. Thank you!' Ang Tshering replied.

'Well, you don't seem fine,' the professor said, as Ang Tshering looked down at his feet and remained silent. 'You should not continue here. You may insist, but this will have serious repercussions on your long-term health. You may even die.'

Ang Tshering remained silent, not knowing what to say, as he knew as a half-doctor himself that whatever the professor was telling him was right.

The professor continued, 'You can either be an ailing doctor all your life or live a healthy life, far from this place. The choice is yours. If you can, seek a transfer to medical colleges in Chandigarh or Mussoorie. It's cooler there and you may be able to cope. If you can't arrange a transfer, I advise you to simply return home.'

Dropping out of college completely seemed like a rather radical move to Ang Tshering, so he sought a transfer to a hilly medical college as his professor had suggested. He took a train to Kolkata and visited the office of journalist Desmond Doig, who had travelled the world with his father and Sir Edmund Hillary with the yeti skull from Khumjung back in 1960.

After explaining the situation to Desmond, Ang Tshering asked, 'Can you manage my transfer to a hilly medical college?'

Without a second thought, Desmond replied, 'Why not? I can make that happen!'

Ang Tshering returned to the cooler Kathmandu and waited for news from Kolkata. Soon after his return, his health problems and allergies disappeared, and he was a healthy man once again.

Back then, the most reliable way people could communicate remotely in Nepal was via messages sent over telex, a fax-like alert system. Ang Tshering's wait stretched from a few days to over eight months, when finally he got a telex from Kolkata through a hotel in Kathmandu – a one-line message, asking him to wait on the telephone line the following day at 2pm.

'Finally,' Ang Tshering heaved a sigh of relief, informed his family and, the following day, went to the telecommunications office.

At around 3pm, the operator finally yelled, 'Who is Sherpa here?'

'It's me, sir!' Ang Tshering said.

'You rush to booth number three,' the operator directed.

It was Desmond from Kolkata.

Desmond said something from the other side, but the line was so disturbed that Ang Tshering did not understand anything.

'I can't hear you, sir. Can you say again, please?' Ang Tshering yelled several times, holding the phone receiver with both hands.

Desmond kept saying something and Ang Tshering pressed the receiver hard on his ear, trying to decipher Desmond's voice against the continuous feedback on the line. Finally, when he hung up, Ang Tshering understood that Desmond had arranged the transfer, but on the condition that he would have to repeat his studies right from the first year. 'I am still not sure I understood that conversation right,' Ang Tshering told us.

'My parents and all other family members still wanted me to go to the medical school,' Ang Tshering said. 'But I decided the opposite. I didn't want to be lingering in the first year with juniors, while my contemporaries passed out as doctors the following year. I finally dropped out.'

*

During his long wait for the message from Kolkata, Ang Tshering had made his way into tourism once again. His brother-in-law had started a trekking company, where Ang Tshering had already started working as a manager. 'After quitting my studies, I fully devoted myself to a career in trekking and tourism,' Ang Tshering said. 'The dreams that I had weaved as a teenager in the 1960s were finally coming true, and I was happy about that.'

After working for three years as a manager in his brother-in-law's company, in 1982 Ang Tshering heard that two politicians were looking

Furdiki Sherpa and Nima Doma Sherpa, whose husbands both died on Everest, on top of Everest in 2019. Photo courtesy: Furdiki Sherpa.

Members of the first female Sherpa Everest expedition. Pasang Lhamu Sherpa (far left), the first Sherpa woman to summit Everest, who died on descent, with (from left to right) Nanda Rai and Lhakpa Futi Sherpa. Photo courtesy: Lhakpa Futi Sherpa.

The village of Beding. Photo courtesy: Pradeep Bashyal.

The village of Na. Photo courtesy: Pradeep Bashyal.

The village of Khumjung. Photo courtesy: Pradeep Bashyal.

Kinjum Sherpa (Pemba Gyalze Sherpa's mother) in Beding. Photo courtesy: Pradeep Bashyal.

Phurba Tashi Sherapa (who has summited Everest 21 times) with his wife and daughter. Photo courtesy: Pradeep Bashyal.

Phurba Tenzing Sherpa, Pemba Dorje Sherpa, Dawa Diki Sherpa and Phurba Thiley Sherpa achieving a unique record – the highest number of siblings arriving at any 8,000-m (26,247-ft) peak at the same time. Photo courtesy: Phurba Tenzing Sherpa.

Phurba Tenzing enjoying chhyang with local Sherpa women in Rolwaling. Photo courtesy: Phurba Tenzing Sherpa.

The village Khumjung at night.
Photo courtesy: Ang Tshering Sherpa.

Ang Tshering Sherpa's parents, Konjo
Chumbi Sherpa and Ang Pali Sherpa.
Photo courtesy: Ang Tshering Sherpa.

Ang Tshering Sherpa with
Sir Edmund Hillary.
Photo courtesy: Ang Tshering Sherpa.

Babu Chiri Sherpa, who set a record in 1999 by spending 21 hours at the Everest summit. Photo courtesy: Ravi Manandhar.

Nima Dorjee Sherpa, nicknamed 'Boka Lama', a priest and religious leader in Makalu. Photo courtesy: Salina Bhattarai.

Tashi Lhakpa Sherpa, Mingma Sherpa and Chhang Dawa Sherpa, the three brothers who own Seven Summits, in Antarctica during their 2021 South Pole expedition. Photo courtesy: 14 Peaks Expedition.

Ang Rita Sherpa, nicknamed 'Snow Leopard', who climbed Everest 10 times without supplementary oxygen.
Photo courtesy: Chakra Karki.

Apa Sherpa, nicknamed 'Super Sherpa' who held the world record of 21 Everest summits, until this was equalled by Phurba Tashi Sherpa and broken by Kami Rita Sherpa.
Photo courtesy: Chakra Karki.

A crevice in Khumbu Icefall. Photo courtesy: Kuntal Joisher.

The Western Cwm, which must be passed on the route between Camp 1 and Camp 2. Photo courtesy: Kuntal Joisher.

Apa Sherpa ('Super Sherpa'), Lhakpa Gelu Sherpa and Dr Scott McIntosh during the 2007 study into Sherpas' physiologies. Photo courtesy: Super Sherpa Expeditions.

Kami Rita Sherpa, who holds the record for the highest number (26) of Everest summits. Photo courtesy: 14 Peaks Expedition.

Dawa Finjhok Sherpa, who led a high-profile expedition to recover the body of Goutam Ghosh in 2017. Photo courtesy: Dawa Finjhok Sherpa.

Vegan mountaineer Kuntal Joisher on the Third Step on the North Face of Everest.
Photo courtesy: Mingma Tenzi Sherpa.

Namgyal Sherpa, who died on the North Face of Everest in 2013, his widow
Doma Sherpa has tried unsucessfully to retrieve his body from the mountain.
Photo courtesy: Chakra Karki.

for a buyer for their trekking company. He reached out to them and said he was interested in buying their company.

'During that time, it was very difficult to get a trekking licence. The two politicians had registered a company called Asian Trekking, but as they lacked any knowledge about trekking and tourism, they were unable to run the company. They did not have any clients and the company had been silent right from its registration,' he said. As he had earned good money through trekking engagements with his brother-in-law, Ang Tshering was able to buy their licence for 200,000 rupees (about 20 million rupees by today's standards) and take over the company.

Soon after Ang Tshering took over Asian Trekking, he started getting lots of clients. 'My father and uncles had a good reputation in mountaineering, and their goodwill got me clients from the very first year,' he recalled, explaining how his family's history in mountaineering, from the time of his grandfather, helped him gain an instant trust among the climbing community. 'Word about my company spread very quickly, and the foreign friends of my family did all they could to land me as many clients as they could.

'For several years after starting the company, I hardly slept four hours every day. We did not have enough human resources in the company and I had to type clients' profiles and itineraries myself, all manually with a typewriter,' he said. 'It's easy these days due to computers. Back in those days, all we could use to copy itineraries was carbon print papers. The carbon papers could copy only two sheets at a time, and we had to repeat the same process over and over again.'

During his heyday, Ang Tshering himself accompanied his clients up to the higher camps of several 8,000-m (26,247-ft) mountains. 'But I never went to the summit, sometimes by choice and sometimes as the conditions didn't favour it,' he said. 'Rather than climbing peaks myself, I always thought my forte was in managing the business, and that's what I did all my life.'

A leap in the tourism industry had fared very well for Ang Tshering. Just a few years after taking over Asian Trekking, he'd also started a separate rafting company, which he had left for his brothers to run. Then came an opportunity to run a hotel. One of his relatives was looking to rent out his hotel in Kathmandu. One evening, Ang Tshering got a sudden call. The person on the other end of the phone – his relative – was drunk and aggressive.

'What do you think you are trying to do? You had committed to take my hotel and now I hear you've changed your mind. What is this? You know who I am?' the relative said.

Utterly unaware what the fuss was all about, Ang Tshering hung up and went to meet his relative the next morning.

At the very first sight, the relative told him, 'I am so sorry about yesterday. I was trying to call another Ang Tshering, but happened to dial your number. Sorry again. What will you take? Tea?'

Ang Tshering learned that the relative was desperate to lease out his hotel. 'I took an instant decision and leased that hotel as well,' he said, explaining how the hotel started making a good profit soon after he took it over.

Within a decade after starting Asian Trekking, Ang Tshering was already a big name in Nepal's tourism industry. His company had been operating huge mountain expeditions, as well as trekking, rafting and overseas travel, among other things. Now that his hotel business had also taken off, he was ready to take another giant leap – this time expanding into aviation. Once he had his choppers up and running, his empire in the tourism industry would be complete and he would not have to depend on other agencies for most of his affairs.

After all the geopolitical struggle, when he was finally able to bring his Russian-made Mi-17 helicopters to Nepal, he initially faced some difficulties operating them. 'My choppers were labelled giants in the media and people criticized them, referring to them as machines taking over trekking porters' jobs,' he recalled. Ang Tshering's helicopters could easily carry over 4,500kg (4.5t) of weight at once and could easily fly in high altitudes as well. 'This scared existing transport businesses here, hence all the negativity around our choppers,' Ang Tshering said.

But, as they say, any publicity is good publicity. One of the media reports lashing Ang Tshering's helicopters as giants eating up human jobs caught the attention of a hydropower contractor in western Nepal. He came to Kathmandu looking for Ang Tshering's office. He wanted the helicopters to transport construction goods to remote locations, to the places where humans could take several weeks carrying heavy equipment and materials. 'Once they took off, transporting materials to remote construction sites, the helicopters could hardly take any rest,' Ang Tshering said. 'This saved a lot of money for the contractor. For me also, the profit was very high.'

As Ang Tshering's success skyrocketed, some of his friends asked him to invest in an airline company as well. His sister suggested that he take the counsel of a high-ranking Lama in Swayambhu, a major Buddhist shrine in Kathmandu. The siblings went to see this Lama, who at the very first look at Ang Tshering, said, 'You'd better stay away from the machines.'

Ang Tshering was taken by surprise. 'We had not uttered a word about investing in airplanes or any kinds of machines,' he said. 'But as I had already rolled out some money into the airline, I decided to carry on, notwithstanding the Lama's counsel.' However, the Lama's words came true and, in another three years, Ang Tshering's company witnessed five crashes – three helicopters and two airplanes. He again went to the same Lama, this time alone. 'So many people visit this Lama every day. It's impossible for him to remember everyone by face,' he said. 'But as soon as I sat down before him, he said how he had warned me three years ago.' After returning from the Lama's abode, Ang Tshering made up his mind to pull back from the aviation business. He sold all his aircraft, ended his journey in the air and retreated to the ground, limiting his affairs to his areas of passion – trekking and mountaineering.

Because of all Ang Tshering had contributed to the evolution of climbing and trekking in Nepal, and his active involvement in the country's tourism industry, he was trusted to lead the Nepal Mountaineering Association (NMA), Nepal's only alpine club, for over a decade from 2002. The NMA is a powerful mountaineering body recognized by the government of Nepal and authorized to issue permits to climb 27 peaks across the country. Ang Tshering has also chaired the Union of Asian Alpine Associations several times throughout his career.

Asian Trekking is still active today and is popular as a pioneer mountaineering company operating major expeditions in Nepal and Tibet. Ang Tshering is now over 70 years old and has several people, including his brothers and children, to run the company. Yet, he still goes to the office almost every day; he likes to see what's happening. He functions as a proud and beloved guardian angel to hundreds of climbers and guides who have flourished over an era under his shade. There may be many companies in the mountain scene today, but Ang Tshering is the name that stands as steady and unshaken as the rocks at the bed of Everest; for since the age of ten, when he walked down to Kathmandu with his father to take part in the American Everest expedition, Ang Tshering has been an undisputed champion of the business.

Chapter 10

SEVEN SUMMITS BEYOND

In January 2022, three Sherpa brothers from Nepal's Himalayas – Mingma, Chhang Dawa and Tashi Lhakpa – made headlines, this time not from the top of Everest, but from a faraway sea of ice and snow: the South Pole in Antarctica. Becoming the first people from Nepal to reach the Geographic South Pole, the brothers' extreme adventure was poles apart, literally, from what they had been practising in the mountains all their life.

Several oceans away from home, the three brothers landed in the southernmost country of the world – the Republic of Chile – sometime in mid-December 2021. That same week, they flew four hours further south to land on the Union Glacier Blue-Ice Runway, located in the Heritage Range of Ellsworth Mountains. Boeing 757 aircrafts can land on huge runways marked on the blue ice of the Union Glacier formed over several hundreds of thousands of years.

The Union Glacier – sitting 3,000km (1,860 miles) by land from the southern tip of Chile – is the farthest point that most tourists visiting Antarctica usually reach. The glacier is the only place in the continent that offers tourist camps and is visited by just over 50,000 people every year, mostly between November and January. For most of these visitors, the Union Glacier, where -1°C (30°F) is the warmest it could get at best, is the last destination. For mountain climbers, their endpoint could be Mount Vinson Massif (4,892m, 16,050ft), the base camp of which is another 45-minute flight from the glacier. A handful of some other keen adventurers head further south from the Union Glacier to explore the Geographic South Pole – a wild journey into an endless sea of ice. From the Union Glacier, the South Pole is 1,138km (707 miles) away, and five more hours of flying, to an approximate latitude of 89 degrees south. From there begins the sluggish seven-day, last-degree trek on skis, measuring 111km (69 miles) in distance. This was exactly where the brothers from Nepal were headed.

'The temperature must have been less than -30°C (-22°F) when we landed near the South Pole,' one of the three siblings, Tashi Lhakpa, told us at his home in Kathmandu, nearly two weeks after his return. Black marks of healing frostbite on his cheeks were still clearly visible. 'As soon as we stepped out of the plane, it felt as if we had arrived in an alien space outside the universe. The wind was extraordinarily strong and gushed like an irritating high-pitched squeal,' he said.

The brothers knew they had a long trek towards the south to reach the South Pole. However, how would they know which direction was south? The brothers stood in what resembled the middle of nowhere. 'All we could see was a vast plain of ice in all directions. There were no milestones, no references, no human-made tracks or a way that we were supposed to follow,' Tashi Lhakpa described the wilderness to us, the experience of which was still fresh in his memory. 'Even though we had our compass and GPS devices, the view of it and the place where we stood sent chills down our spines.'

Being the kind of mountain adventurers they are, the brothers had not hired local guides to help them navigate the South Pole. They neither had porters like in Everest, nor a member in the team familiar with the route and directions. Undeterred, the brothers fixed ski blades on to their boots and headed southward with the use of their navigation devices, dragging behind them sleds loaded with supplies of food, tents, gear, equipment and suits. 'Each one of us had our own sled, which weighed up to 100kg [220lb],' Tashi Lhakpa said.

The trek to the Geographic South Pole was a tricky one. Because the trip was unguided, the Sherpa brothers had to keep a constant watch on their compass. Since there was no trail, just the unending plateau of white ice, if they did not follow the right way, there was a possibility that they could walk several days and end up at the exact point from which they had started. 'The compass was our only guide and taking it out of our pocket every now and then to check the direction was particularly difficult because of the cold,' Tashi Lhakpa said.

Each time the brothers took out the compass for navigation, the device's screen would quickly be covered in a layer of ice. 'We would wipe the ice and make sure that we were heading in the right direction,' Tashi Lhakpa told us. 'Because of the cold, we could not even talk with each other when we were walking. Our breath as we walked was forming a mist that would quickly transform into ice particles on our suits. Talking too much could easily worsen that, making our movement more difficult.'

The weather was deceptive too. The days were mostly sunny, and the light reflecting on the sea of white snow emanated incredible brightness, making it seem as though it should be warm. However, the notion of the warmth of the sun was beyond the brothers' imagination. 'As we were so far from the equator, the daylight was too thin, just like oxygen up in the mountains,' Tashi Lhakpa said. 'The sun barely seemed to have any heat down there – not enough even to dry some of our clothes, wet due to sweat and body mist. When we camped for the night, we had to dry our clothes by squeezing them inside the sleeping bag.

'As the light never fell, it seemed like continuous broad daylight for 24 hours. We would figure out it was night by looking at the time. We did not have daily destinations, so whenever we were tired or when it was evening, wherever we were, we would take out our tents, fix them in the snow and retreat,' Tashi Lhakpa said. Inside the tent, they would light up the camping stove and boil together whatever they got their hands on – burgers, potatoes, corn, rice, buckwheat, pickles, salt, pepper, meat...'We do this sometimes in Everest as well,' he giggled. 'We call it the food-mass.'

On the last day of 2021, the brothers stopped 25km (15.5 miles) from the planet's absolute southern frontier, set out their camp and rested. 'One more day,' Tashi Lhakpa told himself, and took out an expensive Scotch – a

Blue Label, which he had bought in Chile. For the first time in their lives, the brothers saw whisky frozen in its bottle due to extreme cold. 'Until then, I did not know that whisky froze,' Tashi Lhakpa laughed.

The day deserved a celebration. It was New Year's Eve, and the three brothers were far from home. 'That day, we did not boil random food. We took out the best we had – salmon, dry meat and rice,' Tashi Lhakpa said. 'It took us a while to warm the whisky, but we finally managed to pour it in our glasses.'

The bottle of Scotch did not last long. 'We were barely tipsy and the bottle was already empty,' Tashi Lhakpa said. 'Then we took out two bottles of French wine and finished them both. We drank until 2am, but even the cocktail of Scotch and wine failed to take our senses away, probably because of the cold.'

After a short two-hour nap, the brothers got up early the next morning and headed further south to explore what awaited them at the edge of the world. When they finally arrived at the South Pole and looked at their compass, they were flabbergasted to see all directions facing 'North'. The GPS coordinates only offer a latitude of 90 degrees south – and all lines of longitude meet there.

The South Pole expedition is very different from a mountain expedition. The mountain risks associated with high altitude, technicalities around the use of ropes and gear while climbing, avalanches and crevasses, are simply non-existent in the polar region. The only physically adverse aspects at the pole are extreme cold and tricky navigation. What is scarier about planning a trip to the southern frontier is its associated expenses. The arrangement of logistics, visas, travel permits and costs of travelling across the globe all involve about US$100,000 – a cost prohibitively expensive even for the citizens of industrialized nations.

After returning from the South Pole to the Union Glacier, the brothers started another mission. This time, they had been hired by a group of Russian climbers to take them to Vinson Massif.

The siblings run Nepal's largest expedition company, Seven Summit Treks, trusted by climbers all over the world. The company has clientele in all fourteen 8,000-m (26,247-ft) peaks across the world as well as the highest mountains in all seven continents. After ticking off their private mission to the South Pole, as well as the Vinson Massif expedition with the Russians, Chhang Dawa and Tashi Lhakpa returned to Nepal and began gearing up for the 2022 spring Everest expeditions. Meanwhile, Mingma set out on a climbing tour across the world. He went from Antarctica to South America, guiding a group of climbers in Mount Aconcagua (6,960m, 22,835ft) in Argentina. Then he travelled to San Francisco in the US and rested a couple of days there, before travelling again to Africa's Tanzania, leading another expedition in Mount Kilimanjaro (5,895m, 19,340ft).

Mingma is the first Nepali and South Asian to bag all 14 8,000-m (26,247-ft) peaks – all achieved in his first attempt, which is a separate record held by him. Likewise, Mingma and brother Chhang Dawa hold another world record for the world's first two brothers to successfully summit these 14 peaks. Meanwhile, Tashi Lhakpa is the youngest person to climb Everest without supplementary oxygen (see page 252).

With unquestionable climbing qualities, leadership, planning and strategies catering to the needs and limitations of mountaineering clients all over the world, the Sherpa brothers have formed an empire in the global mountaineering industry today. To understand and explore the roots of their growth and success, we travelled to their home village in the remote eastern district of Sankhuwasabha in Nepal, home to Makalu (see page 128) and the famous Makalu Barun National Park.

*

On our way to the Sherpa homes in the Makalu region, we first landed at Tumlingtar Airport in the Sankhuwasabha District. Tumlingtar is a 45-minute flight from Kathmandu, which connects to the road networks further up north. Sankhuwasabha is also accessible by road, a 12-hour ride passing through the plains of Nepal to the city of Biratnagar (see page 132), then up into the hilly region of eastern Nepal.

It had been raining for several days when we were planning our trip to Makalu. On the day of the flight, luckily the weather in Kathmandu had cleared and we were fortunate to board the afternoon flight on time. Tumlingtar was also bright and sunny when we landed there. The airport was bigger than we had expected, in comparison with other mountain airstrips in Nepal, including the one in Lukla, the gateway to the Everest region.

From Tumlingtar, we travelled in a taxi to the district's headquarters in Khandbari. To our surprise, the road was tarmacked, but was broken in many places, signifying there had not been any recent repair or maintenance works. As the taxi travelled uphill, passing through villages on the way, the air got cleaner and colder, forests on the hill towards the left grew wider, and there we were, all set to explore what lay ahead.

We had asked the taxi driver to help us find a car we could hire to take us to a place called Num Bazaar, our destination for the day. 'It's already late-afternoon and there might not be regular passenger jeeps going there today,' the taxi driver warned us, as he called his friend in Khandbari, asking to reserve a vehicle for us. The person on the other end of the phone apparently agreed and the taxi driver told us, 'You guys are lucky. We have found a vehicle that has agreed to take you to Num today.'

After a 30-minute drive from Tumlingtar, we arrived in Khandbari, where, by the main highway intersecting with a smaller road leading to the marketplace, we found our ride waiting for us – a rugged Bolero jeep, one of the most trusted machines to run on the off-roads of hilly Nepal. It was already early evening and, without wasting any time, we quickly thanked the taxi driver, jumped into the jeep and headed north, on our way to Num Bazaar.

'The highway has disturbances a little ahead from here,' the driver, a young man probably in his 20s, told us and proposed to take a detour through Khandbari's market area. We happily agreed to the detour as we also wanted to see the market. Plunging along the narrow passage through the market, with shops and houses on both sides, we met the highway again and took a turn onto a bumpy off-road to Num. The driver connected his smartphone with the Bluetooth music player installed in his jeep and turned on his playlist. One of the songs that we heard on the way to Num, interestingly, was about Sherpas. It was a modern upbeat number with some clumsy rap lyrics glorifying Sherpa culture and the deeds of Tenzing Norgay and Pasang Lhamu. 'This is a nice song about Sherpas,' we complimented the driver, who we learned belonged to the Chhetri caste, found mostly in the mid-hills. He told us, 'I come from mountain villages past Num, where you are headed. There are many Sherpas in my village as well.'

The ride got bumpier as we rolled on. The road was paved with uneven stones in many places to prevent vehicles from getting stuck in the mud. The stones made it all even jerkier. We tightly gripped the passenger handles and tried to keep ourselves as steady as we could. Yet, on occasion, when the jeep rode over inevitable holes on the way, we were shaken in our seats, jumping sometimes to such an extent that our heads touched the ceiling of the jeep.

At some point on the way, we phoned our contact in Num – Ming Temba Sherpa, a mountaineer from the Makalu region. 'It's raining here in Num,' Ming Temba said over the phone. 'If the rain catches you on the way, you will arrive here late – probably after 7pm. I have booked your accommodation at the Sherpa Guest House. Your driver will know the place. I will meet you guys early tomorrow morning.'

Soon after Ming Temba hung up, we got caught in the rain that he had warned us of. It was a massive storm with hail the size of small pebbles. 'The road ahead will be slippery,' the driver told us. 'I hope the hail does not trigger a landslide on the way. We will now have to travel on four-wheel drive mostly, which will slow us down. But we will reach Num by 7.30pm at the latest.' We kept on clinging tightly to the grip handles and prayed for safety.

When we finally arrived in Num, at around 7.15pm, the village was already at rest. There was no movement visible along the way, all the shops had closed, the houses were shut and there were just one or two people on the streets whom we could see via the vehicle's headlights. The driver took us straight to the Sherpa Guest House and escorted us inside, where we were received by a Sherpa man, probably in his 60s. We greeted him and told him, 'Ming Temba said he has booked us a room here for tonight.' Somewhat surprised, he asked, 'Really?' Confused as to whether we had come to the right place, we were about to call Ming Temba, when the Sherpa man said, 'He must have talked with my son. He has gone outside with friends. I will call him. Why don't you make yourselves comfortable? I will make you some coffee.'

Relieved, we sat down in the dining room, observing the old man's family photos on the wall.

'Is that you with the climbing suit in one of these photos?' we asked him.

He replied, 'No. It's my elder son. He is a mountaineer and lives in Kathmandu. My younger son also studies in Kathmandu, but he is home at the moment. He will be the one cooking today for all of us.'

'What's your name?' we asked him, trying to socialize, while we waited for his son to return.

The old Sherpa proudly said, 'Nobody recognizes me by my name. You go outside and you say you met Japanese Sherpa, and even a stray dog will know.'

According to him, when he was young, Sherpas from Makalu were not as much into trekking and mountaineering as they are today. 'It was all about Sherpas from Khumbu back then. I got an opportunity to go trekking only once. Later, I went to Japan to work and spent many years there. That's why people call me Japanese Sherpa.'

Soon after, a young boy in his mid-20s rushed in and welcomed us. By then, Japanese Sherpa had already showed us our room, and we had changed our clothes and were ready to dine. The last meal we had had was in the airport in Kathmandu, and we were starving.

The boy asked, 'Would you like some meat? We only have pork today.'

'One of us is a vegetarian and the other will eat absolutely anything,' we joked and, while we waited, we talked about the Sherpa villages we would be visiting the following day. We told Japanese Sherpa we were headed towards Walung – an area predominantly inhabited by Sherpas in Makalu, home to the family of Mingma, Chhang Dawa and Tashi Lhakpa, and Kushang Dorjee Sherpa, whom we had met in Darjeeling.

Japanese Sherpa and his son seemed to know everybody we mentioned. 'We are relatives of the family of Mingma, Dawa and Tashi,' the old man said. 'We all come from the same village called Nurbuchaur. The famous Kushang Dorjee Sherpa is also from Nurbuchaur.'

*

Unlike many other Sherpa villages in Nepal, some of the Sherpa villages in the Makalu region, which we were about to visit, are accessible by road. The road connecting Num Bazaar with northern villages inhabited mostly by Sherpas was constructed after 2014, with the inception of the 900-MW Arun-III hydropower project, which is currently under construction. The road was built to serve as an access network to the hydro project. Until the road construction started here, the village people could not even imagine travelling out of their homes in a motor vehicle.

Despite being rich in high-current river resources fit for hydro projects all over Nepal, the country grappled with acute power shortage until recently. Less than a decade ago, there would be daily power outages for up to 18 hours a day in the capital city Kathmandu. Consequently, people in the cities relied on battery-powered lights for household use, while villages connected with the national gridline used to rely on tiny solar panels, which gave off enough energy to light a bulb and charge phones overnight. Those who could not afford solar panels or battery-powered chargeable lights had to depend on candles and home-made kerosene lamps. After some reforms aimed at controlling electricity leakage and ramping up hydro projects all over Nepal, the power outages gradually started decreasing after 2016. As of now, the electricity authority of Nepal claims the country's electricity production remains in surplus for half the year and is enough to be exported outside Nepal. Upon completion, the electricity generated by Arun-III will also be exported to India.

Speaking of electricity access, most of the Sherpa villages of the Makalu region beyond Num Bazaar are still off-grid. In the Khumbu region, the national electricity grid is accessible only up to Khumjung, and in Rolwaling Valley, Simigaun. The off-grid Sherpa settlements depend upon tiny household solar panels for lighting bulbs and charging mobile devices. During expedition seasons, the mountain base camps are also powered by solar technology and petroleum generators.

The following morning, we were received at the Sherpa Guest House by Ming Temba, a 30-year-old, well-dressed, handsome, smiling Sherpa, wearing an adventure smartwatch on his wrist and carrying an expensive little 'Sonam' backpack, a popular Nepali trekking brand with premium outlets in Kathmandu and other major cities.

From Num, we were about to share a ride with locals in a passenger jeep headed to Walung. There are several tiny Sherpa villages in Walung. We were headed first to Nurbuchaur, the village of our Sherpa friends Mingma, Chhang Dawa, Tashi Lhakpa, and Kushang Dorjee.

Sharing the jeep with us were a Sherpa couple and their two-year-old daughter; a Sherpa donning gumboots (wellingtons), who had come to Num to get supplies for his shop in the village; Ming Temba himself; and a rookie chain-smoking driver with curly hair wearing tight jeans and a slim-fitting windproof jacket. As soon as he sat in the driver's seat and started the engine, he lit a cigarette, pinched its butt between his lips and sucked the smoke as both his hands alighted on the steering wheel.

Walung is a three-hour drive from Num Bazaar. Soon after we left Num Bazaar, our jeep crossed paths with a young couple on a motorcycle. The driver exchanged smiles with the rider and told those of us on the front seat, 'This guy is a Brahmin from Khandbari, and the girl a Sherpa. He had gone to the girl's village with some work. Don't know if his work got done, but he sure did run away with this girl and got married. Ha ha ha… They returned to the village only recently. I hear the girl's parents have already accepted this relationship.'

The road was as bumpy as it had been the day before, when we were travelling from Khandbari to Num. As the driver danced on his steering wheel, weaving his way between the potholes, his phone rang. 'This must be my wife,' he said. 'I don't know how, but she has to call me always, exactly when I am trying to take a tricky turn like this. I will have to miss this call and explain later.'

Once we were about halfway to Walung, we stopped for a quick snack at a small Sherpa village. Along with noodles, a lady in the hotel brought a kettle full of *chhaang* and a bowl each for all of us. *Chhaang* is a Nepali and Tibetan alcoholic beverage, like beer, brewed by fermenting millet seeds, rice, barley or other grains. We were reluctant to drink at first. But, as we refused, everyone else in the group, even the driver and the two-year-old girl, held their bowls and started gulping the liquor as if it were milk. Just as the lady took our empty bowls away, we called her back. The group burst into laughter, and there we were, drinking *chhaang* on an empty stomach, before our first meal of the day. *Chhaang* is said to be a remedy for severe cold in the mountains and is believed to heal the common cold, fever and allergies, among other things. According to Sherpa folklore, *chhaang* is also a favourite drink among the yetis, who reportedly used to raid Sherpa villages for it.

A little further on, we arrived at the home of the Sherpa couple and their daughter who were travelling with us. Along with them, all the other Sherpas in the vehicle, including Ming Temba, stepped out to help unload their stuff and even carried it all down to their home. 'The Sherpas are just like this. Very united and very helpful, especially to the people from their own community,' the driver told us, as he lit yet another cigarette. A woman, probably the mother of the man travelling with us, came out of the house with a kettle of *chhaang* and started distributing it to the group, which everybody gracefully accepted. 'This is their way of returning a favour,' the driver said. 'To them, *chhaang* is just like tea offered to visitors at home.' The *chhaang* was again offered to the three of us in the front seat, including the driver. How were we supposed to avoid such a gracious gesture?

The bumpy ride quickly came to an end and we finally arrived in Walung. Ming Temba led us into one of his relative's houses by the roadside. 'I have asked them to prepare lunch for the three of us. Let's quickly have something here and get going. Nurbuchaur is about 45 minutes' slow walk from here,' he said.

In the house, we sat on the balcony and waited for the food to arrive. However, before it came, we were served *Tongba*. *Tongba* is another millet-based mountain liquor – fermented millet grains are stuffed tightly in a pot, hot water is poured over the top and the juice is sipped through a straw. 'Not again,' we thought, yet pulled the *Tongba* pot closer and started sipping.

Over lunch, we were accompanied by Ming Temba's relative, who has been working in Everest expeditions as a base camp cook for over a decade. 'I specialize in European delicacies,' he said. 'But all I can offer you here is a basic Nepali meal and as much *Tongba* as you want.'

We thanked the cook for our mouth-watering Nepali lunch – an expansive plate of rice, lentils, green vegetables, tomato pickle and meat – and set off on our way to Nurbuchaur. Soon after we started walking, it began to rain. Hoping that our down jackets really were waterproof, as the storekeeper had guaranteed us in Kathmandu, we kept moving. Ming Temba quickly fetched a 'Gore-Tex' rain- and snow-proof jacket from his bag and put it on, checking that we were okay to walk in the rain. We all wanted to reach Nurbuchaur before sunset, so sitting out the rain was not an option.

About 30 minutes later, we arrived at a small stream rushing towards the Barun River to our distant right. Above the stream was a small wooden bridge, leading to an uphill trail. Ming Temba led us that way and, just a few steps uphill from the bridge, we discovered a village with houses scattered all over the hill from its top to the bottom. 'This is Nurbuchaur.' Ming Temba pointed with his finger towards the hilltop. He told us our stay for the night was somewhere towards the top and, when we arrived what must have been midway to our shelter, he suggested we take cover under the balcony of one of the houses, as the rain was getting heavier. None of the houses had any fence or wall surrounding them, so we just rushed towards the house nearest to us. The tin-roofed mud house was reinforced with wooden planks to support the structure. The ground floor had an open storage area and an exterior wooden staircase led to a balcony in the upper floor, where there were rooms, padlocked from the outside. Soaked by the rain and curious as to whether we'd be able to dry ourselves by a fire if the house owners were nearby, we asked Ming Temba, 'Whose house is this? Do you know?'

'This is the house of Nawang Gyalze Sherpa – the sibling of Mingma, Chhang Dawa and Tashi Lhakpa,' he replied. 'He has now settled in Belgium with his family. Nobody lives here.'

There are altogether eight siblings in the family: six brothers and two sisters. The eldest, Karma Tenzing, spends village life in Nurbuchaur and remains untouched by the wonders of mountaineering and trekking. After Karma Tenzing and sister Kidoma, comes Mingma, the third child of the family, and the second son. Mingma is followed by Nawang Gyalze, Chhang Dawa, sister Chhiri Pangmu, Tashi Lhakpa and, youngest of all, Pasang Phurba. Four of them – Mingma, Chhang Dawa, Tashi Lhakpa and Pasang Phurba – currently run the Seven Summits.

After the rain slowed a little, we got moving again, but before we could arrive at our shelter, it again intensified and forced us into another house on the way – this time with a burning chimney and full of people. Ming Temba greeted the members of the house and we found our way into the kitchen towards the fireplace, where everyone was seated. By then, we had understood that it was customary practice throughout the region to greet visitors with *chhaang*. This time, we held our cups without any hesitation and started socializing. When we said we were there to see the village of the owners of the Seven Summits, one of the elder members there proudly associated himself with the eldest of the siblings, Karma Tenzing. 'My boy is married to Karma Tenzing's daughter. This is their child,' he said, pointing to a puffy-cheeked, six-month-old girl playing with an empty cup of *chhaang* by the fire. 'We had never thought those boys from our village – Mingma, Tashi and others – would make it this big. They are known everywhere, even outside the country. But the boys are not arrogant. They are decent. They come here, pay us a visit and greet us as elders every time they are in the village.'

After several rounds of *chhaang* and a rich conversation on a range of topics – from politics, to mountaineering, to the weather and COVID-19 – the rain finally stopped. It was already nearly dark and we had somewhere else to go to spend the night. We stepped out and followed Ming Temba towards a pre-primary government school with a tiny badminton court on its grounds. On a plot of land overlooking the school was the house of a revered young Lama of the village, also a mountain climber himself and the friend of Ming Temba.

We entered the house, went past the storage area on the ground floor and took a wooden staircase to the upper floor, where we were escorted straight into a room to change out of our wet clothes, then to the kitchen with a burning fireplace and a metal chimney sticking out of the roof, smoking unceasingly in the dark windy night. Our day, which had started with a bowl of *chhaang* on our way to Walung from Num, ended over a strong coffee cocktail called 'Mustang Coffee', made by boiling millet liquor in butter, coffee and sugar, and seasoned with deep-fried cumin seeds.

*

After a good night's sleep, we awoke to a bright, sunny morning and, from the balcony, we could see the hilly settlement of Nurbuchaur. The weather had cleared and the morning sunlight falling over the village was full of hope, excitement and optimism.

Nurbuchaur stands at little over 2,500m (8,200ft) and grows a vast range of agricultural crops. Towards the top of the hill, villagers grow potato and barley, and towards the bottom grows millet, buckwheat and other grains. The community forest areas nearby offer plenty of firewood to the villagers. When we saw unprotected firewood visibly stacked on the un-walled ground floor of many houses there, which is used as storage, we asked the Lama in whose house we had rested the night, 'Is this safe from theft?' Theft, however, is an alien concept in the village. 'We are all Buddhists here and people are honest. On top of that, supplies of firewood and seasonal crops grow in abundance for everybody. There is simply no need for theft,' the Lama told us.

Nurbuchaur also has a peculiar trait when it comes to livestock. The houses towards the hilltop mostly keep yaks, while other houses towards the bottom keep cows, buffaloes, sheep, goats and chickens. Nearby forests are used as grazing fields for most of the livestock, while yaks are taken to the high-altitude pastures for grazing during spring and monsoon.

'By the grace of God, our village is blessed with prosperity. If it was not for the mobility and curiosity of the outer world, people wouldn't have to travel outside the village to simply survive,' Tashi Lhakpa said to us, in an interview at his bungalow in Kathmandu's expensive residential area of Budhanilkantha. In Kathmandu, owning land and a home is a clear sign of prosperity and a dream for many. Tashi Lhakpa's south-facing bungalow stands in an abundance of property, with room for his expensive Mitsubishi Pajero. There is enough parking for two other big SUVs and a garden to sunbathe in during the winters. The house somehow resembles the pious Boudhanath Stupa (see page 55), with colourful prayer flags fluttering on the terrace.

In Nurbuchaur that same morning, we visited Tashi Lhakpa's ancestral home. At the time of our visit, the house was empty and the rooms were padlocked. However, as in other houses in the village, the stock of firewood stored on the ground floor just lay there, for anybody to access. Tashi

Lhakpa's mother lives in this village home most of the time, but when we were there, she was in Kathmandu, in her son's Budhanilkantha home, skipping the winter.

With a blue tin roof and two floors – one used for storage and one for living – Tashi Lhakpa's mud house in the village is just like any ordinary house in the region. But there is a little something that other houses don't have – a helipad in the courtyard. Seven Summits currently owns two helicopters, and the brothers land in their village home at least once a year to conduct annual rituals to please the family deities.

From Tashi Lhakpa's home, we headed upward to meet the family of our other friend, Kushang Dorjee, from Darjeeling (see Chapter 5). In the same house where Kushang Dorjee grew up, and from where he travelled to Dharan, then lost his way into Bhutan and finally found fortune in Darjeeling, we met his mother, now in her 90s. A woman of few words, she was happy to know we were Kushang Dorjee's friends. She generously offered us some *chhaang*, which we graciously declined to save the old woman the troubles of hospitality. We sat down with her, exchanged greetings, asked about her health and left the place, making our way to another house upward at the hilltop, where Kushang Dorjee's younger brother, Nima Dorjee Sherpa, lives with his family.

Ming Temba introduced us to Nima Dorjee, who goes by the nickname 'Boka Lama' all over the region. 'Boka' refers to a male goat in Nepali and signifies Nima Dorjee's grey goatee fluttering down his chin. The term 'Boka' is also used colloquially to refer to playboys, especially in the cities, but our Boka Lama, who is a revered priest and religious leader in Makalu, is definitely not that! 'Very few people know me by my real name,' he laughed, looking over the village of Nurbuchaur from the courtyard of his home at the hilltop. 'It's a beautiful morning. We have seen bright sunlight in many days. Otherwise, it has been raining all the time this winter.'

Boka Lama's wife brought us *chhaang* and insisted we take it as a good-morning greeting. That was an offer we could not refuse and, over the liquor early that morning, we started unfolding Boka Lama's account of Makalu's growth into tourism and the mountaineering industry. Boka Lama has summited Everest 12 times and was the Sirdar in the team of the legendary Babu Chiri, who is known for spending 21 hours on the summit of Everest and his former record 16-hour and 56-minute ascent of Everest (see page 10).

'During those days, in the 1990s and even until the early 2000s, there were only a couple of mountain-climbing Sherpas from Makalu,' Boka Lama said. 'Sherpas from Khumbu would mostly get the chance, while us from Makalu were a little unfortunate, as we neither had a network, nor experience in trekking like the Khumbu Sherpas.'

Sometime in the early 1990s – Boka Lama does not remember the year exactly – he was distraught after an unpleasant stint with a mountaineering company in Kathmandu. With one Everest summit to his name already, Boka Lama had been hired to go to the summit of Everest for the second time. While returning from the summit, the group of Sherpas, of which Boka Lama was part, happened to lose some of the tents in a higher camp. The expedition company deducted their pay for this loss, blaming them for what was perceived as theft. Being punished for a mistake that he had not committed, Boka Lama took a vow to himself not to associate with that company again. Soon after, someone told him that Babu Chiri Sherpa was looking for an Everest summiteer to include in his team. Boka Lama knew where Babu Chiri lived – in a rented room in Chhetrapati in downtown Kathmandu. One morning, he stood at Babu Chiri's doorstep asking for work. 'During that time, there were not many Everest summiteers,' Boka Lama recalled. 'When I told him about my Everest summit, he took me in without any further questions.'

In the years that followed, Boka Lama aided Babu Chiri in his expeditions, and gradually became promoted as his Sirdar in every Everest expedition taking place. 'He was my boss, but we became like friends,' Boka

Lama recalled. 'He rode a motorcycle and would pick me up at my place near Boudha, whenever he had some work.'

In 1999, when Babu Chiri was planning to spend the night at the top of Everest, Boka Lama was his closest aide. Mountain Hardwear, an American sportswear company, had designed a customized tent for Babu Chiri to use at the top of Everest. In an interview published in outinunder.com, the designer of the tent, Martin Zemitis, recalled how some people criticized him for designing the world's highest coffin for Babu Chiri, as there were only a few who actually believed he could make it overnight at the summit of Everest.[1]

'It was a lightweight blue tent with strong layers to avoid extreme cold and wind. I carried it on my back to the summit of Everest and fixed it for Babu Chiri. We had also taken about half a dozen little gas stoves to heat the tent, which we left there for his use over the night,' Boka Lama explained.

On 6 May 1999, Babu Chiri reached the summit of Everest at around 9am. As planned, he stayed there while other Sherpas of his team returned to Camp 4. Early the next morning, when Boka Lama and the other Sherpas sneaked out of their tents and looked towards the summit, there he was – Babu Chiri was returning. 'We believed in our leader like anything. But we knew what he was setting out to do was madness. To see him returning in one piece, fit and fine, with the tent on his back, was a huge relief to us,' Boka Lama recalled. Babu Chiri had spent 21 hours at the summit of Everest, a record nobody had ever attempted before – or since.

'Later that day, we went to the top again to clean and collect the leftovers,' Boka Lama said. 'I found a mattress, on which Babu Chiri had scribbled the names of all his daughters. He must have missed them throughout the night.'

1   Zemitis, M., 13 Sep. 2017. Martin Zemitis on designing a tent for Babu Chiri Sherpa. OutInUnder. Available at https://www.outinunder.com/content/ martin-zemitis-designing-tent-babu-chiri-sherpa.

After the record of 1999, Babu Chiri caught the world's attention. There were headlines about him in national and international media and he became a huge sensation. 'He only operated with premium clients, even before 1999, and would charge US$60–70,000 for an expedition,' Boka Lama said. 'He loved us all, treated everyone fairly, and thus brought fortune to all of us.'

In 2001, Babu Chiri's team was taking a group of American climbers to the top of Everest. The team, of which Boka Lama was Sirdar, arrived at Camp 2 on 29 April for a rest day. Boka Lama was sleeping in his tent, which he shared with Babu Chiri's elder brother, Dawa Sherpa, who was also part of that expedition. Sometime in the afternoon, Babu Chiri sneaked into the tent and called to Boka Lama, 'Hey! Hey Lama! Boka Lama! Get up. Let's go and make some tea in the kitchen.' The kitchen tent was right next to the tent where Boka Lama was sleeping. 'I woke up, but refused to go to the kitchen, as I wanted more sleep. He said okay and went outside, probably towards someone else's kitchen camp, looking for tea.'

As it was a rest day and there wasn't any climbing to do, Boka Lama recalls Babu Chiri was not wearing crampons when he left the tent. Only a little further up from the tent where Boka Lama was sleeping, Babu Chiri apparently happened to step on a crevasse that was deceitfully covered in a layer of snow, making the 30-m (98-ft) crack on the ice invisible. 'Babu Chiri fell down into the crevasse and, for quite some time, nobody was aware of it,' Boka Lama said, caressing his goatee. 'There was a strong wind that day at Camp 2. Everyone was inside their tent. Nobody could have imagined anything bad had already happened outside.'

It was only at about 5pm, when the wind stopped and everybody came outside and went to their kitchen camps for snacks, that someone asked for Babu Chiri. 'He was nowhere in sight. Initially we thought he must be sleeping. Someone went looking for him in his tent, but as he was not there, the entire Camp 2 quickly became alarmed.' After several minutes of searching, someone spotted him in the crevasse, still and already dead.

'One of the Sherpas at Camp 2 went into the crevasse, but was unable to pull him out,' Boka Lama recalled. 'He tied a rope around Babu Chiri's feet and came back.' The following morning, everyone gathered and pulled the body to the surface, which was then airlifted to Kathmandu. 'I was left with three clients to guide to the summit of Everest,' Boka Lama told us. 'That was going to be my last mission with Babu Chiri and I did not want to let him down. I took the clients to the summit and returned to Babu Chiri's after-death rites in Boudhanath a few weeks later.

'It's been several years, but I still see Babu Chiri in my dreams sometimes,' Boka Lama recalled. 'If I had agreed to go with him to our own kitchen that day for tea, the mishap would never have happened. If only he had escaped that fateful day, today, I am sure, half the records on Everest would be in his name.'

Despite the tragedies he has seen in Everest, today, Boka Lama is proud of having had the opportunity to go to the mountains during his youth, while most Sherpas like him from the Makalu region could only dream of it. 'I must say I was the rare lucky mountaineer representing Makalu from my generation,' he smiled. 'Things started getting easier for us, only when some little boys from our place made it big and started giving jobs to the underrated Makalu Sherpas.'

We asked if it was Mingma and his brothers to whom Boka Lama was referring. 'Yes, yes. Those little boys. I remember how they struggled to even wipe their noses properly. It feels like yesterday that they herded animals in those forests.' Boka Lama pointed in the direction where, according to him, Mingma's family had grazing fields. 'I am proud that they have made it this far. If it was not for them, our boys would still be struggling to go to the mountains.'

*

As Mingma grew up with his brothers, spending time farming and herding animals, Makalu was still not a celebrated tourist destination, unlike Khumbu or Rolwaling. Yet, the villagers would catch sight of a few foreigners every now and then whenever there was an expedition on Mount Makalu. Early on in his life, Mingma had started weaving dreams of going to Everest one day, whenever he heard news about the expeditions on the radio. However, getting a chance to become a porter, even in Makalu expeditions, was rare for Sherpas from the region, let alone Everest.

'I put my name down to become a porter in Makalu expeditions, but got rejected twice,' Mingma recalled. 'On my third time, when I was around 15, I got selected. But they allowed me to carry only 15kg (33lb) of weight, while the maximum limit was 30kg (66lb).'

Carrying half the load would mean earning half of what other Sherpas were earning. However, as the opportunity meant more than money to Mingma, he happily took the job. Having got his first taste of the mountains, Mingma decided that was what he wanted to do for the rest of his life. After returning from that expedition, he travelled to Kathmandu and started looking for porter jobs in trekking and expeditions. Some companies took him on as a porter in trekking, but mountaineering was still a far-fetched dream for him. 'I had to do all sorts of jobs to sustain my life in Kathmandu,' he told us. 'Occasional trekking opportunities would provide only peanuts, and I started taking up any job that I could get my hands on. Sometimes, I worked as a labourer, sometimes a porter and sometimes cleaning dishes. I must have been surviving on less than a dollar a day during those times.'

Finally, after five years of struggle, in 2000, Mingma got his first major break, in a Manaslu expedition. After this 8,000-m (26,247-ft) summit, things started getting a little easier for him. In the years that followed, he started getting more opportunities and, between 2000 and 2004, he summited nine mountains, including Everest. 'During that time, without proper networks and a proven track record, it was difficult to land summit opportunities,' Mingma recalled. 'However, once you stood on the summit of an eight-thousander, you would quickly grab the attention of expedition companies.'

Just as Mingma's career was taking off, in 2005 he was given the opportunity to seek his fortunes abroad. However, Mingma was slightly luckier than the hundreds of thousands of other Nepali migrant workers in that his destination was not the heat of the Middle East and Malaysia, as it is for the majority of Nepalis, but Japan. One of Mingma's relatives from Makalu, who had settled in Japan by then, sent sponsorship letters for visit visas for Mingma and his wife.

Several weeks after their arrival in Japan, the visa expired, but they didn't return as planned. Mingma had taken up a job with Toyota, assembling machine parts, and his wife ended up with a job in a hair salon. 'We had initially planned to return after a few months, but the prosperity of Japan stopped us from returning,' Mingma told us at a premium coffee shop on the outskirts of Kathmandu. 'Our combined savings would be far higher than what I had been earning in Nepal, climbing one or two mountains a year. Living conditions were good and, above all, there was going to be a regular income throughout the year.'

Four years quickly passed by, and Mingma and his wife had already decided to settle in Japan. However, one day in 2009, the Japanese immigration authorities detained his wife for illegally overstaying and deported her. Mingma was not caught, but the separation from his wife brought an end to his Japanese dreams. He came back to his roots – the mountains – just a week after his wife's return to Nepal.

By 2009, two of Mingma's younger brothers – Chhang Dawa and Tashi Lhakpa – had already been immersed in the climbing world, following their elder brother's footsteps. Chhang Dawa was introduced to mountaineering by Mingma in 2001 after the latter's Manaslu success of 2000. When Mingma returned from Japan, Chhang Dawa had six 8,000-m (26,247-ft) summits to his name, including Everest. Likewise, Tashi Lhakpa had also already secured a good place in mountaineering by keeping the world record of the youngest person to climb Everest without supplementary oxygen, at the age of 19 in 2005.

Tashi Lhakpa's is an interesting story. In 2005, his second time on Everest, he was part of a Korean expedition. An earlier summit push had been aborted due to strong winds at Camp 4. All the team members, including other expedition groups, had to return to Base Camp and wait for a favourable window. With these turns of events and changes of summit plans, Tashi Lhakpa's expedition group ended up running low on bottled oxygen. 'We were left with only a few bottles, not enough for everyone, for the second push,' Tashi Lhakpa said. 'When my team of four, two Korean climbers, a Sherpa guide and myself, reached our camp at South Col, there were only five oxygen tanks left.' The ideal in the death zone is two oxygen bottles per person, so this was clearly a matter of serious concern.

'We decided to give two bottles each to the two clients,' Tashi Lhakpa said. 'The Sherpa in the team was a senior guide and he took another bottle, while I was left with none. We had agreed that he would give me his oxygen if I needed it at some point. However, nothing happened and I went to the summit and back to safety without extra oxygen. I discovered only later that I had set a record that remains unbroken to this day.'

Therefore, when Mingma returned from Japan in 2009, the seeds that he had sown in the mountains had come to fruition. His younger brothers, Chhang Dawa and Tashi Lhakpa, were fully immersed in climbing. For Mingma too, after Japan, if there was anything at all to look up to in life, it was the mountains. What's more, the brothers were there for each other; they shared a common passion and together saw a dream to somehow make it big in the industry.

However, making it big with a climbing company was not an easy task to pull off back in 2009. There were plenty of western companies, with a good network, reputation and skills, that had been dominating the mountaineering scene in Nepal and beyond. If Mingma was to break that status quo, he had to do something different, as simply registering a company would not be enough. 'I decided to invest what I had earned in Japan in myself,' he told us. 'Before going to Japan, I had done nine of the fourteen 8,000-m (26,247-ft) peaks. In two years after arriving in Nepal, I summited the remaining five mountains, and became the first Nepali to bag all fourteen eight-thousanders.'

Apart from recognition, Mingma's achievement was a major advertisement for his new business venture. More people across the world now knew him and wanted to climb with him. By then, the brothers Mingma, Chhang Dawa and Tashi Lhakpa had identified a pool of young Sherpas from Makalu who were fit to climb. Now that they had clients in their pocket, it was time to take a dive into the riches.

'When everything was set, the easier option for me was to get high-end clients who were ready to spend up to US$100,000, twice to thrice the existing market price,' Mingma said. 'But I had different plans for my company. I had sensed that the craze of mountaineering was growing in the world and middle-class clients, with less than US$30,000 in their pockets, were increasingly interested in scaling the roof of the world. I believed this was a sustainable approach.'

This formula of grabbing the middle-class clients worked wonders for Mingma from the very first year. 'In no time, my company started attracting more climbers from all over the world. My biggest asset in making that happen was the undiscovered Sherpas from my village in Makalu.' When the company was in its infancy, the brothers had taken a vow to produce ten Everest summiteers every year. However, as the years passed by, they ended up overachieving what they had initially aimed for.

According to Mingma, when he started his company, there were only a handful of Sherpas from Makalu who had summited Everest. As his company targeted Makalu Sherpas, trained them and generated employment over the years, at the time of writing, over 300 Sherpas from Makalu have summited Everest and mountains in different parts of the world. Moreover, the number of clients Mingma's company has managed to take to the summit of Everest stands close to 1,000. No company has ever before taken this number of people to the top of the world.

Starting off with the US$30,000 clients – Seven Summits' USP – in no time, the clientele expanded to VIPs, including billionaires and Arab royals. 'This is a clear statement of the trust that we have been able to gain over the years,' Mingma said.

The upward mobility of the success of the company is visible at Everest Base Camp every expedition season. The company's operations of several hundred people seem to be on a war footing – with the most number of tents with multiple kitchens; luxury arrangements for expensive clients, including pubs, DJs, coffee shops, and so on. For the VIP clients, the company has expanded facilities with luxury tents, unlimited oxygen tanks, dedicated rescue teams, and separate kitchens and accommodation, including coffee machines, even up to Camp 2. While many criticize such operations for their contrast with the alpine values and over-exploitation of Sherpa porters, for Seven Summits, all of this seems to have been faring well. 'It's not a matter of values. What's the problem if clients are willing to pay for the comfort?' Tashi Lhakpa says. Indeed, this is how the company that started by paying US$2,000 in tax is now the biggest contributor from the mountaineering sector, paying the government about US$20 million in tax, excluding permit fees.

*

After his latest mountain run across three continents, in Antarctica, South America and Africa, Mingma received a series of welcomes one after another. The week he returned, he attended several celebratory events organized within and beyond the climbing industry. However, one morning, while a number of events were still pending and several people waited in line to meet Mingma and congratulate him in person, he flew by helicopter and landed in the courtyard of his home in Makalu. 'The business is fine, but I am a mountaineer more than a businessman,' he said. 'After working across several time zones in extreme conditions, I needed a break. And there is no better place than your own home to rest.'

Chapter 11

SHERPAS ARE STRONG, BUT MOUNTAINS ARE NOT

Can climbing Everest ever be 'a picnic' for anyone?

Apa Sherpa's 2007 ascent of Everest was, in his own unprompted words, indeed just that. Unlike in previous years, Apa was climbing this time with a group of six of his fellow Sherpas. Including Apa, these seven accomplished climbers had completed a combined total of 52 Everest summits. That year, the Sherpas were their own guides. They didn't carry heavy loads or extra oxygen bottles on their backs. For the first time ever, on the iconic mountain, they were relieved of their usual responsibility of keeping someone else alive. With lighter shoulders this time, they were the last group to leave Base Camp for the summit, and the first to return. Along the way, the Sherpas, with their climbing pace in tune with one another, talked, cracked jokes and enjoyed the view.

'For the first time in all these years, the journey up Everest felt like a recreation to me,' said Apa, who had ascended Everest for a record number of 16 times before 2007. 'It was just like a picnic. I wished it had always been the same.'

The previous year, Apa and his family had relocated to Salt Lake City, in Utah, USA, where his children could access a superior education. Another Sherpa, Lhakpa Gelu (see page 202), was also in Salt Lake City around the same time. The city folk were aware of the presence of these celebrated Sherpas and were proud to host them. The Sherpas were welcomed almost as if they were real-life supermen. The locals were excited and, at the same time, curious about the amazing strength of the Sherpas. They wanted to know how Apa and Lhakpa Gelu were able to go so high and so fast up to the

8,848.86-m (29,031.69-ft) top of Everest, when, by contrast, even small hikes up the 4,000-m (13,000-ft) peaks of Utah were 'a big deal' for the local people.

The widespread curiosity of Salt Lake City's citizens finally took the form of a science project, to explore and examine the Sherpas' strength and resilience in the mountains. Apa and Lhakpa Gelu became the subjects of this study, which would be conducted by high-altitude scientists at the University of Utah and Intermountain Healthcare.

For the pre-study phase of the experiment, Apa and Lhakpa Gelu were taken to laboratories in Salt Lake City to measure their body fat, stamina and oxygen consumption, among other physiological traits.

In one of the experiments, the Sherpas walked on treadmills with about 23kg (51lb) on their backs. A device was then used to measure the amount of oxygen and carbon dioxide being inhaled and exhaled by the Sherpas through the mouth (their noses were clipped). 'This experiment was to tell us how well their bodies use oxygen, and also the maximum amount of oxygen a person's body can use,' Dr Scott McIntosh, a mountaineer himself, who was leading the study, told us in an interview. Dr McIntosh is a physician/ professor at the University of Utah and has a respected reputation in high-altitude medicine. 'They did very well, but at an altitude of just 2,000–3,000m (6,560–9,840ft), their performance was nothing out of the ordinary,' he added.

Similarly, the body fat level of both the Sherpas was more than 25 per cent, which is at the level of 'borderline obesity'. By contrast, most athletes' levels are at 6–17 per cent. According to modern medical standards, an 'acceptable amount of body fat' is between 18 and 24 per cent in a human body.

On the one hand, these pre-study findings, portraying Sherpas as normal human beings, were challenging the glorified expectations of their climbing abilities and fitness. On the other hand, the findings also fuelled the prevailing curiosity on how these experiments could reflect their proven track records on Everest.

The study, however, had only just begun. There was still a long way to go and many more questions – many based on stereotypes – were yet to be answered:

- Are the Sherpas immune to high-altitude complications?
- Do they have bigger lungs, as we hear all the time?
- How can Sherpas manage to acclimatize so swiftly at high altitude, despite spending several months or years at low altitudes?
- Do they really have supernatural strength when it comes to climbing?

In 2007, Dr McIntosh himself joined Apa, Lhakpa Gelu and other Sherpas on an expedition to climb to the top of the world. While seeking answers to all these questions, the Sherpas would also get to enjoy what Apa described as their 'picnic expedition'.

As they flew from Salt Lake City to Nepal's Khumbu, Dr McIntosh's curiosity about the Sherpa world was growing bigger and bigger, and the expedition had already acquired its popular name – 'the Super Sherpas'.

*

Standing atop Everest for the 21st time in 2011, Apa set a new record in the history of climbing. The fast-spreading world of the internet, emerging social media and globalized modes of popular communication platforms all played a part in making Apa the strongest Sherpa, arguably, of all time. While Tenzing Norgay's global popularity as the first man, along with Sir Edmund Hillary, to reach the top of Everest is eternally unmatched, Apa's feat had proven the Sherpas' climbing abilities beyond limitations, and the quick dissemination of this sensational story all over the world made him a new superhero.

The world formed its own glorified opinions about Apa's feat and his characteristics, describing them in hyperbolic terms. While some of these opinions were informed by facts reported in the media, others were exaggerated, involving wild imagination and fantasies:

- Apa Sherpa can 'talk with Mount Everest'. He ferociously stares at the mountain as he sets off from Base Camp, as if to challenge the grandeur of Everest with his own.
- Apa knows no fear when it comes to climbing.
- Apa can literally run all over the mountain, as if it is his playground. No part of Everest ever challenges his skills and confidence.
- Apa does not care about safety while climbing. He simply does not need safety equipment, as he is invincible.

We asked Apa which of these were true. He burst into laughter and told us, 'None.' Debunking these myths, he went on, 'Nobody can ever challenge Everest. Comfort in climbing differs from one year to another, but all these years, there has not been a single time I have not feared Everest. Climbing is very scary, and safety has always been my number-one priority.'

Apa grew up in Thame, a small village in the shadows of Everest. For many Sherpas, climbing is a profession, a way of earning a living and less of a passion. So it is, too, for Apa. 'Climbing Everest may be a person's one-time passion,' he said, 'but for most climbing Sherpas like myself, one can't be foolish to keep climbing the same mountain over and over again out of passion, knowing that it could kill you at any time. For me, and many others like me, it is our livelihood, and nothing more.'

Apa proudly calls himself a family man. Rob Hall, who tragically died on Everest in 1996, was Apa's client during Hall's first ascent of Everest in 1989. The two developed a close bond. When Rob started guiding professionally in the following years, Apa became one of his key Sherpas. 'I was supposed to join the team in 1996 as well, but my wife stopped me; I don't know why,' Apa said. 'We had some pending construction work at home, so my wife asked me not to go to the mountain that spring. The construction work could have been pushed a few months later, but I didn't feel like going against the will of my family. I was lucky to survive that fateful year, all thanks to my wife. Sometimes, I think if I had gone, I could have possibly saved some of my friends, but you never know.' These days in the US, Apa gives motivational speeches and a line that he never misses, referring to this 1996 incident, goes, 'Always listen to your wife.'

After his retirement from mountaineering in 2011, the following year Apa embarked on an adventure, joining a team of friends trekking across the Himalayan foothills all over Nepal, east to west, covering the distance of 1,449km (900 miles) in 99 days. The adventurous trek, covering several mountain base camps, high passes over 5,000m (16,400ft) and trails ranging from lush pine forests in the tropical areas to the dry chilly vegetation of the tundra, is known as the Great Himalaya Trail.

One of Apa's fellow travellers, journalist Saurav Dhakal, had some interesting observations about how connected Apa is with his family: 'The rest of us in the team would not bother much even if we hadn't been able to establish contact with our families in Kathmandu for several days due to bad network,' he recalled. 'But Apa *dai* [a Nepali term for elder brother] had to talk with his family in the US at least once a day.' (Though Apa's phone calls were unusually short and to-the-point: *Hello! How are you? What did you have for lunch or dinner? Okay, see you soon!*)

'Whenever we went several days without a good network, Apa *dai* would start showing signs of irritation and unrest,' Saurav recalled. 'During my 99 days' trekking with the legendary Apa Sherpa, one thing I understood was that he loved big challenges to be accomplished in a short time, so that he could be with his family as soon as he could.'

During our interview with Apa, we talked at length about his family. Now, Apa is permanently settled in Utah with his family: a wife and three children – two sons and a daughter. The eldest son is an accountant; the younger one, a civil engineer; and the daughter, a nurse. 'As a child I always wanted to be a doctor. But the nearest school from Thame was in Khumjung, which was six hours away, and I couldn't keep going to school for a very long time,' he said. 'But I am proud today that my daughter is a medical professional. She has somehow fulfilled the void left in me. I am equally proud of all my family.'

When speaking of his family, Apa refers to his immediate family living in the US and also to his extended family in Nepal – the wider Sherpa community of the entire Khumbu region. Since his retirement from mountaineering, Apa has made himself active in charity work, mainly lobbying for children's access to education in Khumbu through his Apa Sherpa Foundation. He raises funds by trekking in the US and Nepal and delivering motivational speeches all over the world.

Although many believe Apa to be wild and indifferent, he is highly organized and disciplined. Out of his high regard for safety while climbing, he always made it a point to go for the summit push in the very first window of opportunity, each season. Throughout his climbing career, he gave the utmost importance to the appropriate use of gear, oxygen and equipment, and liked to climb the conventional way, mostly during spring, never attempting any unconventional assault on the mountain. 'The fact that you are climbing Everest is "by far enough" of an adventure,' he said. 'Doing odd things that compromise safety is never recommended. If you respect safety, you are respecting the mountain, and that's how you can be successful.'

Apa's companion in the Great Himalaya Trail, Saurav Dhakal, shared another highlight of how organized and conventional he found the legendary Super Sherpa: 'On some occasions, we lost our track and had to camp in the middle of the forest,' he said. 'No matter where we were sleeping, or how badly tired we were, Apa *dai* would wake up early in the morning and make sure to brush his teeth and shave. It's strange for someone to be shaving during a wild trek of several weeks, especially when you are going to spend time with the same set of travellers throughout.

Apa *dai*'s organized way of living is what I think kept him focused on his priorities, all his life.'

On the subject of fear, Apa did not hesitate to admit that the mountains are exhausting and scary. 'Who wouldn't fear climbing the tallest mountain of the world? There are deep crevasses that can engulf you at a single wrong step. There are deadly avalanches on the way, which could fall and easily crush you to rubble in a matter of seconds. There are knife-edge ridges, where ropes are your sole lifeline. If you mistakenly untether yourself, or miss a track, you are gone. No matter how much oxygen you are on, you are not at 100 per cent once you have plunged into the death zone,' Apa went on, stressing how important fear is to keep one concerned and alive on the mountain. 'I may be the legendary Apa Sherpa, but I get exhausted just like others. The act of climbing and its wilderness equally frighten me to the core.'

Dr McIntosh recalled how, during the 2007 Super Sherpa expedition, after a long day of climbing, Apa would sneak into the tent, take long breaths and wittily joke about exhaustion, '. . . ha, I am too old for this'.

'From my early years in mountaineering, each time I returned to the safety of Base Camp from the summit, I would take a vow to myself to not come back again the following year. I always knew the risk was not worth taking,' Apa said. 'But what good is a vow made to yourself when, after a year, your pockets are empty and there are no other jobs at hand? I kept making these promises and then breaking them one year after another.'

For all that this Super Sherpa is, and for the love he holds for his family, it's clear that Apa was not climbing for the world record when he returned to climb Everest every year. Climbing was neither his inner calling, nor was it a passion he wanted to fulfil at any cost. If there was anything that drove Apa to Everest 21 times, it was his need for a livelihood. However, no matter how harsh the realities of life, can poverty and helplessness alone take someone to the roof of the world, not once, not twice, but 21 times?

There is more to this story.

*

When the group of seven Sherpas, including Apa and Lhakpa Gelu, set off from Base Camp for their summit push in 2007, Dr McIntosh followed them. He had been running tests and examinations on the Sherpas. Apa and Lhakpa Gelu were his primary subjects, and he performed similar tests on himself, as a control subject for the experiment. One key experiment, alongside other observations, was the measurement of blood oxygen level.

From Camp 1 to Camp 2 of Everest, the oxygen level of the two Sherpas was 78 per cent, while measuring 64 per cent for Dr McIntosh himself. As they moved higher up, between Camps 2 and 3, the Sherpas' oxygen level reduced to 68 per cent, while it was stagnant at 64 per cent for Dr McIntosh. At Camp 3 during the summit attempt, the doctor plugged into his oxygen mask, while the Sherpas continued to climb without supplementary oxygen support. By the time they reached Camp 4, while Dr McIntosh's oxygen level had hiked up to 76 per cent with the use of bottled oxygen, the Sherpas' oxygen level had reduced to about 63 per cent.

'The results clearly demonstrated the difference between Sherpas and lowlanders like me,' Dr McIntosh explained. 'At Camp 4, without oxygen, Apa and Lhakpa Gelu's oxygen level was about equal to what I had far below at Camp 1. Likewise, with the use of bottled oxygen after third camp, my oxygen level at Camp 4 equalled the level that the Sherpas had at Camp 1.'

Dr McIntosh continued, 'Comparing their results against mine, we know that they had been faring better than me in the thin air of Everest.'

The ideal oxygen saturation for a human body when measured at sea level is between 90 and 100 per cent. At high altitudes, the barometric pressure gets lower. At the top of Everest, the barometric pressure is roughly one-third than it would be at sea level. The oxygen in the lungs, therefore, has much less pressure driving it into the bloodstream. This is the reason that the vast majority of climbers use supplemental oxygen while climbing Everest.

A small number of climbers have reached the summit of Everest without extra oxygen, but this practice is extremely risky and has led to many fatalities. Ang Rita Sherpa from Thame, who climbed Everest ten times without using any extra oxygen, is renouned for this. For his eccentric climbing records between 1983 and 1996, Ang Rita is also known to the world as 'Snow Leopard'.

Apa has fond memories of Ang Rita: 'He was a fine climber, one of a kind, and probably the best I have ever seen. We came from the same village. As I grew up, he was already a celebrated name in climbing. He used to be on the news all the time for climbing Everest without oxygen. That used to inspire us a great deal.'

Apa recalled one of his conversations with Ang Rita, while climbing Everest sometime in the early 1990s:

'Why don't you ever use oxygen?' Apa asked Ang Rita.

'I don't need extra oxygen. Whatever little I get to breathe in the mountain is enough!' Ang Rita replied.

'But it is safer and easier climbing with extra oxygen!' Apa stressed.

'Well, I have heard it's easier with oxygen. But if I wear it, I think the mask and all those hanging pipes will choke me before the thin air there does,' Ang Rita told Apa.

In 2013, a History Channel show called *Stan Lee's Superhumans* ran experiments on Ang Rita, eventually proclaiming that the Sherpa was immune to altitude-related complications. For the show, Ang Rita was taken to the US and, with several other control subjects, put in a hyperbaric chamber of an altitude research facility, where his resilience was tested against high altitude. Running these experiments was none other than Dr McIntosh.

The altitude inside the chamber was taken straight to the same elevation as that of Everest. Minutes later, the control subjects started showing immediate signs of hypoxia – trembling and fainting – warranting quick oxygen support. However, Ang Rita remained calm, showing no signs of any effects of the altitude on him. The elevation was then increased above the height of Everest – over 9,000m (29,500ft) – but even after several minutes without any supplementary oxygen at this altitude, Ang Rita seemed to be faring well, with little to no impact on his body or mind. The show then has the doctors giving up, proclaiming Ang Rita to be altitude immune.

Still quite sceptical about these TV proclamations, we asked Dr McIntosh, 'Is there anything like altitude immunity?'

'I have not seen it,' he replied with a smile.

Referring to the gradual decline of oxygen saturation at high altitude, which was observed in Apa and Lhakpa Gelu during the 2007 experiment, Dr McIntosh said, 'If people were altitude immune, their oxygen saturation would not decline at all, which is not possible biologically.'

We spoke with Ang Rita's son, Chhewang Dorje Sherpa, and grandson, Tenzing Sherpa, who currently live in the USA. According to them, during his last days, Ang Rita had lost his memory, forgetting things, and sometimes even people. 'That could have been a result of his adventures, climbing Everest without oxygen so many times,' Ang Rita's son told us.

We took up this matter with Dr McIntosh, asking if climbing Everest so many times without supplementary oxygen could have resulted in Ang Rita's memory loss in his old age. 'It's surely possible. We don't know for sure in the case of Ang Rita. But our brain needs so much oxygen. When it doesn't get it, it disintegrates,' he said, stressing again how immunity against altitude is beyond possible. 'What's true, instead, is that Sherpas can utilize the oxygen in their body better than us lowlanders. That's how they can adapt in thinner air.'

Sherpas' ability to utilize oxygen better, according to Dr McIntosh, is a result of genetic changes that have come about over thousands of years. 'Over time, Sherpas have developed several coping mechanisms against the harsh environment they live in,' he said.

One major genetic change that the Sherpas have evolved to survive the thin air is the capacity of their lungs. 'Not just Apa and Lhakpa Gelu, but other Sherpas also have a much bigger lung capacity compared to controls,'

Dr McIntosh said. However, that doesn't yet mean that Sherpas' lungs are literally bigger in size. The lung is made up of tiny sacs called alveoli that exchange oxygen with the blood vessels. 'The volume of these sacs is higher in Sherpas than in other people of similar height and body type, meaning that the volume of air that can go in and out and the oxygen exchange capacity of Sherpas' lungs is higher than other people's,' Dr McIntosh explained.

For this, and for many other social and scientific reasons, the Sherpas' acclimatization schedule is also vastly different than it is for other people. Even after living away from a mountain environment for several months or years, say in Kathmandu or even abroad, Sherpas can acclimatize to high altitudes incredibly quickly.

'The process of acclimatization that we gain at Everest Base Camp recedes after four to six weeks of returning to lower altitude. However, even if we return to Base Camp after two to three months, we are likely to do better than someone who didn't go there in those months previously,' Dr McIntosh explained.

Speaking of coping mechanisms, Dr McIntosh believes that there is as much sociology in Sherpas' mountain resilience, as there is science. 'Growing up in such a harsh environment with challenges every day becomes "their normal",' he said. 'Despite all the risks and hardships, they continue to go back to the mountain again and again, as that is their only way of making ends meet.'

This struggle for survival, limited education and lack of opportunities in the outside world, magnified again by the social prestige associated with climbing Everest, are the prevailing sociological conditions that lead Sherpas like Apa to Everest year after year, generation after generation.

As with prolonged acclimatization, the Sherpas climbing again and again comes with a perk of what Dr McIntosh calls 'physiological memories'. According to his understanding, having done the same thing over and over again, Sherpas naturally get accustomed to the act of climbing the routes up Everest and the recurring sets of physical challenges. Putting this more simply, with years and years of practice and experience, 'climbing' to Sherpas becomes what 'football' is to Ronaldo and Messi.

Apa confirmed this understanding: 'I found climbing Everest easier than treading the long and tiring journey of the Great Himalaya Trail in 2012,' he giggled. 'I think I can climb Everest again even after all these years of rest. However, I don't think I can make the trail happen again.'

Saurav Dhakal's observation of Apa, during the Great Himalaya Trail, also resonates with the legend's feelings: 'Maybe it's just my impression, but I found Apa *dai* far more comfortable crossing high passes and walking in the snow, than in the lowlands, crossing forests and rivers,' he said. 'Maybe his body was more accustomed to climbing than simply walking in the lowlands and foothills.'

When Dr McIntosh returned home after his experimental expedition at Everest, he took with him some memories that would last a lifetime, as well as some answers to those questions surrounding Sherpas' climbing abilities. For sure, the Sherpas were just like other human beings, prone to the damages of altitude, yet more resilient to it than other people who live elsewhere. 'There are definite findings – scientific and sociological – that tell us of Sherpas' extraordinary resilience in the mountains,' he said.

Indeed, otherwise climbing Everest could never be 'a picnic' to anyone!

*

After climbing Everest a record number of 26 times, Kami Rita Sherpa, who comes from the same village as Apa, is more convinced than ever that it is not just his strength and resilience that have been backing him all this time in the mountain. He believes it's his luck, destiny and the blessings of the gods that have been sustaining him on Everest all these years.

For the simple fact that he has been there more times than anyone else in the world, Kami Rita knows the mountain better than anyone. And what he knows for sure is that the mountain is changing, growing more and more unpredictable with each passing year. Deep down, somewhere in his heart, beneath all his strengths and skills visible on the surface, there is an appalling hollow, reminding Kami Rita of the fears of climbing. The intensity of this fear is such that as the world awaited their hero's next adventure, in 2021, he withdrew from his planned summit bid, disturbed by 'nothing' but 'just a bad dream'.

'You can feel the changes in Everest in your every step up,' he said. 'It's getting easier in some places and, elsewhere, it has become harder to climb. It's not about how easy or difficult it's getting. Something is off! And I know it's not going right.'

In 1992, when young Kami Rita followed in his elder brother Lhakpa Rita's footsteps to Everest, working as a kitchen helper, he remembers Base Camp was situated a little higher than where it stands today. 'There used to be grasslands only a little below Base Camp, where we would see the yaks grazing,' he said. 'In three decades, Base Camp has shifted several metres below where it used to be, and the grasslands have gone.'

Climber and respected mountaineering archivist, Alan Arnette, backs up Kami Rita's observations with some facts and figures. In an archive, he writes, 'The (Khumbu) glacier has thinned by 12 to 15 meters [39–49ft] over most of the length. Everest Base Camp is lower today due to the ice melting. In 1953 when Hillary and Tenzing summited, EBC was about 5,320 meters [17,454ft]; today it is 5,280 meters [17,322ft].'[1]

So, what does that mean? According to the International Centre for Integrated Mountain Development (ICIMOD), a Kathmandu-based research institute, the Khumbu Glacier is retreating at an alarming rate of 20m (66ft) every year. Kami Rita is one of many climbers who have witnessed this melting and its result in the form of strange alterations in

---

1   alanarnette.com, 15 Mar. 2017. Everest 2017: Why is the Khumbu Icefall so dangerous? [blog]. Available at https://www.alanarnette.com/blog/2017/03/15/everest-2017-why-is-the-khumbu-icefall-so-dangerous/.

the formation of the Khumbu Icefall, the most treacherous part of Everest to climb (see page 22).

The Khumbu Icefall originates with a river of ice releasing from Lhotse Face at around 7,600m (25,000ft). The glacier takes the route of the Western Cwm of Everest for over 3km (2 miles) and then takes a swift plunge to form the Khumbu Icefall for another 4km (2.5 miles) between Camp I and Base Camp. From Base Camp, the river of ice, measuring in width between 500 and 800m (1,640–2,600ft), continues to flow several kilometres southward, up to an altitude of about 5,000m (16,400ft).

'After leaving Base Camp, and before arriving at Camp I, we must zigzag our way through the puzzling Khumbu Icefall, crossing over deep crevasses on ladder bridges and navigating our way through towering ice seracs and avalanches looming over our heads,' he said. 'In recent years, particularly after the 2015 earthquake, crossing this section has become slightly easier. But it seems to be expanding higher up, even above Camp I, which is clearly a tormenting sign for climbers.'

According to Kami Rita, since 2015, the number of ladders that need to be used at Khumbu Icefall has reduced to only about four – before the earthquake, about a dozen were used. 'However, as new crevasses and seracs are appearing between Camps I and 2, our job surely is going to be tougher and riskier in the future. Just imagine having to deal with treacherous Khumbu Icefall conditions at higher altitudes up on Everest.'

Kami Rita's worst fears turned into a reality in 2014, when an avalanche that poured down upon Khumbu Icefall killed 16 Sherpas (see page 29). An Al Jazeera report published after the incident reported that climate change was to blame for the avalanche, citing a warning from the Intergovernmental Panel on Climate Change (IPCC), issued one month before the incident.[2] IPCC's warning quoted in the Al Jazeera report reads,

---

2   Lewis, R., 26 Apr. 2014. Climate change played role in Everest avalanche, scientists say. Al Jazeera America. Available at http://america.aljazeera.com/articles/2014/4/26/everest-climate-change.html.

'. . . warming temperatures caused by man-made climate change have led to less predictable weather conditions worldwide – and the roof of the world is no exception'.

Several Sherpas killed in the 2014 avalanche belonged to Kami Rita and Apa's own village, Thame. One of them was his close relative Ang Chhiring Sherpa, a brother whom he highly regarded. Ang Chhiring was an expedition cook and specialized in Japanese cuisine. Kami Rita remembers him as a rare personality for whom climbing and cooking were a passion rather than a profession. 'Both his sons had been doing well in the climbing business,' Kami Rita said. 'The old man in his 60s didn't have to go to Everest again and again, if it were not for his passion.'

According to Ang Chhiring's son Mingma Sherpa, who operates a trekking and mountaineering outlet called Climbalaya, before the expedition season of 2014, his father had told him it would be his last time on the mountain. 'We had been trying to convince him to stop going to the mountain as he was already old,' Mingma recalled. 'About a month before the expedition season of 2014 began, he had promised me that it was going to be his last time, and that he planned to start his own bakery in the village thereafter. But that fateful year turned out to be the last one, once and for all. My father died doing what he loved the most.'

Mingma decided to quit climbing himself after this incident, but went back again in 2016, guiding two persons with disabilities to the top of the world. 'That was a promise my father had kept with his friends from the US. One of them had lost his legs in a war and another sustained a lifelong disability in an accident,' Mingma said. 'I had to take them to "the roof of the world", and I did it as a tribute to my father.'

After 2014, following the death of their loved ones in the avalanche, Kami Rita's elder brother, Lhakpa Rita, a veteran climber, one of the first internationally certified mountain guides of Nepal and the first Nepali to climb the highest peaks in all seven continents, decided to quit mountaineering. When we arrived at Kami Rita's home in Thame in

February 2021, we talked at length about the two brothers with their father Sirdar Mingma. 'It's good that Lhakpa Rita has quit climbing. I want Kami to do the same, but he says it's all he can do for a living,' Sirdar Mingma told us. 'And I ask him how many Sherpas who don't climb mountains have died starving. But he doesn't listen.'

No matter how much he downplays everyone's counsel not to climb anymore, Kami Rita knows for sure that the horrors of the mountains are going to get worse due to the melting ice and snow: 'We are not scientists, and we can't tell if an outcropping of ice is melting by looking at the surface. We know things have changed only when the bedrock of the mountain works its way out,' Kami Rita said. 'In all these years, I have seen a lot of them, at all places throughout the climbing route of Everest.'

Kami Rita went on, 'When rocks start showing up on the route, that becomes a major headache for us. Our crampons, that are designed to walk on ice and snow, don't hold properly on the rock. These days, on several occasions while climbing, we must take our crampons on and off. Imagine how risky that is, playing around with your boots at that altitude. For instance, what if you fall off while taking the crampon on or off, or if you leave your laces untied, step on them at the very next step and fall off a ridge?'

*

In February 2022, a scientific report made headlines all over the world, claiming that much of the 2,000-year-old ice at South Col Glacier at an altitude of nearly 8,000m (26,247ft) has melted in the last 25 years. A team of scientists, led by Dr Paul Mayewski, had gone to Everest in 2019, curious to discover how the highest point on earth was impacted by global human activities. The team, under one of the world's top glaciologists, was about to observe scientifically the changes in Everest that Kami Rita had witnessed with his own eyes throughout his 30-year career.

'We know climate change has dramatically impacted the Arctic and Antarctic, and that weather patterns have become significantly unpredictable throughout the world. Drought is increasing and, even in the Arctic, the forest fires have been increasing,' Dr Mayewski, Director of the Climate Change Institute and distinguished Professor at the University of Maine, said. He was leading the expedition and was also the science leader of the project. 'We knew the highest part of the mountain was probably no exception in terms of the impacts of climate change, but we could not be sure until we had examined the ice loss and we had reason to believe it was not worse on Everest than in the polar regions.

'The average annual temperature at Everest is -24°C (-11°F),' Dr Mayewski went on. 'We know that the temperature at that elevation in the last three decades has increased by only one degree, so it means it is still below freezing, leaving hopes that records from ice cores would still be preserved at the high altitudes of Everest. But that was not the case. All of a sudden, 2,000 years of ice was missing from as high as 8,020m (26,312ft) on Everest.'

The study, commissioned by the National Geographic Society and Rolex in 2019, was one of a kind, probably the most detailed and scientific examination ever made of the southern side of Everest. The first climate study being conducted over 8,000m (26,247ft) had several different components to it. The scientists drilled ice cores to understand the history of the ice and also looked at water samples – as the glaciers in the Himalayas melt, there is the issue not only of the loss of water but, potentially, an increase of the pollutants which human activity has deposited over hundreds of years, impacting the water quality and the ecosystem downstream. The study also carried out a high-resolution face-mapping with a detailed ground-based approach, and installed five automatic weather stations as high up as the Balcony at about 8,400m (27,600ft). Apart from scientific inquiry, these automatic weather stations will be valuable to the future of climbing, as there will now be more accurate data available for the potential summit windows, as well as the forecast for air pressure, temperature and wind patterns.

Dr Mayewski himself was part of this expedition along with researchers from Nepal, the US and the UK, with a group of Sherpas which included Panuru and his son Lhakpa from Phortse (see page 80). Explaining what may have caused the melting of the 2,000-year-old ice so rapidly, Dr Mayewski proposed the point raised by Kami Rita – the surfacing of the mountain's bedrock beneath its fresh snow and ice. The slight increase in temperature, coupled with winds getting stronger in the mountains, do not let the seasonal snow rest for very long on the surface. In addition, a slight increase in temperature means that the air above the glacier can hold no more moisture and, if the wind is too strong, it will blow that moisture away.

And then comes snow sublimation, which is very critical: 'It removes the glacier surface by evaporation. On top of that, whenever it snows – that might be a few centimetres each year accumulating on the surface – the fresh snow gets easily blown off, exposing the bedrock to solar radiation,' Dr Mayewski said. 'A layer of white snow reflects as much as 100 per cent of the radiation. When it's not there, the darker surface, which is ice or rock, absorbs incoming radiation and stores heat, eventually melting older ice at the core.'

The study has recorded the disappearance of 50–55m (164–180ft) of ice from South Col Glacier in the last 25–30 years. The scientists expect there still may be 40–50m (131–164ft) of ice left, which, at the same rate of melting, will be gone completely in another 25–30 years. 'This opens up the door for people who think that the loss of Himalayan ice is something that is happening only at lower elevations,' Dr Mayewski said. 'We now know that it's actually happening at the top. This is particularly alarming because it's the upper elevations, above 5,000m, where the snow accumulates, forming ice over centuries, and has until recent decades proven to be effectively a water tower, for storing frozen water. These are the sources of water downstream, and losing them means losing water, challenging the entire ecosystem.'

The formation of a glacier begins with snowfall. As snow accumulates and gradually compresses, its density is only about one-tenth that of water. With more and more compression of surface snow, over time, over years, it eventually becomes firm, and arrives at the stage where it's known as 'compacted snow', which is still half the density of water. With time, again, it reaches a stage where it is completely densified into ice, which is about nine-tenths the density of water. 'We would normally have to drill at least 40m (131ft) into the glacier before we encountered ice,' Dr Mayewski said. 'That's how deep it is. That's how long the process is. But South Col glacier is almost all exposed ice – the snow and firm ice is gone for much of the year and is only present temporarily during the winter before wind, sublimation and melt remove that year's accumulation.'

*

So, what does all this mean for mountain climbing? As a mountaineer himself, Dr Mayewski contemplates this question a lot. Just as Kami Rita has been going back again and again to the mountain, Dr Mayewski believes climate change will not bring climbing to an end. 'Whether there is ice or not, the bedrock will still be there, and Everest will still stand tall and magnificent,' he said. 'And humankind will therefore seek to stand at the roof of the world, no matter what. All we can predict is that there will be changes in the ways of climbing, simply because the mountains will no longer be the same.'

Dr Mayewski is aware of the concerns raised by Kami Rita about crampons making it difficult to walk on the rocks that are surfacing on Everest. 'I think there will be innovations. Humankind is good at that. Think of something that works like crampons but has a rubber sole as well, to make walking on rocky surfaces easier,' he said.

Then there is the placement of Everest Base Camp and the route passing Khumbu Icefall. 'Base Camp is built on Khumbu Glacier, with a lot of debris underneath, lakes all over the place and streams flowing right under it,' he said. 'We know for sure that Khumbu Glacier and the Icefall area are going to be more and more volatile with all the melting that is taking place at all elevations. Taking this threat into account, people might have to explore new routes, even avoiding Khumbu Icefall altogether. But even if we continue to take the same routes, there could be more technology and equipment involved, for example, more ladders, advanced upgrades in the gear that is used, cameras and sensors for better predictability. In another possible scenario, helicopters capable of going a lot higher than they can now could come into play, making a conventional landing possible up to Camp 2.'

Similarly, in another 25 or 30 years, people may not be walking above the glacier as they do today, as there might only be snow patches on the mountain. And imagine having to carry all the drinking water from Base Camp, as there would no longer be any ice to melt, boil and drink. Similarly, on steep slopes, due to the melting of ice and snow into the rocks, there will be more risk of sliding, just as it is today on the northern side of the mountain, where, at some places, climbers go up five steps and come back down two by sliding. But there is an upside as well. According to Dr Mayewski, the temperature at the South Col would be higher, due to exposed dark surfaces, which can mean a slight increase in oxygen. 'It would be a whole different experience to climb,' Dr Mayewski said, 'but we'll adapt. We always have adapted.'

With global climate change and its increasing impact on the Himalayas, there are going to have to be a lot of adaptations in climbing, as Dr Mayewski suggested. But who will lead this process? It was the Sherpas who helped the world navigate its way to the top of the world in the first place. If the world enters a whole new era of climbing, it will again have to be the Sherpas who lead the way.

'We may know the science, but it's the local people who must build ways to adapt, as nobody else knows their place better than them,' Dr Mayewski said. 'Just to get semi-comfortable in the areas where Sherpas live takes us at least two weeks. It doesn't make us as well-suited as Sherpas to know the mountains. Beyond any doubt, they know it all better than we do.

'As I have observed in the Antarctic, where just a small swirling in the surface of snow means something to the experienced polar veteran, for Sherpas, there is always a completely unique understanding of the landscape. Some types of snow are good for hunting; some aren't. Some imply storm conditions; some tell them it's safe to climb.' (Mayewski Peak in Antarctica bears Dr Mayewski's name in recognition of his research there.) 'Climate change is real, and the changes in the mountains are even more so. Climbing the mountain through all these changes will surely undergo many upgrades and evolutions. And the Sherpas are going to be at the centre of it, crusading the world's way to the summit of Everest and many other mountains.'

That's why, according to Dr Mayewski, it's important for scientists and climbers to spend time in these places and learn about the existing cultures and lifestyles. As he rightly said, there is a lot more to understand than just getting up and down the mountain, and coming home and saying you did it.

*

In 2019, when Kami Rita landed at Kathmandu's Tribhuvan International Airport after scaling the summit of Everest for a record 24th time, there was a huge reception there to welcome him. Media all over the world were competing to secure an interview with him. Photographers were struggling to get their best shot. People from the climbing community, both Sherpas and non-Sherpas, thronged in a queue with flower garlands to greet him.

Outside the airport, there was a long convoy that took Kami Rita all over Kathmandu city, and finally escorted him to his apartment in Kapan, a place near Boudha, where his family was waiting. All the way, Kami Rita popped his head out of the vehicle's sunroof, smiled at people and waved his hands.

When he finally got home and stood before a crowd of reporters to speak with the world, he sounded rather irritated, as if he wanted to end all the material glory at once. Part of this irritation may be the result of the long day he'd had, all the noise, exhaustion and the slow city tour. Much of it, however, was a rant against the despicable habit of climbers who leave litter in the high camps of Everest and the poor economy of the Sherpas in general – the modest recognition they get versus western climbers and the 'little-to-no' efforts of the government to address things that are not going right on Everest.

While he was saying all this, drawing the government's attention to the cause as much as he could, little did he know that in a long list of things that are not going right on Everest, one – the melting of ice, as high as 8,000m (26,247ft) – was already beyond the reach of his government.

Chapter 12

DESCENT

In 2017, Doma Sherpa flew on a Dubai-bound jet plane from Kathmandu's Tribhuvan International Airport. Unlike thousands of Nepali migrant workers fleeing the country to the Gulf, away from their families and with hopes of returning soon with some cash in hand, for 39-year-old Doma, the flight was a heavy-hearted escape from home. After take-off, Doma's fellow passengers rejoiced with what was probably their first bird's-eye view of the mountains on the northern range. For Doma, however, the view of the mountains meant anything but pleasure. As she struggled to spot Everest, all she had in mind was her husband Namgyal Sherpa, who had been resting a few hundred metres below the top of Everest on the Tibet side since 2013. A celebrated Sherpa, Namgyal had collapsed and died during his descent. After a lot of futile attempts to bring his body down, Doma was now leaving him behind on Everest, trying to go as far as she could from her memories and guilt.

Also in 2017, Dawa Finjhok Sherpa, a young and promising mountaineer with five Everest summits to his name, got a strange offer from the company he was working for. Dawa Finjhok had just returned to Kathmandu from his unsuccessful trip to Cho Oyu, which had been aborted due to bad weather. Soon after he returned, he had a conversation with his employer, who asked him to lead a mission to retrieve a dead body from Everest:

'Hey Dawa! We are bringing down a body from Everest. Are you interested?' the employer asked.

'Oh sure! When is it?' Dawa Finjhok queried.

'There is a body at 8,400m [27,600ft]. You will lead the team of five. We are in a hurry, so you will have to leave tomorrow morning.'

'Oh, okay...'

'I will give you a briefing tomorrow at the airport.'

'Okay then, see you tomorrow!'

'Oh, and one more thing. You can fly directly to Camp 2, where other members of the team will join you from Base Camp.'

'That's great. See you, sir!'

The next morning, Dawa Finjhok arrived at the airport, donning a fluffy down jacket and sunglasses, carrying a colourful rucksack on his back and chewing gum. He met with his employer there, who, under the deafening noise of the chopper's blades and the incoming and outgoing airplanes, briefed him about where Dawa Finjhok's team would find the body in the death zone. Within an hour, Dawa Finjhok had left Kathmandu's green valley on a light utility H125 helicopter and landed at Everest Base Camp, making a sharp altitude gain of some 4,000m (13,000ft). At Base Camp, the chopper was relieved of most of its unnecessary weight, the seats were taken out, the doors were undone and Dawa Finjhok flew in it once more, directly to Camp 2 at 6,400m (21,000ft).

While the act of climbing a mountain follows a predetermined approach, the job that Dawa Finjhok had signed up for had never been done before; what he was going to do that year would set a precedent of its own – a descent from the highest point on Everest a dead body had ever been recovered from. 'I never thought of it too seriously or with too much scepticism. It was just another job for me, and I was confident my team of five Sherpas would be able to pull it off quite easily,' Dawa Finjhok told us. This was the confidence of a man who had never previously recovered a dead body from any mountain.

The expedition that Dawa Finjhok was about to lead was a high-profile one. The body that they were assigned to recover from the death zone belonged to an Indian Bengali policeman, Goutam Ghosh, who had died during his descent in 2016. This 20-million rupee operation had attracted global attention, and the *New York Times* was about to chronicle every tiny bit of it.

*

For most climbers driven by the obvious glories of the summit, their primary goal in an expedition is the ascent. However, for Sherpas, their focus is slightly different. 'While we are excited to share the joy of a successful summit with our clients, we are also equally concerned about the realities of retreat, the importance of touching the ground, no matter what height you have scaled. Therefore, in an expedition, summit is only half the success. If you are unable to return in one piece, what will you do with a summit in your name?' Panuru Sherpa, a 17-time Everest summiteer, who runs a mountaineering school in Phortse (see page 80), told us in a thoughtful tone.

One critical aspect of a descent is the estimation of oxygen consumption against a climber's speed. In charge of a client's success or failure in the mountain, a Sherpa pays close attention to his client's climbing characteristics. 'The key is to take note of the client's pace, and control their bottled oxygen intake during ascent. We must make sure that a client is not overconsuming oxygen in the excitement of reaching the summit, because if you are out of your life-saving gas while returning, there is no way you can make it down.' Panuru shared his wisdom gained over an active mountaineering career spanning three decades. He is renowned for his maturity and high concern for safety. 'I have abandoned expeditions several times from over 8,000m (26,247ft), the closest one being at the South Summit at only about 150m (500ft) below the top,' he added. 'If I'm not confident that my clients can descend, I simply don't go any further. The clients are angry sometimes, but they realize later that it was a decision taken for their own life.'

According to scientific research conducted by Massachusetts General Hospital, 'most deaths happening in the death zone of Everest are during the descent'.[1] The reason for most of these deaths is high-altitude pulmonary

---

1   Massachusetts General Hospital, 9 Dec. 2008. Research team explores causes of death on Mount Everest. EurekAlert! Available at https://www.eurekalert.org/news-releases/828616.

and cerebral oedema, caused respectively by fluid in the lungs and fluid penetration of the blood–brain barrier or cellular retention of fluids. Acute altitude sickness can result in disorientation, lethargy and nausea, that triggers other ailments and soon causes death.

'Most climbers drain all their energy while climbing up as their mission is to get to the top,' Panuru told us. 'For this reason, they are more susceptible to sickness while coming down. It is the Sherpas' job to prevent such situations by planning for a smooth descent right at the beginning of ascent.'

According to Panuru, it is normal for clients to struggle with challenges and difficulties during ascent. 'However, if their speed is on par with the moderate supplement of controlled oxygen intake, and as long as the client is hydrated, you don't have to worry too much. But if by any chance you run out of oxygen during descent, you are in real trouble.'

Panuru was lucky enough to have learned this lesson right after his first summit of Everest in autumn 1993, with a Korean client, from the Tibet side of the mountain. Since it was his first time on Everest, as well as an attempt during an unpopular autumn season, one of his mentors had advised Panuru about the route up to the summit at the North Col at 7,000m (23,000ft). 'North Col offers a clear view of the route up to the summit,' Panuru said. 'I had a clear understanding of the route and headed up with my client.' Before their final summit push, Panuru and his client had been defeated several times due to bad weather. Those ups and downs in that alpine expedition without the help of fixed ropes on the way had worn both of them out. Finally, about a week after the earlier declared summit window, the weather cleared and Panuru and his client headed up and stood on the summit on 6 October. The pair arrived at the summit at about 12.30pm and spent about half-an-hour at the top, as the weather was very good without too much wind that day.

Soon after they began the descent, Panuru's client started showing signs of exhaustion. The northern route of Everest has three steps above its last camp, also known as Camp 3. While descending, when they arrived at the third step – a snowy surface on the ridge of the mountain only 300m (985ft) below the top – the client started getting too slow. After about 100m (330ft) of descending from the third step on about a 20-degree slope, they arrived at the second step, which is the most difficult section of the mountain on the northern route, with 40m (130ft) of vertical ascent/descent on a ladder fixed on the wall. Soon after descending that ladder, the client sat down and refused to move. Panuru got scared and quickly checked his oxygen level. Relieved that there still was enough oxygen in the tank, Panuru concluded that his client must be simply too exhausted. He encouraged the client to keep moving slowly and steadily. Between the second and first steps, there is a spot called 'mushroom rock', where climbers are required to plummet another few hundred metres on a slope of about 30-degrees to arrive at the first step. 'He was too slow and we were running out of time,' Panuru recalled. 'We had already taken several hours to get this far. According to the briefing I had received, we should have reached Camp 3 by then.'

After somehow crawling a little below the first step, which is normally one-and-a-half hours from the last rest camp at 8,300m (27,230ft) on the northern route, the client refused to move any further and passed out. 'We were still about 300m [980ft] away from the camp and it was already about sunset,' Panuru said. 'I literally dragged him the rest of the distance. It took us two-and-a-half hours, but we had finally arrived at the safety of the camp. I gave him warm soup and tea, and he soon recovered after a few hours of rest.' The next morning, the two climbers got up at about 7am and headed downward, passing through Camp 2 at 7,500m (24,600ft), North Col at 7,000m (23,000ft) and finally arriving at the ABC at 6,492m (21,300ft). ABC is situated at the height of Camp 2 on the southern route from Nepal. However, as yaks can get up to ABC, for there is no Khumbu Icefall on the northern route, it is often also regarded as the base camp of the mountain. However, below ABC, there is one more base camp at 5,182m (17,000ft).

Panuru's first experience of descent taught him many things. According to him, the most important was about the use of oxygen. 'We were delayed in the death zone by several hours while descending and, if we had run out of oxygen due to excessive consumption during ascent, it could have complicated many other things and we could have died,' he said. 'There are other factors as well while descending. Apart from exhaustion or altitude sickness caused by breathing thin air, there are constant threats of avalanche, dehydration and extra pressures on the knee joints while descending, among many others. Until you have reached the bottom in full safety, your expedition is still ongoing and it is challenging, be it on the ascent or during descent.'

According to The Himalayan Database, 305 people have died on Everest between 1924 and December 2021, with the death rate standing at 3.5 per cent. Combining all deaths, in the death zone or below, 28 per cent perished during descent.[2] As of 2021, more than 100 dead bodies are reported to be stranded in different parts of the mountain, buried deep in the snow or visible on the surface, probably never to be recovered. One thing is clear for all the bodies engulfed in the belly of Everest – there won't be a descent back home. When bereaved Doma flew to Dubai in 2017, her husband Namgyal was one of them, gone forever.

*

Namgyal and Doma were both 16 when they got married in 1995 in the vicinity of Boudhanath Stupa, a key Tibetan Buddhist shrine in Kathmandu Valley, a UNESCO World Heritage site.

The stupa, which is believed to have been built first in AD 600 and later moved to its present site in the 14th century, attracted thousands of Tibetan refugees who fled to Nepal after Chinese occupation in 1959. They started settling around the locality of the stupa for religious reasons and thus

---

2   The Himalayan Database: The expedition archives of Elizabeth Hawley. Available at https://www.himalayandatabase.com/.

introduced the neighbourhood of Boudha, and the whole of Kathmandu, to the rich cultural heritage of Tibet. The Tibetans not only brought together their culture, skills, craft and values, but also precious Buddhist scriptures, prayer beads and valuable stones, statues and jewellery. In the present day, there are dozens of monasteries in the areas surrounding Boudha, most of which are believed to have been established by the Tibetans who came here as refugees to preserve their religion and scriptures.

After the Tibetans settled around Boudha, the area became a key cultural junction for Buddhists from all over the country. The Sherpas migrating to Kathmandu for studies or work also started thronging in the localities surrounding Boudha, identifying the place as their next home. Today, Boudha is one of the city's downtown neighbourhoods, where youngsters from all over Kathmandu huddle up in the evenings to get a taste of the Tibetan culture, food and solace in the vicinity of the stupa that resonates sacred love and peace.

In 1995, Namgyal, originally from the district of Khotang in eastern hilly Nepal, was studying in Grade 8 at a government school in Boudha. Doma, who also lived in Boudha with her relatives, did not go to school, and had only recently come to Kathmandu from her home in the Solukhumbu District, a region that also hosts Everest. Solukhumbu and Khotang are two neighbouring districts, and it turned out that the families of Namgyal and Doma were distantly related. The relatives of the two families got along very well and started lobbying for the wedding of the handsome young Namgyal and eternally beautiful Doma.

'I had met him earlier as well as in Boudha, and I liked him. When our relatives started pressuring us to get married, neither of us objected,' Doma said with a smile on her face and turned towards the window of the café, staring at the magnificence of Boudhanath Stupa. She had agreed to meet us in Boudha early in the morning over coffee and breakfast. The hustle and bustle of the stupa was yet to start when we met her and, during our long conversation, which was mostly gloomy, given the darkness of death and tragedy we were talking about, Doma occasionally smiled whenever she made reference to her early relationship with Namgyal.

Soon after marriage, Doma discovered that her husband was a hard-working boy with high ambitions in life. 'He was good at studies and martial arts. He was also very conscious about fitness and physical strength from very early in his life,' Doma shared. 'I supported him in every possible way and encouraged him to study as far as he wanted. But he dropped formal education after passing the national board exams of Grade 10 and employed himself as a martial arts instructor of children in the locality.'

Namgyal found his way into mountaineering in 2000, when a senior Sherpa from his village recommended him to an expedition company. His first job in an expedition, as for most other Sherpas, was that of a kitchen helper. However, he was quick to progress further – first as a cook and then as a high-altitude porter – as he was smart, fit, strong, educated and had high ambitions. 'Around 2003–4, when he was a cook, I joined him in a Kanchenjunga expedition and reached base camp,' Doma said, recalling her romantic days with Namgyal. 'It was so cold there, and the journey over base camp looked very scary to me. I asked him if it was risky climbing the mountains, but he just smiled and told me not to worry.'

Finally, in 2006, he got a break as a guide in Everest and made it to the top on his very first chance. 'He was so happy when he came home after his Everest summit in 2006. I didn't know anything about mountains and mountaineering. I still don't know anything. But I was as happy as he was over his success,' Doma said. 'He knew the summit of Everest would bring him more jobs as a guide, and for the first time in his life, he was assured that he was going to make it big one day.'

*

In 2006, 11 years before Dawa Finjhok went on a mission to recover the body of Goutam Ghosh, when Namgyal bagged his first summit of Everest, Dawa Finjhok also got his debut break in trekking, in the foothills of the Himalayas. The debuts of both Namgyal and Dawa Finjhok were those of hope and ambition, which coincided with optimism for the country's political destiny. 2006 was a turning point in Nepal's history. That year, the Maoist militants put down their guns and signed a comprehensive peace agreement with the government, bringing a decade-long armed conflict to an end. With this development, the country leaped forward by ending the 240-year-old monarchy, electing a new constituent assembly and giving way for decentralization of power through federalism. While the country basked in high hopes of peace, development and prosperity, the lives of Namgyal and Dawa Finjhok also took interesting turns. For Nepal as well as the two Sherpas, while some of these hopes held true, others just froze in silence over time.

When Dawa Finjhok started trekking, he had not thought, even in his wildest dreams, that he would be pursuing the mountains someday. He was a 20-year-old boy with little education, seeking mobility in life. A year before his break into trekking, in 2005, he wanted to go to Iraq for labour employment as he had heard the country offered good salaries to the workers. He even processed his labour migration to Iraq with a recruitment agent, who duped him and left him stranded in New Delhi for several weeks. This misfortune cost 160,000 rupees of his mother's hard-earned cash, who was then employed in Korea as a migrant worker.

After a year of trekking in Nepal, Dawa Finjhok decided to try his luck one more time in foreign employment. In 2007, he flew to Malaysia, ending up at a golf course, where he trimmed the grass and bushes for a little while. 'It was not too bad there, but I soon started missing trekking very badly. I returned to Nepal the same year, and started trekking again,' he explained.

In the autumn of 2008, one evening, Dawa Finjhok happened to stumble upon an old friend whom he had met in 2006 on a trek. The two friends sneaked into a tavern. After a few drinks, the friend offered Dawa Finjhok the opportunity to join him in the mountains. 'I have a very impulsive nature. The second before I got that offer, I had no intentions of going to the mountains. Now that I had that offer in front of me, I made up my mind to go to the mountains at any cost,' he said. 'I instantly agreed, and, a few months later, joined him on an expedition to Dhaulagiri.'

During his first summit, Dawa Finjhok had only heard about climbers needing oxygen in high altitudes and, as he did not have access to oxygen, he simply didn't care. 'I just kept gaining height without oxygen. After 7,500m (24,600ft), I started slowing down a little, but I thought that must be due to regular exhaustion,' he said. 'I went to the summit of Dhaulagiri without oxygen on my very first attempt. I probably won't go over 8,000m (26,247ft) without oxygen ever again as now I know that it is risky as hell.'

*

As Dawa Finjhok slowly made his way into mountaineering, Namgyal was starting to progress higher in his profession. After his 2006 Everest summit, Namgyal began landing himself mountain jobs more easily. He also took advanced mountaineering and rescue training in Switzerland and started occasionally guiding in the mountains of Italy as well.

'The financial condition of our family gradually improved,' Doma said. 'He started riding a motorcycle. I started a small clothing store in Boudha and we also bought land in Kathmandu. When we were progressing swiftly, it never dawned on me that all of it would turn ugly.'

Being the ambitious man he was, the jobs in expedition were still not fulfilling Namgyal's inner urge for progress. In 2008, he started his own expedition company and took a vow to create jobs for other Sherpas like himself. Nothing had gone wrong in Namgyal's life thus far; no wonder his expedition company took off in no time. 'He was very outspoken, with great networking abilities,' Doma said. 'That's what gave him the confidence to run his own organization. He had a lot of friends in mountaineering, and everyone helped him get clients.'

Two years after he started the company, Namgyal also launched a clean-up campaign called Extreme Everest Expedition 2010, together with his friend Chakra Karki, a mountaineering journalist. 'He was initially planning to set a record by spending 24 hours at the summit of Everest without oxygen,' Chakra told us. 'When I suggested he look at the broader picture, beyond his individual record, we both came up with the idea of this clean-up campaign. We approached some private institutions and were finally able to secure funds for the campaign.'

Namgyal and his team of 20 men made the clean-up campaign a huge success by bringing down 1,800kg (2t) of waste, straight from the death zone of Everest. They also managed to recover two dead bodies of a Swiss and a Russian climber from above 8,000m (26,247ft), a heart-wrenching irony given how Namgyal himself has been stranded in the death zone for several years. 'I still can't comprehend how ugly this world is and how full of ironies,' said Doma, again looking outside the window, over to the Boudhanath Stupa in silence.

Namgyal's friend Chakra was coordinating the clean-up campaign from the base camp. It was in the middle of the popular climbing season and, to avoid obstructing ways for other climbers on the mountain, the arduous task of bringing the bodies down was planned for the night-time. On the night the team was about to drag the bodies from the death zone, the weather had badly deteriorated. 'There was heavy snowfall that day and the wind was also very strong. Some people blamed us for the bad weather as they thought we had brought bad omens by touching the bodies resting on Everest,' Chakra said. 'Namgyal was already exhausted and was having a very difficult time up there. These rumours broke him further. We had a long conversation over the radio that day. He got very emotional and even cried.'

As the success of this clean-up campaign was widely reported in the media, it brought Namgyal a good deal of recognition, which eventually attracted expedition groups to his company. In the years after the clean-up campaign, he started operating five to six expeditions annually.

Namgyal paralleled his success with his philanthropy. In his remote home village in the Khotang District, even basic amenities like proper healthcare and sanitation were sparse. Soon after he started his company in 2008, he secured some international donors and supported his home community by building toilets for over one hundred households. Additionally, he also built a hospital in the village, which is still running today. Chakra accompanied Namgyal to the village during their goodwill mission of 2008.

'I learned there that Namgyal was neglected as a child when his mother got married to someone else after the death of his father at a young age,' Chakra said. 'When the villagers saw Namgyal there, doing amazing works for the development of his place, a lot of people cried and hugged him. All over the village, Namgyal became an example of and an inspiration for how the sky is the limit for people trying to do a little good.'

Namgyal's village is situated at an altitude of about 2,500m (8,200ft). It is a mixed community consisting of Sherpas as well as other ethnicities. Therefore, unlike other high-altitude Sherpa hubs, someone climbing Everest from this village had come as a matter of surprise and pride for the locals. 'You were abandoned by your own mother. Who would have thought you would climb Everest one day?' Chakra recalled the villagers' words. 'We can't thank you enough for coming back and doing all the good work here.'

Observing Namgyal's love for his village and his unimpeded quest to help people in need, Doma had also come to realize that he loved his indulgence in philanthropy as much as he loved being in the mountains. 'I wonder what he could have achieved, had he somehow been able to escape that fateful year of 2013.'

In 2013, Namgyal's company had signed up for an expedition from the Tibet side of the mountain. This was an expedition that he was supposed to coordinate from the base camp, while he had arranged for another Sherpa to go up with the client. 'He had a recurring problem of gastritis and had been complaining of a stomach ache when he headed to Tibet to coordinate the expedition,' Doma told us. 'That must be why he had decided not to go up that year.'

However, Namgyal's friend, Chakra, told us that, although Namgyal had been pondering over stopping climbing and only operating expeditions from the base camp in those times, in 2013 he had agreed with the client to go up, despite his gastritis problem.

Namgyal left for Tibet in a jeep, taking the route via the Tatopani-Khasa border point, which is just a little over 100km (62 miles) from Kathmandu. Doma received a phone call from her husband's Nepali number for the last time. ' "Hey, I am about to cross the border now. Will speak with you later when I arrive in Tibet",' Doma quoted Namgyal as saying over the phone.

There wasn't another phone conversation for another month. As Nepali sim cards don't work in Tibet, any cross-border conversation must go through a satellite network, which is very expensive. 'One month after we last spoke, I received a satellite phone call from the base camp of Everest.'

'Hey, how are you? Everything okay?' Namgyal asked Doma.

'Yes, everything is fine here. How are you doing?' Doma replied.

'It's fine, but I am not feeling too well. The gastritis, you know.'

'You never eat well. That's why it keeps troubling you. Take medicines and stay well, please. And eat well.'

'It's nothing. I will be fit in no time. Okay, I will have to hang up now. Will talk later.'

'Okay, take care!'

According to Doma, Namgyal had become careless about his eating habits due to his busy schedule. 'Like most Nepalis, his favourite food was rice and lentils, but you don't get that at the base camp. There is western food mostly, and I am sure he had not been eating too well,' Doma told us.

Over a week after their satellite phone call, Doma received another call from the base camp. Someone on the line told her that her husband had passed away while returning from the summit. Doma's eyes turned hazy and it all felt like a bad dream for a moment. When she realized that she was not dreaming, she instantly broke down, not able to utter a single word. 'I had turned numb,' she said. 'When I tried to talk back after several minutes of silence, I realized the phone had already disconnected.'

The news about her husband's death shook Doma to the core. Her world fell apart and she did not know what to do. 'I thought he must have tricked me and gone somewhere,' Doma said. 'But the news was all over already, and all of my hunches trying to convince me that he was alive were short-lived.'

While returning from the summit of Everest, Namgyal had started feeling uneasy. The client was leading the descent and two Sherpas – Namgyal and a junior Sherpa – were slightly behind him. By the time they were at about 8,400m (27,600ft), the distance between Namgyal and the other Sherpa had widened a little. Namgyal did not seem in very good health and had started to slow down. 'Are you okay?' the other Sherpa asked Namgyal, while he just nodded, pointing towards his chest suggesting a little pain, and said, 'You go on. I am following you.'

From a little further down, the other Sherpa turned back again and saw Namgyal sitting down quietly on a rock. 'He must be resting,' the Sherpa thought and marched on towards the camp. As Namgyal had not arrived in the tent over one hour after his other team members, the other Sherpa rushed back to the spot where he had seen Namgyal resting. He had already died. Bereaved and totally shaken, the rest of the team carried on with their descent, while Namgyal waited behind in eternal numbness.

*

Three years after Namgyal collapsed in the death zone on the Tibetan side, Goutam Ghosh, a Bengali climber from the Indian Police, collapsed at around the same altitude, on the southern face of the mountain in Nepal. Goutam's dreams of Everest had been dashed for two consecutive years – in 2014 due to the Khumbu Icefall avalanche and in 2015 due to the earthquake. Finally, he could march up Everest on his mission in 2016, together with his team of four climbers, accompanied by Sherpas.

Unfortunately, as they ascended in the death zone, the team became very slow, and a mismanagement of coordination and poor communication among the team members and Sherpas led them to scatter in the death zone. All four Bengali climbers suffered from high-altitude sickness, and three of them, including Goutam, died on different parts of the mountain. Goutam, who was last seen at 8,700m (28,550ft) late in the afternoon, was found dead the next day at the Balcony, sitting silently without an oxygen mask. One member of the team died in a tent at Camp 4 and another while descending below that. The lone survivor of the team later claimed that she and Goutam had reached the summit of Everest together that day, and that Goutam got left behind while descending, as she was quicker. However, her summit claim was not approved due to lack of evidence.

One year later, at the request of the Indian government, Dawa Finjhok had been hired to lead the team to retrieve Goutam's body. Having flown straight to Camp 2 in a chopper, Dawa Finjhok waited two days for the other members of his team to arrive. When the team finally assembled, they briefly exchanged names and moved on with their mission. 'I bet all of us had forgotten everyone's name by the time we returned from that trip. Maybe that was because the expedition was a hard one, or simply because we were all too casual,' Dawa Finjhok said, bursting into laughter.

Dawa Finjhok was taken by surprise when the boys joined him at Camp 2. 'They were teenagers, without any prior experience in an extreme rescue like that. With no offence – I was no good either. I had some theoretical knowledge on the use of ropes to bring an object down in the mountain, but with no practical experience,' he offhandedly told us at his hookah bar in Boudha.

Dawa Finjhok currently holds a partnership at a restaurant in Boudha, where he manages its hookah section. At the hookah bar, he gets busy in the evenings, when youngsters come there in groups to enjoy drinks and flavoured hookah – double apple, mint, grapes, paan (betel leaf), among others. Dawa Finjhok had invited us to this restaurant one evening. We took a seat out in the open near a bonfire. In the middle of the interview, Dawa Finjhok got up and prepared a special hookah for us.

'Which is your favourite flavour?' Dawa asked us.

'Any will do. What is the best here?'

'Let's mix double apple and mint. That's my favourite,' Dawa Finjhok replied.

'Lovely.'

Dawa took several minutes and came back with a double-hosed hookah tower. 'This is an expensive gadget – the most expensive hookah that I have. I usually don't serve this to the customers, but you guys are my guests,' he laughed, and we started inhaling gracefully, making thick clouds of hookah smoke, as if to cloak the moon that seemed unusually bright that evening. 'It's just like the fog covering up the peaks of the mountains up there,' we told him.

After assembling at Camp 2, the team briefly planned their activities. Apart from regular mountaineering equipment, they only had ropes to tie the body and make passages down the cliffs while descending. Dawa Finjhok's checklist of equipment for this mission also had a stretcher, but they did not carry it from the lower camps, as he was told there was one at Camp 4 for their use.

'As a leader, my job was to take photos, videos and coordinate the dead body descent,' Dawa Finjhok said. 'But as we came down with the body, our roles blurred in the snow. I did not have the luxury to enjoy the leadership, and it was all four of us engaged in managing that difficult job.'

The team left Camp 2 the same day at around 1am. After walking through the night, they arrived at Camp 4 at 8,000m (26,247ft) at about 8am. At Camp 4, Dawa Finjhok looked for the stretcher that he was told would be there. 'But there seemed to have been some miscommunication,' he said. 'There was no stretcher.'

They took a brief rest, munched some dry fruit and chocolate, and drank hot water. 'In my backpack, I had also carried a bottle of cola, which had already frozen. I took it out, cut the bottle across the middle with a knife, and boiled the icy cola in a stove. We all took a few sips of that, and left Camp 4 at around 9am to locate the body.'

It took them about an hour and a half to reach the Balcony at about

8,400m (27,600ft), where they found the mortal remains of Goutam Ghosh. 'He was seated at the Balcony, resting his lower back on a small rock, facing west,' as Dawa Finjhok described the scene. 'He was facing up, and it looked as if the weight of his head was pulling the body backward, forming an arc of almost 180 degrees, with his eyes taking an upside-down look at Pumori to the east.

'I had not done any research on the size of Goutam's body. When I took my first look close up, I was baffled. It was huge. A massive non-moving object that must have been 183cm [6ft] tall and over 100kg [220lb],' he added. 'For several minutes, we had no idea how we were going to even start.'

When Dawa Finjhok's team met with the body of Goutam Ghosh, his face was not covered by a mask. The eyes were open, teeth clenched as if in pain, and the face extremely sunburned. 'The look of the body was very disturbing, especially with a face exposed like that in the snow,' he said. 'First things first, I covered his face with the cap attached to his down jacket and tied it nicely to make sure it did not disturb us again in the middle of our work.'

The body was so heavy that it took them more than an hour just to move it around, trying to wrap it up. We had harder plastic wraps that did not seem to cover the body well enough for us to attach harnesses to it. 'We started looking around for any objects we could use to wrap the body,' Dawa Finjhok said. 'We found plastic tarps and sleeping pads left on the mountain by climbers. We used them to wrap the body and tied it tightly in many places from head to toe with rope.'

To make sure that the arduous effort of dragging a dead body down Everest did not obstruct the way for other climbers, the descent of Dawa Finjhok's team and Goutam Ghosh was planned for the last window of the season. On the day of the descent, the weather had already started to deteriorate – the wind was 40kmph (25mph) – and, for Dawa Finjhok's team, the journey was long.

*

Soon after her husband put himself to rest in the death zone of Everest, for Doma, life started becoming as ugly and challenging as it could get. The unprecedented death of her beloved had created a huge vacuum in her life. Wrestling with this, she realized how badly she had become dependent on her husband's shadow. Doma had enjoyed Namgyal's growth and success, and had shared together with him their lift from rags to riches. When Namgyal was suddenly gone, Doma was pulled down to the harsh realities of life – from hopelessness and desperation, to despair and destitution.

On the one hand, there was a painful pit of sorrow in her heart, dug by the loss of her loving partner. On the other, there were several mountains to climb. 'First, I had to try to bring my husband's body down from Everest,' Doma said. 'Second, there was the burden of his legacy that I had to carry forward. Then there was this financial setback, which I was supposed to grapple with all alone.'

By 2013, Namgyal's expedition company had seen exponential growth, operating five to six mountain expeditions annually. For someone who had a very humble beginning, working as a porter and a cook less than a decade before, this was nothing short of impressive. After Namgyal's death, Doma had to take care of the company and its promising growth, but she simply didn't know how. 'It was always all about Namgyal and, when he was gone, our company also lost its key strength,' Doma said. 'On top of that, I didn't know anything about the company and expeditions. All I had done so far was stand by my husband in all his efforts. But I didn't have any idea about running a company.'

Doma knew she could do nothing to save the company. Still, for two years after Namgyal's death, she kept the office. There was no business, but she kept paying the rent out of her own pocket. Then, finally, she gave up. She sold all the office assets, from the tables and chairs to the climbing gear and equipment, to a travel agency. 'I missed him very badly that day,' Doma said.

'I knew he would have wanted me to save his company, but there was nothing I could do. I had failed.'

As per Sherpa tradition, Doma completed all her husband's after-death rituals within 49 days of his death. However, as she had not seen his body and as there was no funeral, she couldn't shake the thought that her husband was still alive. Namgyal's motorcycle, a fashionable Pulsar 220cc, popular among the city's young boys, stood quietly in the yard of their rented apartment in Boudha. 'When there was the noise of a motorcycle passing by on the road outside, I thought it must be him,' Doma said. 'It happens to me sometimes even today.'

After Namgyal's death, the mammoth task before Doma was to bring his body down from Everest. 'My husband had himself brought two bodies down from Everest in 2010. I had never thought the job was so difficult until I started trying to arrange his last descent myself,' Doma said. The obvious hurdle that stood before her was money. Hiring a company to drag down bodies from Everest is three times more expensive than simply climbing the mountain. This is because recovering a dead body and dragging it down takes several Sherpas. For instance, if five Sherpas are employed for the removal of a body, you will have to pay for all their climbing permits, insurance, gear, oxygen and other equipment. What's more, for the time and effort involved in recovering a body from deep into the death zone, the Sherpas or companies charge several times more than for any regular expedition.

No matter how expensive the descent, money was no object for Doma when faced with the chance to say a final precious goodbye to her beloved. She sold land and properties, accepted the help of friends and family and, after one year, accumulated a sum that was still barely enough. Some of Namgyal's old clients had also committed to donating some money and Namgyal's friends in mountaineering had vowed to support in kind, arranging the oxygen bottles and equipment.

'I did not leave any stone unturned in trying to arrange funds for my husband's descent. I held a press conference, lobbied for the government's help and support, and even asked for help from national and international mountaineers,' Doma said. 'Finally, with the support pledged and committed from all parties, I was confident about the recovery of the body.'

Beyond the financials, another major hurdle was limited access to Tibetan authorities. Namgyal had died in the Tibetan territory and Doma had to gain permission from Chinese authorities to launch her mission. 'After several rounds of efforts, the Tibetan authorities granted permission to extract the body in 2015,' Doma said. 'But imagine how unlucky I must have been – the same year, there was an earthquake. The mission got cancelled.'

A year later, the dynamics relating to the retrieval of Namgyal's body had drastically changed. The money that Doma had thought she would spend on her husband's descent had thinned due to her everyday expenses. Friends and sponsors, who had pledged their support earlier, had lost interest as everyone's priorities had shifted after the earthquake. Therefore, it was impossible for Doma to summon the same spirit and support in bringing her husband's body down from Everest. 'It was not just about bringing his body down,' Doma said. 'I was running out of money and there were limited helping hands. Even if we had recovered the body, it would have been impossible for me to pay for his death rituals.'

Doma felt broken by the situation. 'I tried my best to put everything together to gain support from all quarters, as in 2015,' she said, 'but nothing worked out. In another two years, I had no money left. I had failed again and there was no way ahead.'

Battered and defeated, Doma gradually came to believe that her husband was at peace in the mountain he loved, and that it was absurd trying to bring him back. 'I had somehow made up my mind to let him rest there forever,' she said. 'But how was I supposed to escape the enquiries of family and friends?' Whenever Doma met with a friend or a relative, they would ask her, '. . .any progress with Namgyal's body?'

'I had miserably failed, and with no answers to give anybody,' Doma said.

*

Soon after Dawa Finjhok and his team had finished wrapping the body of Goutam Ghosh, they realized the mammoth task they had signed up for. 'We were struggling to even move the body on its side so that we could fix the ropes,' Dawa Finjhok recalled. 'It did not take us more than five minutes to realize that this descent was going to be several times more challenging than climbing up.'

No matter how dreadful the journey, Dawa Finjhok had to take it. Abandoning this responsibility could have consequences – first, he would lose his payment; and second, it could ruin his name and reputation in the climbing world. 'I was convinced that climbing down Everest with an over 100-kg [220-lb] frozen human body was a hard nut to crack,' he said. 'But not even for a second did I think about abandoning it. I had my own interests attached to this mission, and I had to complete it any way I could.'

Dawa Finjhok used the rope pulley technique to slowly move the body downwards on the sloped terrain in the death zone. He initiated the process by looping a rope through a pulley that he had created by fixing an anchor to a rock. Then he attached the body's harnesses to the same rope he was controlling. As he released the rope, steadily gliding the body downwards, other members of the team created support for the body from all sides so that it did not lose track while moving down. 'Once we started working with the pulley, the whole process looked practically doable,' Dawa Finjhok said. 'I regained all my confidence and we kept going, repeating the same rope technique several times.'

The team reached Camp 4 at around 12.30pm, about eight hours after finding the body. With a dead body lying motionless in its wraps on the snow beside them, Dawa Finjhok and his team took another quick break, made some tea and sipped it, discussing their journey so far and the way ahead. 'We were all having very different feelings,' he said. 'We had returned so close from the summit, and it felt very weird. If we had gone further up for another two or three hours, we would have had another summit in our name, but here we were, returning so close from the summit, and with a dead body.'

A little below Camp 4, before arriving at the Yellow Band of the Lhotse Face over Camp 3, there is a flatter surface called the Geneva Spur, a rock buttress leading towards the South Col of Everest and neighbouring Lhotse. 'The Geneva Spur is relatively flatter and does not offer enough slope to use the same technique, using earth's gravity to pull the body down while controlling its movement with a rope,' Dawa Finjhok recalled. 'It was clear that we had to carry the body, but how? The walking trail was too narrow for two climbers to fit on two sides of the body. A single person could not carry the body as it was way too heavy. We could not drag it as, on the rock surface without snow, the body could be easily damaged.'

The only way out of the Geneva Spur, therefore, was for two people to lift the body from the front by its toes and two people to do the same at the back with the upper part of the body. 'It was an awkward position. This way, we could walk only one or two steps at a time. We would put the body down and repeat, hopping another one or two steps at the count of three,' Dawa Finjhok explained.

The Geneva Spur is only about 1km (0.6 miles) long, which usually takes no more than an hour for Sherpas. That day, Dawa Finjhok and his team took nearly five hours to cross it. 'Never in my lifetime had I thought it could be so difficult to move on a flatter surface on a mountain,' Dawa Finjhok recalled. 'As we counted "one, two and three", or we gasped or panted, I felt alive and it reminded me of the critical mission that I was part of.'

The team faced similar hurdles every time they came across narrow flat surfaces on Everest. 'It could have been so easy if only we had a stretcher. At places where we could not use rope techniques, we could have simply dragged the body, with a stretcher underneath it ensuring that no damage was caused to the body,' he said. 'But we did not have a stretcher and we had to live with this limitation.'

On a similar narrow walking trail, as they hopped the body one step at a time, the body would often lose its track, slipping its way on the ridge. Each time the body slipped, it would send chills down Dawa Finjhok's spine.

'After coming this far, if the body fell and we lost it, all our efforts would be in vain. Besides that, the more I interacted with the body of Goutam Ghosh, the more I felt connected with his family, who I knew were sitting somewhere, waiting for their beloved to come home for one final goodbye,' he said. 'It was still purely a job for me and my only true motivation was money. However, the emotions that came attached to that were somehow holding me more and more accountable.' Dawa Finjhok asked his boys to be extra careful and stay close to the body as they lifted and thumped it on the ground, to prevent it from falling off the ridge.

Before arriving at Camp 3, Dawa Finjhok called a cook stationed at Camp 2 over the radio:

'We will reach Camp 3 in another hour. Can you please come up there with some food?' Dawa asked the cook.

'Okay. I will try to make it,' the cook replied.

'Great. Please come. We are extremely exhausted and hungry. If you meet us at Camp 3, five of us will pay you 5,000 rupees each. Please!'

'Okay no problem. I will see you there.'

'Parts of this route that would normally take us a couple of hours to cross had taken many more this time. It was already midnight and we had been working continuously for 24 hours already, with limited food and water. We did not have any energy to take another step, but we also did not have the luxury to camp somewhere and spend the night,' Dawa Finjhok recalled. As this expedition was planned for the last summit window, the major risk was the weather, which was fast deteriorating. With a dead body to take care of, Dawa Finjhok and his boys did not want to stop on the way and had been aiming to reach Camp 2 by morning, at any cost.

When Dawa Finjhok, his boys and the body of Goutam Ghosh arrived at Camp 3 at about 1am, the cook was already there with noodles, cola, juice and water. 'No food has ever satisfied me more than what we ate at Camp 3 that night. We munched the raw noodles and gulped them down our dry throats with chilled cola,' Dawa Finjhok remembered, smiling. 'I have also never paid so much for a packet of noodles and a soft drink. But if we did not have it that day, all of us would have collapsed.'

After 20 minutes of rest at Camp 3, the team descended further. In another three hours, they finally arrived at Camp 2. They took the body straight to the spot where helicopters land in Camp 2, laid it down, then sneaked inside their sleeping bags in a tent, had several cups of warm water and an omelette, and slept.

*

After a year-long wait, when Goutam Ghosh descended Everest, his loved ones finally convinced themselves that he was really gone. Emerging out of the vacuum of absence and numbness, they could at last embrace the painful process of bereavement. For Dawa Finjhok, who had made it all possible for Goutam Ghosh and his loved ones, the many emotions that the descent had triggered gradually slipped away when he and his team received a substantial sum of money for their efforts.

Meanwhile, on the other side of the mountain, Namgyal was stuck in the death zone. After several futile attempts to instigate a final descent for her husband, shattered and devastated, Doma gave up the same year that Dawa Finjhok orchestrated the dramatic descent for Goutam Ghosh. For another three years, Doma worked in the hotels and restaurants of Dubai, Bahrain and Saudi Arabia. She has now returned to Kathmandu. 'I have lost all hope of his descent,' Doma said. 'If at all possible, I will go there myself someday, meet him by the snow under the top of the world, and ask why it is all so ugly after all.'

EPILOGUE

The painful story of Namgyal's suffering to provide for his family must have left you in utter angst. We are also left agitated and restless over this mountain of grief, exacerbated by the fact that Namgyal's wife Doma will probably never be able to scale Everest and recover her husband's body.

Having told so many stories in this book, however, we have come to a strange understanding of the realities of life that spur on the Sherpas. They know the mountains can kill, yet they partake in someone else's dreams of standing on the roof of the world, driven by the hopes and prospects of pursuing a better life for their families. A lot of them survive these odds, but for many, like Namgyal, just when life is starting to seem comfortable, the ugly blow of fate breaks the wheel of hope and happiness once and for all. This story is often repeated, and yet the Sherpas keep climbing.

After heading up from the last camp at the South Col, climbers take a slight descent to get to the Triangular Face and, from there, look straight up to see the line of climbers' headlamps passing along the ridges of Hillary Step and the South Summit. This procession resembles stars on a march for the summit of Everest, a view that most climbers cherish for life. The same starry illusion in the night sky of Everest's death zone, however, is also a reminder of how high it is going to get and all the horrors associated with a summit attempt. For first-timers, the adrenaline, coupled with their starry dreams, often overpowers these horrors, but, for Sherpas, there is a burgeoning sense of unease every time they set out from Base Camp, yearning for their beloveds waiting at home and overcoming mountains in their minds that are several folds higher than Everest.

A few weeks before the spring expeditions of Everest in 2022, as his colleagues set up tents and ferried oxygen and equipment at Base Camp, we sat with Tendi Sherpa over lunch one Saturday on the balcony of a top restaurant in Kathmandu, overlooking tree leaves sombrely falling on our cars in the car park below. In the past year, after our last meeting with Tendi, he had travelled the world, guiding clients to the mountains in several different continents – from Asia to Europe, and America to Antarctica. Back in Nepal, before gearing up for Everest, he had found some time to relax, going on a short break with his family, and had been meeting friends over lunch and coffee almost every day. One of the best mountaineers, renowned globally, handsomely paid and with a career at its absolute peak, Tendi revealed to us his rather melancholic feelings: 'In two years, I will be 40 and will have completed 20 years in active climbing,' he said. 'Then, I think I should take a long break from this profession. I want a peaceful family life, and there can be no peace as long as I am climbing. Nothing – absolutely nothing – can ever beat the delight of being with family.' It's a luxury for Tendi to be able to even plan for a break. For many other Sherpas like him, this may not be a possibility and they may even perish in the numbness just like Namgyal, long before relishing family moments once again.

It's clear by now that the Sherpas' romance with the mountains and the act of climbing is attached to their love stories back home. That's what we think this book is all about – the restless love stories of our characters, for whom the upward trail leading to the starry illusion of the cold icy night on Everest is never going to end.

LIST OF PERSONS
AND FAMILIES FEATURED

CHAPTER 1: FOOTPRINTS

- Tendi Sherpa: an internationally-certified mountain guide, who has been on the summit of Everest 14 times so far.
  - Interviewed several times in Kathmandu between 2015 and 2022.
- Babu Chiri Sherpa: set a record in 1999 by spending 21 hours on top of the world without bottled oxygen. Also had a record to his name for a speed ascent of Everest, taking only 16 hours and 56 minutes to reach the summit in 2000. Died in 2001.
- Tenzing Norgay Sherpa: the first person to summit Everest with Sir Edmund Hillary in 1953. Died in 1987 (see Chapter 4).
- Kanchha Sherpa: at 19 years old, was part of the team of the first successful Everest expedition.
  - Interviewed in Namche Bazaar and Kathmandu in 2014 and 2021.

CHAPTER 2: ANGRY GODS!

- Mingma Sherpa: one of the surviving Sherpas at the Icefall when the avalanche hit on 18 April 2014.
  - Interviewed in Phortse in 2021.
- Tenzing Gyalzen Sherpa: arrived at Base Camp shortly after the avalanche on 18 April 2014.
  - Interviewed in Phortse in 2021.
- Nima Sonam Sherpa: was at Base Camp when the earthquake hit on 25 April 2015.
  - Interviewed in Phortse in 2021.
- Nima Chhiring Sherpa: was at Camp 2 when the earthquake hit. Ten-time Everest summiteer. Was left at Camp 2 by the rescue helicopters to make his own way down the mountain with other Sherpas.
  - Interviewed in Phortse in 2021.
- Sirdar Mingma Chhiring Sherpa: 90 years old, a first-generation Sherpa living in Thame (see also Chapter 3).
  - Interviewed in Thame in 2021.

- Lakpa Rita Sherpa: the eldest son of Sirdar Mingma Chhiring Sherpa and a 17-time Everest summiteer. He quit the climbing profession after the avalanche of 2014.
  - Phone interview in 2019.
- Kami Rita Sherpa: the youngest son of Sirdar Mingma Chhiring Sherpa. Holds the record for 26 Everest summits – the highest number in 2021.
  - Interviewed several times in Kathmandu between 2019 and 2022.

CHAPTER 3: BECOMING SHERPA

- Sirdar Mingma Chhiring Sherpa: we met this first-generation Sherpa from Thame in Chapter 2. Here, we explore him working as a trader between Nepal and Tibet and Nepal and Darjeeling, initially employed as a porter and a railway track labourer, then as a trekker. Left Darjeeling in the mid-1950s with his wife and two daughters and returned to the Khumbu region, continuing his work as a trekking guide until his retirement in 1992 at the age of 62.
  - Interviewed in Thame in 2021.
- Pasang Diki Sherpa: Sirdar Mingma's wife.
  - Interviewed in Thame in 2021.
- Tenzing Norgay Sherpa: met in Chapter 1 (and we meet him again in Chapter 4). He trained Sirdar Mingma at a climbing school in Kerala.
- Lakpa Rita Sherpa: the eldest son of Sirdar Mingma Chhiring Sherpa. Met in Chapter 2. Summited Everest 17 times and was the first Sherpa to summit the highest peaks in all seven continents. He retired in 2014 and moved to Seattle with his family. He now manages and operates expeditions from Base Camp every season.
  - Phone interview in 2019.
- Kami Rita Sherpa: the youngest son of Sirdar Mingma Chhiring Sherpa. Met in Chapter 2. Holds a world record of 26 Everest summits.
  - Interviewed several times in Kathmandu between 2019 and 2022.
- Mingma David Sherpa: at 32 years old, has climbed all 14 of the 8,000-m (26,247-ft) peaks across the globe, making him the youngest person to do so. Eight Everest summits to his name and a member of the first successful winter expedition of Mount K2 in Pakistan in 2021.
  - Interviewed several times in Kathmandu between 2020 and 2022.
- Dorjee Khatri: three-time Everest summiteer, from Mingma David's home district of Taplejung. Mingma's mentor. Died in the 2014 Khumbu Icefall disaster.

- Panuru Sherpa: a mountain-climbing guide from Phortse. Runs an academy called Khumbu Climbing Center in Phortse. Seventeen-time Everest summiteer. We meet him again in Chapters 11 and 12.
  - Interviewed several times in Kathmandu and Phortse between 2021 and 2022.
- Pasang Diki: Panuru Sherpa's wife.
  - Interviewed in Phortse in 2021.
- Lhakpa Sherpa: Panuru's son. Has climbed Everest twice. Wants to descend Manaslu on a snowboard, then cycle all the way to Kathmandu.
  - Interviewed several times in Kathmandu and Phortse between 2021 and 2022.

CHAPTER 4: REVISITING TENZING NORGAY

- Tenzing Norgay Sherpa: the first person to summit Everest, with Sir Edmund Hillary, in 1953. Died in 1987. First met in Chapter 1.
- Jamling Sherpa: Tenzing Norgay's son. Summited Everest in 1996. Operates a mountaineering company.
  - Interviewed twice in Darjeeling in 2021.
- Ang Tharkay Sherpa: a veteran climber and contemporary of Tenzing Norgay. Died in 1981.
- Dawa Futi: Tenzing Norgay's first wife. Died in 1944.
- Ang Lhamu: Tenzing Norgay's second wife. Died in 1964.
- Dakku: Tenzing Norgay's third wife. Died in 1992.

CHAPTER 5: 'YOU WILL BE THE KING ONE DAY'

- Kushang Dorjee Sherpa: the first man to summit Everest from three points of the compass, a record that remains unbroken.
  - Interviewed several times in Darjeeling and over the phone between 2021 and 2022.
- Sange: Kushang Dorjee's younger brother.
- Pinky: Kushang Dorjee's second wife.

CHAPTER 6: THE MOUNTAINS OF THE SHERPA WOMEN

- Pasang Lhamu Sherpa: the expedition team leader for the women's Everest expedition in 1993. She summited on 12 April 1993, but died near the South Summit when a storm hit.
- Lhakpa Futi Sherpa: a member of the 1993 women's team who remained at Camp 2 while Pasang Lhamu summited. After Pasang's death, she decided never to climb mountains again.

○ Interviewed in Kathmandu in 2021.
- Nanda Rai: a member of the 1993 women's team who suffered from high-altitude sickness at Camp 2 and had to return to Base Camp.
- Nimi Sherpa: part of the Indo–Nepali expedition group, also aspiring to become the first Nepali woman to climb Everest.
- Ang Rita Sherpa: had climbed Everest without oxygen seven times by 1993. (See also Chapter 11.) Died in 2021.
- Sonam Tsering Sherpa and Pemba Norbu Sherpa: guides for Pasang Lhamu's summit. Sonam Tsering died with Pasang Lhamu at the South Summit.
- Furdiki Sherpa: the eldest daughter of veteran Icefall doctor Ang Nima Sherpa, married Mingma Sherpa (who later died on Everest), ran a teahouse in Dingboche then started a lodge in Chhukhung, renting yaks to transport goods from Namche Bazaar to the village and sometimes Everest Base Camp. After her husband died, she fundraised and then climbed Everest with Nima Doma (also a widow of a mountaineer) in 2019, in tribute to their beloveds who died on Everest. Is now a full-time trekking guide.
    ○ Interviewed in Kathmandu in 2021.
- Mingma Sherpa: a carpenter from the Solukhumbu District, married Furdiki Sherpa. Would travel with the yaks (as above) and was then employed as an Icefall doctor, like his father-in-law. In 2013, he fell off a ladder and died.
- Ang Nima Sherpa: veteran Icefall doctor and father of Furdiki Sherpa.
- Nima Doma Sherpa: a friend of Furdiki Sherpa and a widow who had lost her husband in the 2014 avalanche. Climbed Everest with Furdiki in 2019.

CHAPTER 7: AN ODD LEGEND

- Phurba Tashi Sherpa: was originally a shepherd and summited Everest 21 times. In his initial years of climbing, he kept it from his parents as they were against it and he had promised only to work as a cook at the base camp. Was on the expedition with Marco Siffredi and David Tait. He retired after the 2015 earthquake.
    ○ Interviewed several times in Khumjung and over the phone between 2021 and 2022.
- Apa Sherpa: known as 'Super Sherpa', as he held a world record of 21 Everest summits, equalled later by Phurba Tashi and broken by Kami Rita.
    ○ Interviewed in Kathmandu in 2014 and via video call in 2022.
- Panuru Sherpa and Dawa Tenzing Sherpa: on the Marco Siffredi expedition with Phurba Tashi.

CHAPTER 8: A FAMILY FROM ROLWALING

- Pemba Gyalze Sherpa: a cook at Camp 4 who was in the blizzard of 1996. Lives in the Rolwaling Valley. Was reluctant to go to the summit, but went with his younger brother – Pemba Dorje Sherpa – in 2000. Retired from the mountains after the death of his brother Phurba Thundu Sherpa in the 2006 Pumori avalanche
- Kinjum: Pemba Gyalze's mother.
- Chhiring Norbu Sherpa: Pemba Gyalze's father.
- Yanjung: Pemba Gyalze's wife.
- Norbu Sherpa: Pemba Gyalze's son.
- Pemba Gyalze's siblings (from eldest to youngest):
    - Phurba Thundu Sherpa
    - Pemba Dorje Sherpa
    - Pasang Futi Sherpa
    - Dawa Diki Sherpa
    - Nima Gyalzen Sherpa
    - Phurba Tenzing Sherpa
    - Lakpa Diki Sherpa
    - Phurba Thiley Sherpa
    - Sonam Temba Sherpa
    - Nima Lhamu Sherpa
    - Different members of the family interviewed in Rolwaling and Kathmandu between 2021 and 2022.
- Pemba Dorje Sherpa: Pemba Gyalze Sherpa's younger brother. Employed in 2000 by a Japanese expedition to go to the summit. Persuaded his brother to go with him. Also set the speed record for the fastest ascent of 8 hours 10 minutes in 2004, although this has been disputed. Known as Pemba 'Speed' in the climbing community.
    - Interviewed in Kathmandu in 2021.
- Dawa Diki Sherpa: Pemba Gyalze's younger sister, fifth of the eleven siblings. Her husband died at Base Camp in the 2015 earthquake. Travelled with the authors to Rolwaling.
    - Interviewed in Rolwaling in 2021.
- Dorje Sherpa: a cook in his mid-20s, hired by Pemba Gyalze's siblings in Kathmandu to help their mother in Rolwaling during the winter.
    - Interviewed in Rolwaling in 2021.
- Phurba Tenzing Sherpa: Pemba Gyalze's brother. Made his debut climb at the age of 17 in autumn 2006 on an expedition to Mount Pumori. Went to Gorakshep to buy camera batteries and witnessed the avalanche that killed his brother Phurba Thundu. Initially promised not to go on the mountain again, but

now has 15 Everest summits to his name at the age of 33. Now owns a trekking/
mountaineering company.
  ◦ Interviewed in Kathmandu in 2021 and 2022.
- Phurba Thundu Sherpa: Pemba Gyalze's brother. Went on the 2006 expedition to
Mount Pumori and died in the avalanche witnessed by his brother Phurba Tenzing.

CHAPTER 9: PLAYING THE LONG GAME

- Ang Tshering Sherpa: had to drop out of medical school due to low altitude health
problems. Owner of Asian Trekking. Led the Nepal Mountaineering Association
for three tenures.
  ◦ Interviewed in Kathmandu in 2021.
- Konjo Chumbi Sherpa: Ang Tshering's father.
- Thukten Philip Sherpa: Ang Tshering's brother.
- Nawang Gombu Sherpa: a nephew of Tenzing Norgay, part of the American team
that reached the summit of Everest on 1 May 1963.

CHAPTER 10: SEVEN SUMMITS BEYOND

- Mingma Sherpa, Chhang Dawa Sherpa and Tashi Lhakpa Sherpa: the first people
from Nepal to reach the Geographic South Pole. Run Nepal's largest expedition
company, Seven Summit Treks. Mingma is the first Nepali and South Asian to bag
all 14 8,000-m (26,247-ft) peaks. Mingma and Chhang Dawa hold a world record
for the world's first two brothers to successfully summit these 14 peaks. Tashi
Lhakpa is the youngest person to climb Everest without supplemental oxygen, at
the age of 19. There are eight siblings in the family:
  ◦ The eldest, Karma Tenzing Sherpa, spends village life in Nurbuchaur and
    remains untouched by the wonders of mountaineering and trekking.
  ◦ After Karma Tenzing and sister Kidoma Sherpa, comes Mingma Sherpa, the
    third child of the family, and the second son.
  ◦ Mingma is followed by Nawang Gyalze Sherpa, Chhang Dawa Sherpa, sister
    Chhiri Pangmu Sherpa, Tashi Lhakpa Sherpa and, youngest of all, Pasang
    Phurba Sherpa.
  ◦ Four of the siblings – Mingma, Chhang Dawa, Tashi Lhakpa and Pasang
    Phurba – currently run the Seven Summits.
  ◦ Interviewed Mingma and Tashi Lhakpa several times in Kathmandu between
    2020 and 2022.
- Ming Temba Sherpa: a mountaineer from the Makalu region. Took the authors to
the villages of Walung including Nurbuchaur.
  ◦ Interviewed during the trip to the Makalu region in 2022.

- Japanese Sherpa: owner of the Sherpa Guest House in Num Bazaar.
  - Interviewed during the trip to the Makalu region in 2022.
- Nima Dorjee Sherpa: Kushang Dorjee's younger brother. Nicknamed 'Boka Lama'. Is a revered priest and religious leader in Makalu. Has summited Everest 12 times and was the head Sherpa in the team of the legendary Babu Chiri.
  - Interviewed in Nurbuchaur in 2022.
- Dawa Sherpa: Babu Chiri's elder brother.

CHAPTER 11: SHERPAS ARE STRONG, BUT MOUNTAINS ARE NOT

- Apa Sherpa: from Thame. Has summited Everest 21 times. Retired from mountaineering in 2011 and undertook the Great Himalaya Trail.
  - Interviewed in Kathmandu in person in 2014 and via video call in 2021.
- Dr Scott McIntosh: professor at the University of Utah, who led the 2007 study on Sherpas' physiologies. He is a renowned name in high-altitude medicine.
  - Interviewed twice via video call in 2022.
- Dr Paul Mayewski: director of the Climate Change Institute and distinguished professor at the University of Maine, who led the 2019 study on the South Col Glacier. He is one of the world's top glaciologists.
  - Interviewed twice via video call in 2022.
- Lhakpa Gelu Sherpa: known for his speedy ascent of Everest in 10 hours, 56 minutes, 46 seconds.
- Ang Rita Sherpa: from Thame, climbed Everest 10 times without using any extra oxygen. For his eccentric climbing records between 1983 and 1996, Ang Rita is known to the world as 'Snow Leopard'. Died in 2021.
- Kami Rita Sherpa: from Thame. Climbed Everest a record number of 26 times.
  - Interviewed several times in Kathmandu between 2019 and 2022.
- Lhakpa Rita Sherpa: Kami Rita's elder brother. A veteran climber, one of the first internationally certified mountain guides of Nepal and the first Nepali to climb the highest peaks in all seven continents.
  - Phone interview in 2019.
- Ang Chhiring Sherpa: an expedition cook who specialized in Japanese cuisine.
- Mingma Sherpa: Ang Chhiring's son, operates a trekking and mountaineering outlet called Climbalaya. He has summited Everest 10 times.
  - Interviewed in Kathmandu twice in 2021.
- Sirdar Mingma: Kami Rita Sherpa and Lhakpa Rita Sherpa's father.
  - Interviewed in Thame in 2021.
- Panuru Sherpa and his son Lhakpa Sherpa: from Phortse, met in Chapter 3. Went on the expedition with Dr Mayewski.

○ Interviewed Panuru and his family several times in Phortse and Kathmandu between 2021 and 2022.

CHAPTER 12: DESCENT

- Doma Sherpa: her husband, Namgyal, died on Everest. She tried to arrange a descent for him several times, but never achieved it and his body remains on Everest.
    ○ Interviewed in Kathmandu in 2021.
- Namgyal Sherpa: Doma's husband. First Everest summit in 2006. Launched the Extreme Everest Expedition 2010 with Chakra Karki. Built a hospital in his home village in the Khotang District. Died on Everest in 2013. His body is still up there.
- Dawa Finjhok Sherpa: has five Everest summits to his name. Led the expedition to recover the body of Goutam Ghosh.
    ○ Interviewed in Kathmandu in 2021.
- Panuru Sherpa: met in Chapters 3 and 11. Seventeen-time Everest summiteer.
    ○ Interviewed Panuru and his family several times in Phortse and Kathmandu between 2021 and 2022.

OTHER NOTABLE PEOPLE

- Sharad Kulkarni: a climber from Mumbai, whose wife, Anjali, died on Everest.
- Sir Edmund Hillary: a New Zealand mountaineer who, with Tenzing Norgay Sherpa, became the first climbers confirmed to have reached the summit of Everest on 29 May 1953.
- Colonel John Hunt: the team leader of the 1953 expedition.
- Russell Brice: a New Zealand climbing operator who, in 2012, cancelled all expeditions of his company, citing the related risks of an avalanche from the west shoulder.
- Lama Sangwa Dorje, Khenwa Dorje and Rolwa Dorje: three brothers with supernatural powers who, over 350 years ago, established monasteries in Pangboche, Thame and Rimijung.
- Lama Geshe: of Pangboche monastery and the most senior-ranking monk in the region. Would bless climbers on their way to summit Everest. Died in 2018 at the age of 87.
- Lama Ngawang Paljor: Lama Geshe's successor at Pangboche monastery.
- Eric Shipton: an English mountaineer.
- Marco Siffredi: a celebrated French snowboarder and mountaineer, guided by Phurba Tashi Sherpa, disappeared on 8 September 2002 while making a snowboard descent from Hornbein Couloir.

- David Tait: a British climber, guided by Phurba Tashi Sherpa, abandoned the double traverse.
- American Scott Fischer and New Zealander Rob Hall: died in the death zone of Everest in the blizzard of 1996.
- Chetna Sahoo: a female Indian climber rescued by Mingma David Sherpa.
- Nimsdai Purja: owns an expedition company with Mingma David Sherpa; author of *Beyond Possible*, about his summits of 14 peaks measuring over 8,000m (26,247ft) throughout the world in just six months. Netflix has made a documentary based on the book.
- Dawa Thondup: the leader of the group who travelled to Darjeeling in 1933, including Tenzing Norgay.
- Dorje Latu: senior instructor at the HMI, appointed Kushang Dorjee as his personal assistant.
- James W Whittaker: the first American to summit Everest in 1963.
- Desmond Doig: a journalist, who travelled the world with Konjo Chumbi Sherpa and Edmund Hillary with the yeti skull from Khumjung in 1960.
- Saurav Dhakal: a journalist who travelled with Apa Sherpa on the Great Himalaya Trail.
  ◦ Interviewed in Kathmandu in 2021.
- Alan Arnette: a climber and respected mountaineering archivist.
- Elizabeth Hawley: mountain archiver who started Himalayan Database.
- Goutam Ghosh: Indian Bengali policeman, who died during his descent in 2016, and whose body Dawa Finjhok Sherpa recovered.
- Chakra Karki: a mountaineering journalist. Launched Extreme Everest Expedition 2010 with Namgyal Sherpa.
  ◦ Interviewed in Kathmandu in 2021.

INDEX

Dawa Futi Sherpa 107, 109
Dawa Thondup Sherpa 103–4
dead bodies 11, 155, 279–80, 284
death zone 3–4, 7, 11, 281
deaths 6, 281
Denman, Earl 113
descent, importance of 281–4
Dhakal, Saurav 261, 262, 268
Dharan 132–3
Dhaulagiri, Mount 75–7
diet 185–6
Dingboche 36–7, 157
Doma Sherpa 279, 284, 285–6; husbands
    death 291–2, 296–7; plans to retrieve
    husband's body 297–9, 302
Dorje, Khenwa 47–8
Dorje, Lama Sangwa 47–9
Dorje, Latu Sherpa 146
Dorje, Rolwa 47–8
Dorjee Khatri 70–1, 74

E
earthquakes 44–6, 298
education in Nepal 67–72, 220, 222–6
Elizabeth II 214–15
environment: cleaning/litter removal
    53–4, 278, 288–9; climate change 23,
    192–3, 269–76
equipment 120, 272, 275; carried by
    sherpas 7, 43
Evans, Charles 114–15
Everest expeditions 14–15; 1920s 16–17,
    102; 1924 Mallory-Irvine 103–4; 1935
    reconnaissance 107–8; 1936 British
    expedition 108; 1947 Swiss expedition
    113; 1951 reconnaissance 21, 106–7;
    1952 Swiss expedition 17, 21, 113; 1953
    first conquest 13, 18–19, 114–15, 117–19;
    1963 American Expedition 215–18;
    1993 women's expedition 149–57; 1999
    Kangshung Face 125–7; 2000 Japanese

expedition 190; 2007 double traverse
    expedition 178–81
Everest, George 3
Everest, Mountain: access through
    Nepal 17, 21; access through Tibet 16;
    avalanches 40–2, 44–5; The Balcony
    5, 273; base camp 12, 32–42, 44–5,
    269; blizzard (1996) 185–9; Camp 2:
    38, 45–6; Camp 3: 39; Camp 4: 3,
    10–12, 185–9; cleaning up 53–4, 278,
    288–9; climate studies 273–5; death
    zone 3–4, 7, 11, 281; earthquake (2015)
    44–6, 298; Geneva Spur 300; Hillary
    Step 9, 303; Kangshung Face 125–7;
    Khumbu Icefall 21, 29–32, 40–2, 160,
    269–71; name origins 3; North Col
    282–3; optimum time to reach summit
    5; record at summit without oxygen 10;
    record number of summits 55; record
    numbers of deaths 6; routes to summit
    8, 125, 178–82; sacred nature of 20–1,
    51–5; South Col 21, 115, 126–7, 272–6;
    South Summit 9, 78, 114–15; The
    Triangular Face 4, 303

F
Fischer, Scott 186–7
fluid intake 11
Furdiki Sherpa: climbs Everest 164–6;
    fundraising to climb 162–3; and
    Mingma Sherpa 157–62; and Nima
    Doma 162–6

G
Gaurishankar Conservation Area 193
Geneva Spur 300
Geshe, Lama 49–50
Ghosh, Goutam 292–5, 299–302
Gokyo Trail 172–3
Gombusungjen 49
Great Himalaya Trail 261–2, 268

ACKNOWLEDGEMENTS

As we look back on this project, we are filled to the bottom of our heart with humility and gratitude. A project that started with our limited knowledge of Sherpas and mountaineering soon became an ocean of overwhelming stories, the telling of which could not have been possible without what we think of as divine intervention. The unfolding of the characters of this book and their stories was so immaculate and spontaneous that, if we were to plan it all over again from scratch, we simply wouldn't know how.

We are indebted to all the Sherpas who unconditionally trusted us with their emotions and stories. Without them, and their families, this book would not have been possible. In the course of writing this book, we met with so many Sherpas from different generations. While some made their way onto these pages, there are many others whom we were unable to include. In the Sherpa homelands, there were people who showed us the way to the villages, people who partook in our conversations in the background, people who told us folklores, and so many more. Together, we would like to call them the hidden characters beneath the surface, upon which our book rests.

This book has made us a lot of new friends. One of them is our agent, Ben Clark from The Soho Agency, who helped us put together our ideas and conceive this book. He is the one who exposed us to the whole new world of book-writing and introduced us to our commissioning editor, Trevor Davies from the Octopus Publishing Group. Trevor has always been extra-sensitive to and highly respectful of our work. No matter how many deadlines we missed in the process, he never raised the alarm or indicated any hiccups. We believe the creative space that Trevor built for us was key to our self-accountability and honesty. Then came our project editor Pauline Bache and copyeditor Julia Kellaway, whom we cannot thank enough for bearing with our non-native English writing, checking our facts and bringing the text to where it stands today. There are many more hands who have worked directly and indirectly on our book, conducting legal checks, designing the layout, proofreading the text and sketching maps, among others. The level of unconditional trust and support we have received from people several oceans apart, people whom we have never met, gives us goosebumps.

We were blessed to have a guardian angel in this project – Karen White, who lives in Canada, without whose spiritual guidance throughout the process, we would not have been able to bridge all the cultural differences and treat our subjects with the utmost sensitivity. She was as invested in this project as we were and was always looking to contribute to every aspect of our book-writing.

We are also thankful to our friend Gyanendra Shrestha, a mountaineer himself, who served as the Nepalese government's liaison officer for Everest expeditions continuously for over a decade. He helped us identify Sherpas, and even reached out to them on our behalf.

As we went on writing, we scoured a lot of archives available on the internet. These were critical in our fact-checking and helped us tell the stories with certainty and confidence. We thank the late Elizabeth Hawley for archiving the entire history of mountaineering in The Himalayan Database, which many also refer to as the 'Bible of Everest'. The archives of Alan Arnette were also useful to find facts to support the flow of our story.

In the same process, respected climber Reinhold Messner, whom we met in Kathmandu, was kind enough to tell us about the growth of climbing Sherpas that he has witnessed over several decades.

Vegan mountaineer Kuntal Joisher has been with us from the very beginning. We thank him for bearing with our silly mountaineering questions when we were just starting out with our proposal for this book.

There are some other people whose positive energies, wisdom and blessings have always helped us pursue a better version of ourselves with every new work we do. With book, or without book, Kumar Nagarkoti,

Khem Lakai, Shailendra Sigdel, and Deepak Adhikari are among a few people who are always by our sides.

There is a long list of friends and colleagues we should thank for always encouraging us formally or informally. In the context of this book, however, there are a few names that we should not miss out. Krishna Dangi took us to the Everest region for the first time in 2014 and Keshav Koirala, Ram Bahadur Rawal, Rabindra Manandhar, Sanjeev Giri, Man Bahadur Basnet, and Mingma G were brutally honest with their suggestions and feedback whenever we sought their review on bits and pieces of our work.

For as long as we were invested in this book, we don't know how many weekends we had to skip, how many family dinners we had to miss and how many times we were zoned out during family chitchats. It's only because our families bore the little responsibilities that should have fallen on our shoulders that we were able to think of our stories and write them in elaborate sections.

We cannot imagine the ordeals our partners – Salina (Ankit's wife) and Injina (Pradeep's wife) – and Neilmani (Pradeep's son) had to go through, enduring lonely weekends while we travelled to meet our interviewees or to writing camps for weeks at a time. No matter how often we were not standing by them in times of need, Salina and Injina have always made us feel complete and fulfilled.

When we shared with Ankit's mother that we were pitching a book proposal, she said, 'I will keep a fasting to pray for your success.' Mothers may not know what our work is all about, yet they are the first to stand up, unconditionally supporting their children. We dedicate this book to our mothers, Gita Sharma (Ankit's mum) and Renuka Bashyal (Pradeep's mum), whose prayers and blessings have brought us to where we stand today.

Lastly, for both our fathers, a book is the highest embodiment of a person's intellect. This may be debatable, but with this book, our fathers Jagannath Sharma (Ankit's dad) and Khagendra Prasad Bashyal (Pradeep's dad), are probably the proudest dads in the universe. This book is as much theirs as it is ours.